Men of Arms

# Deinfringe

The Truth About Our Rights and
Answers to the Myths That Have Been
Spread About Them

Joshua Baker
2019

# Table of Contents

# Preface

It was 2014, when I first applied for my Federal Firearms License (FFL), part of my plan was to conduct courses for a Concealed Pistol Licenses (CPL). At that time two instructors were charged for not doing the full eight-hour course. I felt that the solution for this was to follow how the American Heart Association taught Basic Life Support (BLS). When I was a BLS instructor, we played a DVD that we would pause when prompted and give supplemental instruction or hands-on training. A DVD as an aid seemed like a viable option for a CPL course so that everything was covered, but I didn't personally want to create the video series, nor did I have the know-how.

What I did know, however, was how create a great PowerPoint, yeah it wasn't going to be as impressive as a video, but just as useful! I set out with crucial points that I wanted to make sure were covered and especially hit on those points that the course material was lacking. The critical point was that it needed to cover gun rights. After all, you have a room that has multiple different backgrounds and political beliefs, yet they all recognize the need for a firearm, so why not start by reinforcing their idea and have them better equipped to tell people why they choose to carry, after all, knowledge is power.

I got caught up in doing so many other things; Gunsmithing, cerakote, and sales that I never actually took the instructor class, that PowerPoint was seemingly for nothing, but it turned out to be the initial rough draft of this book. I morphed it into a quick sixteen-page PDF document that I saved on my website, so I could easily link to it on social media instead of having the same argument a million times over and I could just say, "read this." The problem was I kept thinking of more stuff to add, so what started as a few PowerPoint slides became sixteen pages, then thirty, then forty-five and now four times that size.

# Introduction

*"Read not to contradict and confute; nor to believe and take for granted; nor to find talk and discourse; but to weigh and consider."* -Francis Bacon

After all the changes and rewrites of this book, I believe my main message has stayed intact. That is and was to show that:

- Gun rights are natural rights
- Owning a gun is normal
- Firearms are an evident and appropriate tool for self-defense

Everything else is just filler and builds on these points. I could summarize this book this way: The firearm is an extension of the natural right of self-defense. It is perfectly normal for people to own and defend themselves with all types of firearms to ensure they can adequately defend themselves. The founders attempted to secure that right and remove government interference by drafting the Constitution and the Bill of Rights.

That pretty much explains it. Of course, just saying that doesn't seem to satisfy the naysayers, so I tried to lay this out as best as possible throughout this book.

Lastly, throughout the book, I use the term Anti-Self Defense Movement (ASDM): This encompasses Anti-gun groups and persons looking for government control of firearms. Saying Anti-gun does not quite relay their real position; they are, in fact, against self-defense. For example, England was "Anti-gun" and when that didn't produce the correct result. They became "Anti-knife" and now some places are charging people for using pepper spray to defend themselves. When gun control doesn't work, they will add another item they want to control.

# Section 1: Natural Rights

This writing intends to lay a foundation of understanding, and one of the most foundational pieces to the gun debate are Natural Rights. One of the reasons that they are so crucial to this debate on gun rights is that the founders based so much of this country on natural rights. Our Declaration of Independence, Constitution, Bill of Rights, and the writings of many of the founders all exude this fundamental belief. To understand those documents, you must grasp their motives. The other more crucial reason is that Natural Rights supersede these founding documents and any government; after all, if the 2nd amendment didn't exist or if overturned, there would be very few who would turn in those firearms, so why is that?

## Natural Rights are a Result of Natural Law

> *"All acts of legislature apparently contrary to Natural Right and justice, are...considered as void"* -George Mason [1]

Natural Rights and the term natural law are often used interchangeably. Sometimes they are referred to by period such as Natural Rights being Aristotle, Socrates, Plato, Aquinas, and others before the 17th century. Natural Law being referred to by Locke and others in the Age of Enlightenment. Others view this as a debate between John Locke (Natural Law) and Thomas Hobbes (Natural Rights). It is not important enough to compare these two: Locke Vs. Hobbes. Still, others use one to describe the moral theory and the other for legal theory. At the basic level, the ideas cross regularly and are used interchangeably. For this book, we are using them as such, and we are not focusing on their differences.

Natural Law is the nature of man in the world. It is man's state of nature without government. To put it another way, Natural Laws are moral truths that apply to all people regardless of class or geographical location — discovered by reason alone. The authority of legal standards derives, in part, from considerations having to do with the moral merit of those standards.

According to the Wikipedia definition:

> *Natural law (Latin: ius naturale, lex naturalis) is a philosophy asserting that certain rights are inherent by virtue of human nature, endowed by nature— traditionally by God or a transcendent source—and that these can be understood universally through human reason. As determined by nature, the law of nature is implied to be objective and universal; it exists independently of human understanding, and of the positive law of a given state, political order, legislature or society at large. [2]*

## Natural Law Theorists and Founding of America

It makes sense to introduce briefly some of the philosophers that shaped Natural Law theory, especially considering what was said about some of them by Thomas Jefferson in his letter to Henry Lee:

> *When forced therefore to resort to arms for redress, an appeal to the tribunal of the world was deemed proper for our justification. this was the object of the Declaration of Independence. not to find out new principles, or new arguments, never before thought of, not merely to say things which had never been said before; but to place before mankind the common sense of the subject; [. . .] terms so plain and firm, as to command their assent, and to justify ourselves in the*

*independent stand we [. . .] compelled to take. neither*
*aiming at originality of principle or sentiment, nor yet*
*copied from any particular and previous writing, it was*
*intended to be an expression of the American mind, and*
*to give to that expression the proper tone and spirit*
*called for by the occasion. all it's authority rests then*
*on the harmonizing sentiments of the day, whether*
*expressed, in conversions in letters, printed essays or in*
*the elementary books of public right, as Aristotle,*
*Cicero, Locke, Sidney Etc. the historical documents*
*which you mention as in your possession, ought all to be*
*found, and I am persuaded you will find, to be*
*corroborative of the facts and principles advanced in*
*that Declaration. be pleased to accept assurances of my*
*great respect and esteem."* [3]

## Aristotle (384-322 BC)

*"Universal law is the law of Nature. For there really is,*
*as everyone to some extent divines, a natural justice and*
*injustice that is binding on all men, even on those who*
*have no association or covenant with each other."*
*Aristotle* [4]

## Marcus Tullius Cicero (106-43 B.C.)

Assassinated for condemning the tyranny of Mark Anthony.
Referred to as the "exalted patriot" by Thomas Jefferson.

*"law in the proper sense is right reason in harmony*
*with nature."* [5]

*"there will not be one such law in Rome and another in*
*Athens, one now and another in the future, but all*
*peoples at all times will be embraced by a single and*
*eternal unchangeable law."* [5]

*"many harmful and pernicious measures are passed in human communities—measures which come no closer to the name of laws than if a gang of criminals agreed to make some rules."* [5]

*"the men who administer public affairs must first of all see that everyone holds on to what is his, and that private men are never deprived of their goods by public acts."* [5]

*"First of all, Nature has endowed every species of living creature with the instinct of self-preservation, of avoiding what seems likely to cause injury to life or limb, and of procuring and providing everything needful for life — food, shelter, and the like."* [6]

John Adams on Cicero

*"all the ages of the world have not produced a greater statesman and philosopher united in the same character; his authority should have great weight."* - [7]

## *Thomas Aquinas (1225-1274)*

*"By nature, all men are equal in liberty, but not in other endowments."* [8]

*"The highest manifestation of life consists in this: that a being governs its own actions. A thing which is always subject to the direction of another is somewhat of a dead thing."* [9]

*"the natural law is nothing else than the rational creature's participation of the eternal law"* [9]

*"It is evident that all things partake somewhat of the eternal law, in so far as, namely, from its being imprinted on them... Wherefore it (human nature) has a*

*share of the Eternal Reason, whereby it has a natural inclination to its proper act and end: and this participation of the eternal law in the rational creature is called the natural law."* [10]

## Algernon Sidney (1622–1683)

Beheaded in 1683 for allegedly conspiring to kill King Charles II. Inspired both the Glorious Revolution in 1688 as well as our American Revolution.

> *"The strength, virtue, glory, wealth, power, and happiness of Rome proceeding from liberty, did rise, grow, and perish with it. Whilst liberty continued, it was the nurse of virtue; and all the losses suffered in foreign or civil wars, were easily recovered: but when liberty was lost, valor and virtue were torn up by the roots, and the Roman power proceeding from it, perished"* [11]

> *"The common Notions of Liberty are not from School Divines, but from Nature . . .,"* [12]

> *"Man's natural love to Liberty is tempered by Reason, which originally is his Nature,"* [11]

> *"That which is not just, is not Law; and that which is not Law, ought not to be obeyed."* [13]

Thomas Jefferson issued this statement:

> *"Resolved, that it is the opinion of this Board that as to the general principles of liberty and the rights of man, in nature and in society, the doctrines of Locke, in his 'Essay concerning the true original extent and end of civil government,' and of Sidney in his 'Discourses on government,' may be considered as those generally approved by our fellow citizens of this, and the United States."* [14]

*"Ense petit placidam sub libertate quietem [By the sword we seek peace, but peace only under liberty]."* Adopted by Massachusetts as the state motto. [15]

## *John Locke (1632-1704)*

Like Newton with gravity, Locke did not invent Natural Law; he was merely the discoverer. Locke was a legal clerk, doctor, philosopher, and theologian whose pivotal work "Two Treatise on Government" was vital to the American revolution. There is zero chance you can get away with a discussion on Natural Rights and not bring up John Locke.

These ideas of limited government, the consent of the governed, equality, self-ownership, individual liberty, the right of revolution, and religious tolerance were all blended into Natural Rights; these were discussed centuries before the American Revolution and our Constitution. We tend to focus and look to the Constitution when we talk about our rights, but we forget our Constitution has a basis. We can see this in the way the founders worded the Bill of Rights. For example, the 1st amendment is "the" freedom of speech. 2nd is "the" right of the people to keep and bear arms. 4th is "the" right of the people to be secure in their persons. All these mention that they existed before government: "the right," and not "a right." They were not establishing rights; they were intending on securing them. Therefore, when people talk about changing the 2nd amendment, they are not just attacking our well-established rights in this country; they are attacking our Natural Rights!

Life, Liberty, and Property

> *"Men being by nature all free, equal and independent, no one can be put out of this estate and subjected to the political power of another without his own consent."* [16]

*"To understand political power aright, and derive it
from its original, we must consider what estate all men
are naturally in, and that is, a state of perfect freedom
to order their actions, and dispose of their possessions
and persons as they think fit, within the bounds of the
law of Nature, without asking leave or depending upon
the will of any other man."* [17]

*"But though this be a state of liberty, yet it is not a state
of license; though man in that state have an
uncontrollable liberty to dispose of their own person or
possessions . . . The state of Nature has a law of Nature
to govern it, which obliges everyone, and reason, which
is that law, teaches all mankind who will but consult it,
that being equal and independent, no one ought to harm
another in his life, health, liberty, or possessions"* [18]

*"Though the earth and all inferior creatures be
common to all men, yet every man has a 'property' in
his own 'person.' This nobody has any right to but
himself. The 'labor' of his body and the 'work' of his
hands, we may say, are properly his.
Whatsoever, then, he removes out of the state that
Nature hath provided and left it in, he hath mixed his
labor with it, and joined to it something that is his own,
and thereby makes it his property. It being by him
removed from the common state of Nature, it hath by
this labor something annexed to it that excludes the
common right of other men. For this 'labor' being the
unquestionable property of the laborer, no man but he
can have a right to what that is once joined to . . ."* [19]

*"the great and chief purpose of men's uniting into
commonwealths and putting themselves under
government is the preservation of their property... the
supreme power can't take from any man any part of his
property without his consent. What men enter into
societies with governments for is the preservation of*

*their property; so it would be a gross absurdity to have a government that deprived them of that very property! So men in society have property, which means that*
> *•they have such a right to the goods that are theirs according to the law of the community, and*
> *•nobody has a right to take any part of those goods from them without their own consent.*
*Without that second clause they would have no property at all; for something isn't really my property if someone else can rightfully take it from me against my will, whenever he pleases."* [20]

*"...for nobody can transfer to another more power than he has in himself; and no Body has an absolute Arbitrary Power to . . . take away the Life or Property of another . . .. and having in the State of Nature no Arbitrary Power over the Life, Liberty or Possessions of another, but only so much as the Law of Nature gives him to the preservation of himself; . . . this is all he doth, or can give up to the Commonwealth . . . so that the Legislative can have no more than this."* [20]

As Ron Paul describes his view of Liberty in the Lockean tradition:

*"Liberty means to exercise human rights in any manner a person chooses so long as it does not interfere with the exercise of the rights of others. This means, above all else, keeping government out of our lives. Only this path leads to the unleashing of human energies that build civilization, provide security, generate wealth, and protect the people from systematic rights violations. In this sense, only liberty can truly ward off tyranny, the great and eternal foe of mankind."* [21]

### *Thomas Paine (1737-1809)*

His Work "Common Sense" is said to have inspired the American Revolution, and his work," Rights of Man," was the central text behind the French Revolution and was almost executed in England as well as France. Unfortunately, Paine was not as respected at the end of his life with his obituary saying:

*"He had lived long, did some good and much harm."*

Only six people showed up to his funeral (three of which were freed slaves). He was hated by politicians and the church alike for his writings because he still called out injustices even after America's independence. He spoke out on slavery, and the treatment of Native Americans, and wrote about how to abolish these in his work "A serious thought." He pushed Thomas Jefferson to add the abolition of slavery to the constitution which Jefferson added to the first draft. He received no money from his pivotal work "Common sense" and asked for the money to go to the war effort. Federalists like John Adams and Alexander Hamilton disliked him, which is a badge of honor. Ultimately, he kept to his principles and was betrayed by his countrymen.

*"Hitherto we have spoken only of the natural rights of man. We have now to consider the civil rights of man, and to show how the one originates from the other. Man did not enter into society to become worse than he was before, nor to have fewer rights than he had before, but to have those rights better secured. His natural rights are the foundation of all his civil rights. But in order to pursue this distinction with more precision, it will be necessary to mark the different qualities of natural and civil rights."* [22]

*"A natural right is an animal right...and the power to act it, is supposed, either fully or in part, to be mechanically contained within ourselves as individuals."* [23]

## *America's Founders*

I get that there are numerous theories of rights, and inside these are further theories, the spiderweb is limitless. Part of the reason we've focused so much on Lockean tradition, following that lineage, is because this was who the founders looked to. So, if you want to look at the Constitution, you should look at who and what helped formulate their beliefs.

We can start with the Declaration of Independence:

> *"When in the Course of human events, it becomes necessary for one people to dissolve the political bands which have connected them with another, and to assume among the powers of the earth, the separate and equal station to which the Laws of Nature and of Nature's God entitle them, a decent respect to the opinions of mankind requires that they should declare the causes which impel them to the separation.....We hold these truths to be self-evident, that all men are created equal, that they are endowed by their Creator with certain unalienable Rights, that among these are Life, Liberty and the pursuit of Happiness... That to secure these rights, Governments are instituted among Men, deriving their just powers from the consent of the governed."* [24]

> *"The very first sentence of the of the actual Declaration roundly states that certain truths are—crucial words— self-evident. This style—terse and pungent, yet fringed with elegance—allied the plain language of Thomas Paine to the loftier expositions of John Locke..."*- *Christopher Hitchens, book: Thomas Jefferson* [25]

The Declaration of Independence isn't merely a quote or statement; it is actual law quoted numerous times by the Supreme Court and codified in the United States Code under Organic Law. Since these are the organic laws, you would think all subsequent laws would have to meet the criteria set, "endowed by their creator with certain unalienable Rights, that among these are <u>life, liberty</u> and the <u>pursuit of happiness</u>."

Unalienable defined:

> *"unable to be taken away from or given away by the possessor"*

Among those rights that they cannot take away are those underlined above (Life, liberty, and property) Again this is a statement declaring self-ownership, property rights; you're permitted to do what you want as long as it does not conflict with another person's life, liberty, and property. This is the reason government was formed, to protect those very things and government is considered illegitimate when it goes beyond this.

It is to be noted though, that, Thomas Jefferson changing property to pursuit of happiness isn't a deviation from Locke. It's almost further solidifying Locke's ideas as "pursuit of happiness" comes from Locke's book "An Essay Concerning Human Understanding" in it he says:

> *"The necessity of pursuing happiness is the foundation of liberty. As therefore, the highest perfection of intellectual nature lies in careful and constant pursuit of true and solid happiness; so the care of ourselves that we mistake not imaginary for real joy is the necessary foundation of our liberty. The stronger ties we have to an unalterable pursuit of happiness in general, which is our highest good, and which, as such, our desires always follow, the more are we free from any necessary determination of our will to any particular action..."* [26]

In short, Locke and Thomas Jefferson, are saying we get to make our own decisions, we get to pursue our interests and needs.

Locke and the founders also knew the key to us being free was limited government, as Thomas Jefferson said.

*"Our legislators are not sufficiently apprised of the rightful limits of their power; that their true office is to declare and enforce only our natural rights and duties, and to take none of them from us."* [27]

A limited government was never supposed to have the power to take our guns away or dictate how we can obtain them. If the government grew to a size where they were infringing on these rights, we have a Natural Right to resist tyrannical rule; Locke considered it a moral obligation to rebel.

*"whenever the Legislators endeavor to take away, and destroy the Property of the People, or to reduce them to Slavery under Arbitrary Power, they put themselves into a state of War with the People, who are thereupon absolved from any farther Obedience, and are left to the common Refuge, which God hath provided for all Men, against Force and Violence. Whensoever therefore the Legislative shall transgress this fundamental Rule of Society; and either by Ambition, Fear, Folly or Corruption, endeavor to grasp themselves, or put into the hands of any other an Absolute Power over the Lives, Liberties, and Estates of the People; By this breach of Trust they forfeit the Power, the People had put into their hands, for quite contrary ends, and it devolves to the People, who have a Right to resume their original Liberty."* [28]

### Lysander Spooner (1808-1887)

*"Children learn the fundamental principles of natural law at a very early age. Thus they very early understand that one child must not, without just cause, strike or otherwise hurt, another; that one child must not assume any arbitrary control or domination over another; that one child must not, either by force, deceit, or stealth, obtain possession of anything that belongs to another; that if one child commits any of these wrongs against*

*another, it is not only the right of the injured child to resist, and, if need be, punish the wrongdoer, and compel him to make reparation, but that it is also the right, and the moral duty, of all other children, and all other persons, to assist the injured party in defending his rights, and redressing his wrongs. These are fundamental principles of natural law, which govern the most important transactions of man with man. Yet children learn them earlier than they learn that three and three are six, or five and five ten. Their childish plays, even, could not be carried on without a constant regard to them; and it is equally impossible for persons of any age to live together in peace on any other conditions."* [29]

Lysander Spooner was a Natural Law proponent, legal theorist, and he was an abolitionist who believed the south had the right to secede. What makes him different from many of the other Natural Right proponents, was his disbelief in a social contract.

The idea of a social contract or social agreement has probably been around since the first government, certainly from ancient Greece onward. The "social contract" is the view that persons' moral and political obligations are dependent upon a contract or agreement among them to form the society in which they live. Social contract theorists generally believe that individuals have consented, either explicitly or implicitly. Spooner, however, did not believe in implied consent. In other words, those who agreed to the Constitution could not obligate others to also obey; this would include future generations.

Thomas Paine put it this way

*"There never did, there never will, and there never can, exist a Parliament, or any description of men, or any generation of men, in any country, possessed of the right or the power of binding and controlling posterity to the "end of time," or of commanding forever how the world shall be governed, or who shall govern it; and*

*therefore all such clauses, acts or declarations by which
the makers of them attempt to do what they have neither
the right nor the power to do, nor the power to execute,
are in themselves null and void. Every age and
generation must be as free to act for itself in all cases as
the age and generations which preceded it. The vanity
and presumption of governing beyond the grave is the
most ridiculous and insolent of all tyrannies. Man has
no property in man; neither has any generation a
property in the generations which are to follow."* [30]

So why even cover the social contract here? Because even if gun
rights in this country did not exist from its founding and gun
rights were not intended to be protected by the Constitution; we
still would hold that it is our Natural Right to own property such
as firearms, and we would also agree that we never signed over
any of our rights to someone else's control.

Lysander fought against slavery, saying it is wrong based on the
Constitution, and he also fought against slavery, saying it was
wrong despite the Constitution. We should see gun rights the
same way.

### *Classical Liberalism to Libertarianism.*

*"Classical liberalism" is the term used to designate the
ideology advocating private property, an unhampered
market economy, the rule of law, constitutional
guarantees of freedom of religion and of the press, and
international peace based on free trade. Up until
around 1900, this ideology was generally known simply
as liberalism." -Ralph Racio* [31]

Locke, Thomas Paine, Frederic Bastiat, Condorcet, Tocqueville,
Herbert Spencer to H.L. Mencken, Mises, Albert Jay Nock,
Hazlitt, Hayek, and Rothbard are just a few of the classic
liberals who have advocated for Natural Rights or at least a
version of rights that do not originate with government. Also,
they argued for limited government power and individual

freedoms. It's no real surprise that so many were also economists, they saw what happened to individual freedoms when central planning and government monopolies took over.

This tradition is what America was founded on, although it went astray quickly because as we know power routinely corrupts, and this belief is still active in America. Gun owners now look to republicans as the answer, yet they are, as Michael Malice would say, "just progressives driving the speed limit [32]." Both of the major parties look for the government to provide solutions to issues they have no business with, both groups advocate for inefficient government monopolies at the expense of the governed, both advocate violence to those who do not comply with government demands.

We live under constant threat to our Natural Rights, firearms are just one of those items that have been infringed and are under constant threat, it is more worrisome to wonder what type of attack our rights will be under as they further take our guns. I included this section on classical liberalism to show that our yearning for our rights is nothing new, and we are not an isolated group. Throughout this book, I have added hundreds of names and quotes; my purpose in this is so that you will continue to research and learn about these topics beyond this writing.

## Utilitarianism (basically the alternative to Natural Rights theory)

Popularized by John Stuart Mill and founded by Jeremy Bentham, unfortunately, utilitarianism seems to be winning in the circle of public opinion, at least that's what media would have you believe. Most politicians over the past twenty years have embraced a view similar to this. A belief that tells people, "it is the greatest happiness of the greatest number that is the measure of right and wrong." Or put more simply, "the greatest good for the greatest amount of people." No doubt, with the rise of socialist ideas, this line of thinking will continue to flourish, that is until a socialist society collapses, once they collapse they all seem to be individualist and believe in Natural Law, almost like it's, um... natural.

Thomas Sowell points out this divide in his book "A Conflict of Vision," where he compares these two ways of thinking as "constrained," which would be the utilitarianism vision and "unconstrained" would be the Natural Rights vision. Sowell makes the statement in this book "there are no solutions; there are only trade-offs [33]." When it comes to the gun debate, the firearm proponent may say that it is their right to own firearms, it is their right to possess and defend themselves, their family, and their country. They side with men like Benjamin Franklin who also mention the tradeoff:

> *"They who can give up essential liberty to obtain a little temporary safety deserve neither liberty nor safety."* [34]

and Thomas Jefferson:

> *"I prefer dangerous freedom over peaceful slavery."* [35]

Therefore, the bad argument made by Utilitarian gun grabbers "how many people must die before you give up your guns" is not only a fallacy it is also a pointless argument to make when you look at the two visions.

The pro-gun crowd gets roped into these arguments trying to defend their views using the ASDM point of view. In many ways, when we say that "more guns equal less crime," we are making a utilitarian argument. You can watch almost any gun debate online or any case made by the media, and you see utilitarian statements with gun advocates having to defend themselves from this point of view.

The greatest good for the greatest amount of people has always failed, and the opponents to this line of thinking have been responsible for the greatest revolutions and most significant advancements in freedom. When you look at the attacks against Natural Rights by utilitarian founder Jeremy Bentham you can almost better grasp what Natural Rights are; his criticism is pluses. George Smith explains what Bentham's said of natural rights: "anarchical fallacies that encourage civil unrest, disobedience, and resistance to laws, and revolution against established governments." That is true, look at what the founders said, and you can see the spirit of resistance, hell, our countries history is not just built on the "spirit" of resistance but actual resistance and revolution, and we encouraged others to do so in places such as France.

 "Rights of Man" by Thomas Paine is to the French revolution as "Common Sense" was to the American Revolution, the utilitarian philosopher Edmund Burke called it a "digest of anarchy." Josiah Tucker said of Natural Rights:

> *"is a universal demolisher of all governments, but not the builder of any."* [36]

Well yeah, Americans weren't looking to replicate the British empire or establish a large government here.

The utilitarian problem is that it relies too much on the legislature, believing that law comes solely from that institution. Thomas Hodgskin puts it this way:

> *"Bentham and Mill, both being eager to exercise the power of legislation, represent it as a beneficent deity, which curbs our naturally evil passions and desires (they adopting the doctrine of the priests, that the desires and passions of man are naturally evil) which checks ambition, sees justice done, and encourages virtue. Delightful characteristics! — which have the single fault of being contradicted by every page of history."* [37]

It seems to be the overriding theme of utilitarians in that they have placed themselves above nature. They get to determine rights; right to education, right to healthcare, right to free housing, and right to a living wage (whatever that means). The danger of this line of thinking is grave; again, Hodgskin explains:

> *"To me, this system appears as mischievous as it is absurd. The doctrines according too well with the practice of lawgivers, they cut too securely all the gordian knots of legislation, not to be readily adopted by all those who, however discontented with a distribution of power, in which no share falls to them, are anxious to become the tutelary guardians of the happiness of mankind. They lift legislation beyond our reach and secure it from censure. Man, having naturally no rights, may be experimented upon, imprisoned, expatriated or even exterminated, as the legislator pleases. Life and property being his gift, he may resume them at pleasure; and hence he never classes the executions and wholesale slaughters, he continually commands, with murder—nor the forcible appropriation of property he sanctions, under the name of taxes, tithes, etc., with larceny or highway robbery. Filmer's doctrine of the divine right of kings was rational benevolence, compared to the monstrous assertion that 'all right is factitious, and only exists by the will of the lawmaker."* [38]

Locke argued against a supposedly divine monarchy and yet, now utilitarians (basically the modern-day left, especially ASDM gun-grabbers) have determined once again the government is divine as if somehow 1,000 legislators imposing their will is better than one monarch. We will cover this throughout, but the belief that someone else is responsible for your life and your safety is a farce, simply an unrealistic fantasy.

# Natural Right of Self Defense and Firearms

> *"This may be considered as the true palladium of liberty.... The right of self-defense is the first law of nature: in most governments it has been the study of rulers to confine this right within the narrowest limits possible. Wherever standing armies are kept up, and the right of the people to keep and bear arms is, under any color or pretext whatsoever, prohibited, liberty, if not already annihilated, is on the brink of destruction."*
> *-St. George Tucker, Blackstone's Commentaries on the Laws of England, 1803* [39]

> *"If a man by the terror of present death, be compelled to do a fact against the Law, he is totally Excused; because no Law can oblige a man to abandon his own preservation." -Thomas Hobbes* [40]

Natural law philosophers believed Natural Rights were self-evident, evident from reason alone. I don't think any right could be as apparent as the right to defend yourself and your family. Murray Rothbard explained it in the context of property:

> *"if every man has the absolute right to his justly-held property it then follows that he has the right to keep that property — to defend it by violence against violent invasion....for if a man owns property and yet is denied the right to defend it against attack, then it is clear that a very important aspect of that ownership is being denied to him. To say that someone has the absolute right to a certain property but lacks the right to defend it against attack or invasion is also to say that he does not have total right to that property."* [41]

One may say that it is self-defense to limit the access of firearms to specific individuals or the type of weapons. For example, is it an act of self-defense to impose background checks because it could preemptively stop someone who wishes to harm you.

Well, Rothbard answers this question for us again in his book, The Ethics of Liberty, in which, Rothbard uses the example of alcohol prohibition. The legislation based on a perceived threat; it was considered "defensive" based on what people could do under the influence of alcohol. It was brutally invasive of the rights of person and property. He explains:

> "In the same way, it could be held that
>
>> A: the failure to ingest vitamins makes people more irritable, that
>> B: the failure is therefore likely to increase crime, and that therefore
>> C: everyone should be forced to take the proper amount of vitamins daily.
>
> Once we bring in "threats" to person and property that are vague and future — i.e., are not overt and immediate then all manner of tyranny becomes excusable. The only way to guard against such despotism is to keep the criterion of perceived invasion clear and immediate and overt. For, in the inevitable case of fuzzy or unclear actions, we must bend over backwards to require the threat of invasion to be direct and immediate, and therefore to allow people to do whatever they may be doing. In short, the burden of proof that the aggression has really begun must be on the person who employs the defensive violence." [41]

Aristotle also explains self-defense as being natural

> "Now it must be wrong to say, as some do, that the structure of man is not good, in fact, that it is worse than that of any other animal. Their grounds are that man is barefoot, unclothed, and void of any weapon of force. Against this we say that all the other animals have just one method of defense and cannot change it for another: they are forced to sleep and perform all their actions with their shoes on the whole time, as one

*might say; they can never take off this defensive
equipment of their nor can they change their weapon,
whatever it may be. For men, on the other hand, many
means of defense are available, and he can change them
at any time, and above all he can choose what weapon
he will have and where. Take the hand: this is good as a
talon, or a claw, or a horn, or again, a spear or a
sword, or any other weapon or tool; it can be all of
these, because it can seize and hold them all. And
Nature has admirably contrived the actual shape of the
hand so as to fit with this arrangement."* [42]

The Dutch Scholar Hugo Grotius takes a similar stance as
Aristotle:

*"For all animals are provided by nature with means for
the very purpose of self-defense. See Xenophon, Ovid,
Horace, Lucretius. Galen observes that man is an
animal born for peace and war, not born with weapons,
but with hands by which weapons can be acquired.* [43]

Cicero also explains that self-defense is natural and so is the use
of weapons.

*"There exists a law, not written down anywhere, but
inborn in our hearts; a law which comes to us not by
training or custom or reading but by derivation and
absorption and adoption from nature itself; a law which
has come to us not from theory but from practice, not by
instruction but by natural intuition. I refer to the law
which lays it down that, if our lives are endangered by
plots of violence or armed robbers or enemies, any and
every method of protecting others is morally right.
When weapons reduce them to silence, the laws no
longer expect one to await their pronouncements. For
people who decide to wait for these will have to wait for
justice, too and meanwhile they must suffer injustice
first. Indeed, even the wisdom of the law itself, by a sort
of tacit implication, permits self-defense, because it*

*does not actually forbid men to kill; what it does instead, is to forbid the bearing of a weapon with the intention to kill. When, therefore, an inquiry passes beyond the mere question of the weapon and starts to consider the motive, a man who has used arms in self-defense is not regarded as having carried them with a homicidal aim."* [44]

Thomas Hobbes the Natural Right philosopher also said:

*"For the right men have by nature to protect themselves, when none else can protect them, can by no covenant be relinquished."* [45]

Numerous philosophers and founders also explain the right to bear arms as a natural defense, which is the difference between free men and slaves, which I would also equate to a form of self-defense, and that is being in control of one's life. Again, going back to Aristotle:

*"Hippodamos planned a city with a population of ten thousand, divided into three parts, one of skilled workers, one of agriculturist, and third to bear arms and secure defense. The farmers have no arms, the workers have neither land nor arms; this makes them virtually the servants of those who do possess arms. In these circumstances, the equal sharing of offices and honors becomes and impossibility. Those who possess arms must be superior in power to both the other sections"* (This would breed inequality) [46]

Algernon Sidney explains the natural right of self-defense in maintaining liberty against tyranny and injustice:

*"Nay, all the laws must fall, human societies that subsist by them be dissolved, and all innocent persons be exposed to the violence of the most wicked, if men might not justly defend themselves against injustice by their own natural right, when the ways prescribed by*

*public authority cannot be taken. Let the danger never be so great, there is a possibility of safety while men have life, hands, arms and courage to used them; but that people must be certainly perish, who tamely suffer themselves to be oppressed."* [47]

And Samuel Adams in 1772 said:

*"Among the natural rights of the Colonists are these: First, a right to life; Secondly, to liberty; Thirdly, to property; together with the right to support and defend them in the best manner they can. These are evident branches of, rather than deductions from, the duty of self-preservation, commonly called the first law of nature.*

*All men have a right to remain in a state of nature as long as they please; and in case of intolerable oppression, civil or religious, to leave the society they belong to, and enter another.*

*When men enter into society, it is by voluntary consent; and they have a right to demand and insist upon the performance of such conditions and previous limitations as form an equitable original compact.*

*Every natural right not expressly given up, or, from the nature of a social compact, necessarily ceded, remains.*

*All positive and civil laws should conform, as far as possible, to the law of natural reason and equity."* [48]

---

## Summary: Natural Rights

We should always relay that our rights were not given to us by the Constitution; the government is not divine and did not grant them. They've existed since time immemorial; the purpose of our government was only implemented to preserve these rights. Unfortunately, the leviathan overgrew, those who wanted power preyed on the weak and began promising absolute security. The government, however, cannot give what it did not take; it is not a producer. It attempts to provide safety by taking the rights of others, like all government programs, it is grossly inefficient and ineffective; its history of failures is limitless.

> "False is the idea of utility that sacrifices a thousand real advantages for one imaginary or trifling inconvenience; that would take fire from men because it burns, and water because one may drown in it; that has no remedy for evils, except destruction. The laws that forbid the carrying of arms are laws of such a nature. They disarm those only who are neither inclined nor determined to commit crimes. Can it be supposed that those who have the courage to violate the most sacred laws of humanity, the most important of the code, will respect the less important and arbitrary ones, which can be violated with ease and impunity, and which, if strictly obeyed, would put an end to personal liberty - so dear to men, so dear to the enlightened legislator - and subject innocent persons to all the vexations that the quality alone ought to suffer? Such laws make things worse for the assaulted and better for the assailants; they serve rather to encourage than to prevent homicides, for an unarmed man may be attacked with greater confidence than an armed man. They ought to be designated as laws not preventive but fearful of crimes, produced by the tumultuous impression of a few isolated facts, and not by thoughtful consideration of the inconveniences and advantages of a universal decree."
> -Cesare Beccaria (1738-1794) [49]

> "law, like language, is (at least originally) not the product in general of an activity of public authorities

*aimed at producing it, nor in particular is it the product of positive legislation. It is, instead, the unintended result of a higher wisdom, of the historical development of the nations" Carl Menger* [50]

*"When we inquire, casting aside all theories and suppositions, into the end kept in view by legislators, or examine any existing laws, we find that the first and chief object proposed is to preserve the unconstrained dominion of law over the minds and bodies of mankind. It may be simplicity in me, but I protest that I see no anxiety to preserve the natural right of property but a great deal to enforce obedience to the legislator. No misery indeed is deemed too high a price to pay for his supremacy, and for the quiet submission of the people. To attain this end many individuals, and even nations, have been extirpated. Perish the people, but let the law live, has ever been the maxim of the masters of mankind. Cost what it may, we are continually told, the dominion of the law, not the natural right of property, must be upheld." -Thomas Hodgskin* [51]

*"Human behavior reveals uniformities which constitute natural laws. If these uniformities did not exist, then there would be neither social science nor political economy, and even the study of history would largely be useless. In effect, if the future actions of men having nothing in common with their past actions, our knowledge of them, although possibly satisfying our curiosity by way of an interesting story, would be entirely useless to us as a guide in life." -Vilfredo Pareto* [52]

*"Life, liberty, and property do not exist because men have made laws. On the contrary, it was the fact that life, liberty, and property existed beforehand that caused men to make laws in the first place."- Frederic Bastiat* [53]

# Section 2: The Constitution

The US constitution's first draft was in 1787 and finally ratified by all thirteen states by 1790. Written with the intent of strengthening the central government that men, like Alexander Hamilton, believed did not have enough power under their current Articles of Confederation.

To understand the Constitution, you must look at the ratifying debates, looking at only the articles of the Constitution or only the Bill of Rights will have you miss the context. It is important also to look at the three years of ratifying debates by the states. For example, why did Rhode Island hold out for so long, as the state only approved the US Constitution by two votes? And that was after the government threatened, they would be treated as a foreign power. Why were so many Virginians against the Constitution? If they could've voted to join the US, why couldn't they vote themselves out (e.g., the south seceding)? Why do the states have their own Constitutions and their own Bill of Rights, many of which also contain a right to bear arms?

## Why Should We Care?

If we are honest with ourselves, we can see the constitution has failed, as Lawrence Hunter points out:

> *"Americans tend to idolatrize the Constitution as sacred and infallible rather than recognizing it for the stumbling, trial-and-error experiment in self-government that it is, created by flawed human beings who acknowledged their frailties and never expected their experiment in constitutionalism to succeed. They were right; it has failed. The longer Americans remain in denial about this demonstrable fact and refuse to*

*think seriously about what to do about it, the more likely this constitutional failure will result in tyranny."* [54]

Or how Lysander Spooner put it:

*"But whether the Constitution really be one thing, or another, this much is certain - that it has either authorized such a government as we have had or has been powerless to prevent it. In either case it is unfit to exist."* [55]

After what I said at the end of our chapter on Natural Rights and our first paragraph, you may wonder, why should we even care about the Constitution? Well, for one, it is still a document that most of the population and politicians care about, at least they pretend they do. The Constitution seems like a nice reprieve from the tyranny we have currently. I am not much for lesser evils, but I doubt there will be much change to our country without first appealing to the Constitution to attempt to constrain the current government and then continue to limit it from there. Fighting for states' rights and using the 10th amendment which we will cover later is a good start.

Gun owners, constitutionalists, etc.… need to work with local governments to enact these changes at the lowest level. If you think this won't work, look at how liberals took over. They started in things like parent groups, community organizations, school boards, city councils, and formed into full-blown politicians. Look at Feinstein, Pelosi, Ocasio-Cortez, Sanders, Frederica Wilson, Warren, and countless others they started at the bottom, some as schoolteachers.

Lucas Botkin and T.Rex Arms (trex-arms.com) did just this and worked on local laws; they tested themselves to see how hard was it to lobby or enact legislation at the lowest level, the result was overturning an old Tennessee tax on ammunition. They document this whole process in a YouTube video [56], this is inspiring, and hopefully, we will see more of this.

Yes, that sounds like the cliché argument, "Don't like it; change it from the inside." I know, and I know we've seen this fail over and over, but at some point, you have to look at the options for change, in a Frederick Douglas pseudo scale, they range from the ballot box to the cartridge box. Unless you are ready to lock and load, then guess what, you'll have to care about the Constitution. While people say they are ready to Boogaloo the fact they haven't proves they are not.

## Bill of Rights

Patrick Henry was against the Constitution as he believed (and he was correct) that the Constitution gave the central government too much power over the states. His arguments were countered by the federalist assuring them that they would add a Bill of Rights once the Constitution passed.

In many ways, when it comes to the Bill of Rights, both the federalist and anti-federalist were right. The federalists believed that the Bill of Rights was not needed, as any power not explicitly granted to the federal government belonged to the state. They also thought that any list of rights could be seen as exhaustive, as if the Bill of Rights would be seen as the ONLY rights granted. Alexander Hamilton explains this in Federalist 84:

> *"I go further, and affirm that bills of rights, in the sense and in the extent in which they are contended for, are not only unnecessary in the proposed constitution, but would even be dangerous. They would contain various exceptions to powers which are not granted; and on this very account, would afford a colorable pretext to claim more than were granted. For why declare that things shall not be done which there is no power to do? Why for instance, should it be said, that the liberty of the press shall not be restrained, when no power is given by which restrictions may be imposed? I will not contend*

*that such a provision would confer a regulating power;*
*but it is evident that it would furnish, to men disposed to*
*usurp, a plausible pretense for claiming that power."*
[57]

Anti-federalists, however, still insisted on more precautions; they held that if it weren't written down, then the central government would be twisted into thinking it was fair game for them to control.

So again, who was right? Both. The anti-federalists believed we needed it to protect those rights from federal power, and they were right as people always claim their "1st amendment rights" or their "right to bear arms shall not be infringed!" Hint: you don't have a 1st amendment right or a 2nd amendment right, etc.... you have the right to free speech, you have the right to assemble, you have the right to bear arms. This is true without the Bill of Rights.

The federalists were right in their premonition as well; when we look at a common argument made by the ASDM, "the 2nd amendment doesn't cover_____." Of course, we know, it doesn't matter that it doesn't specifically say it, as it is not a list of enumerated rights, nor was that its purpose. As many of the founders said.

> *"In all societies, there are many powers and rights*
> *which cannot be particularly enumerated. A bill of rights*
> *annexed to a constitution is an enumeration of the*
> *powers reserved. If we attempt an enumeration,*
> *everything that is not enumerated is presumed to be*
> *given. The consequence is, that an imperfect*
> *enumeration would throw all implied power into the*
> *scale of the government, and the rights of the people*
> *would be rendered incomplete." - James Wilson of*
> *Pennsylvania* [58]

> *"But when it is evident that the exercise of any power*
> *not given up would be a usurpation, it would be not only*

*useless, but dangerous, to enumerate a number of rights which are not intended to be given up; because it would be implying, in the strongest manner, that every right not included in the exception might be impaired by the government without usurpation; and it would be impossible to enumerate every one. Let anyone make what collection of rights he pleases; I will immediately mention 20 or 30 more rights not contained in it." - James Iridell of North Carolina* [58]

*"My own opinion has always been in favor of a bill of right; provided it be so framed as not to imply powers not meant to be included in the enumeration." -Thomas Jefferson* [58]

Good time to point out the often-forgotten 9th amendment:

*The enumeration in the Constitution, of certain rights, shall not be construed to deny or disparage others retained by the people.* [59]

---

## Ratification

*"On every occasion [of Constitutional interpretation] let us carry ourselves back to the time when the Constitution was adopted, recollect the spirit manifested in the debates, and instead of trying [to force] what meaning may be squeezed out of the text, or invented against it, [instead let us] conform to the probable one in which it was passed." -Thomas Jefferson* [60]

For this topic, the central fact that we should see from these ratification debates was the intent of the states not to give more power to the central government than they alone possessed. James Madison, in federalist 39, attempted to assure the people that they would still be independent states:

> *"composing the distinct and independent States to which they respectively belong. It is to be the assent and ratification of the several States, derived from the supreme authority in each State, the authority of the people themselves. The act, therefore, establishing the Constitution, will not be a NATIONAL, but a FEDERAL act. That it will be a federal and not a national act, as these terms are understood by the objectors; the act of the people, as forming so many independent States, not as forming one aggregate nation...Each State, in ratifying the Constitution, is considered as a sovereign body, independent of all others, and only to be bound by its own voluntary act. In this relation, then, the new Constitution will, if established, be a FEDERAL, and not a NATIONAL constitution."* [61]

In 1783 British acknowledged the states were independent; they had 13 individual peace treaties. Given that each state had a constitution of its own also makes it clear that they viewed themselves as an independent. Also, look at the end of the Declaration of Independence:

> *"these united Colonies are, and of Right ought to be Free and Independent States, that they are Absolved from all Allegiance to the British Crown, and that all political connection between them and the State of Great Britain, is and ought to be totally dissolved; and that as Free and Independent States, they have full Power to levy War, conclude Peace, contract Alliances, establish Commerce, and to do all other Acts and things which Independent States may of right do."* [62]

The Bill of Rights also makes no mention of applying to the states. The preamble of the Bill of Rights focuses on the constitution and does not push itself on the individual states.

> *"The Conventions of a number of the States, having at the time of their adopting the Constitution, expressed a*

*desire, in order to prevent misconstruction or abuse of its powers, that further declaratory and restrictive clauses should be added: And as extending the ground of public confidence in the Government, will best ensure the beneficent ends of its institution."* [63]

We also have case law that we can look to such as Chief Justice John Marshall's opinion in Barron v. Baltimore 1833

*"The constitution was ordained and established by the people of the United States for themselves, for their own government, and not for the government of the individual states. Each state established a constitution for itself, and in that constitution, provided such limitations and restrictions on the powers of its particular government, as its judgment dictated. The people of the United States framed such a government for the United States as they supposed best adapted to their situation and best calculated to promote their interests. The powers they conferred on this government were to be exercised by itself; and the limitations on power, if expressed in general terms, are naturally, and, we think, necessarily, applicable to the government created by the instrument. They are limitations of power granted in the instrument itself; not of distinct governments, framed by different persons and for different purposes.*

*If these propositions be correct, the fifth amendment must be understood as restraining the power of the general government, not as applicable to the states. In their several constitutions, they have imposed such restrictions on their respective governments, as their own wisdom suggested, such as they deemed most proper for themselves. It is a subject on which they judge exclusively, and with which others interfere no further than they are supposed to have a common interest."* [64]

# Incorporation and Federal Control

> *"The Constitution of most of our states (and of the United States) assert that all power is inherent in the people; that they may exercise it by themselves; that it is their right and duty to be at all times armed." -Thomas Jefferson* [65]

It is unfortunate, but this topic is not usually covered when looking into gun rights, after all, most gun rights groups look to the federal government or a better term for today would be "National government" to act on the state legislature. It is hard to blame them since many gun owners in unfriendly states have found "success" by appealing to the supreme court. Our point in this section is to look at what cost those "successes" have had.

## *14th Amendment*

If you mention that the 2nd amendment does not apply to the states, you may come across the reply that the Bill of Rights does in fact apply to the states according to the 14th amendment. So, the question is, does the 14th amendment incorporate the Bill of Rights?

Before we go forward and answer that question, we need to lay more foundation and understand how we got the 14th amendment. The 14th amendment spawned from a post-civil war America, as Tom DiLorenzo explains:

> *"When a fair vote was taken on it in 1865, in the aftermath of the War for Southern Independence, it was rejected by the Southern states and all the border states. Failing to secure the necessary three-fourths of the states, the Republican party, which controlled Congress, passed the Reconstruction Act of 1867 which placed the entire South under military rule.*

*The purpose of this, according to one Republican congressman, was to coerce Southern legislators to vote for the amendment "at the point of a bayonet." President Andrew Johnson called this tactic "absolute despotism," the likes of which had not been exercised by any British monarch "for more than 500 years." For his outspokenness Johnson was impeached by the Republican Congress.*

*The South eventually voted to ratify the amendment, after which two Northern states-Ohio and New Jersey-withdrew support because of their disgust with Republican party tyranny. The Republicans just ignored this and declared the amendment valid despite their failure to secure the constitutionally-required three-fourths majority"* [66]

It was forced, unconstitutionally, but it is an amendment, now did it incorporate the Bill of Rights to the states? For this, we should look at what was said at the time; after all, this was a huge switch that would drastically reduce state sovereignty. If this were the case, then surely, they would have made the claim that the Bill of Rights now applies entirely to the states, but they did not, and subsequent cases since the 14th amendment was "passed" also say otherwise.

Starting with the Slaughterhouse case 1873, Associate Justice Samuel F. Miller, for the majority, declared that the 14th Amendment had "one pervading purpose," which was the protection of emancipated blacks [67]. The amendment did not shift control over all civil rights from the states to the federal government.

Chief Justice Waite in United States v. Cruikshank in 1875 decided:

*"The particular amendment now under consideration assumes the existence of the right of the people to assemble for lawful purposes and protects it against*

*encroachment by Congress. The right was not created by the amendment; neither was its continuance guaranteed, except as against congressional interference. For their protection in its enjoyment, therefore, the people must look to the States. The power for that purpose was originally placed there, and it has never been surrendered to the United States."* [68]

He continues:

*"The right there specified is that of 'bearing arms for a lawful purpose.' This is not a right granted by the Constitution. Neither is it in any manner dependent upon that instrument for its existence. The second amendment declares that it shall not be infringed; but this, as has been seen, means no more than that it shall not be infringed by Congress. This is one of the amendments that has no other effect than to restrict the powers of the national government"* [68]

In 1922 in Prudential Ins Co. v. Cheek the court ruled:

*"the federal constitution imposed no restriction on the states protective of freedom of speech, or liberty of silence, or the privacy of individuals or corporations."* [69]

Then just a few years later in 1925 Gitlow v. New York and then in 1927 Fiske v. Kansas, the courts started to rule that the federal constitution applied to the state. Then again in 1941 National Labor Relations Board v. Virginia Electric and Power. These were small potatoes however and never said the Bill of Rights were incorporated into the states.

Two decades later in Adamson v California 1947 with Justice Frankfurther concurrence:

*"Between the incorporation of the Fourteenth Amendment into the Constitution and the beginning of*

*the present membership of the Court -- a period of seventy years -- the scope of that Amendment was passed upon by forty-three judges. Of all these judges, only one, who may respectfully be called an eccentric exception, ever indicated the belief that the Fourteenth Amendment was a shorthand summary of the first eight Amendments theretofore limiting only the Federal Government, and that due process incorporated those eight Amendments as restrictions upon the powers of the States"* [70]

In the 1968 case Duncan v Louisiana Justice Harlan in his dissenting opinion wrote:

*"I believe I am correct in saying that every member of the Court for at least the last 135 years has agreed that our Founders did not consider the requirements of the Bill of Rights so fundamental that they should operate directly against the States. They were want to believe rather that the security of liberty in America rested primarily upon the dispersion of governmental power across a federal system. The Bill of Rights was considered unnecessary by some, but insisted upon by others in order to curb the possibility of abuse of power by the strong central government they were creating...A few members of the Court have taken the position that the intention of those who drafted the first section of the Fourteenth Amendment was simply, and exclusively, to make the provisions of the first eight Amendments applicable to state action. This view has never been accepted by this Court. In my view, often expressed elsewhere, the first section of the Fourteenth Amendment was meant neither to incorporate, nor to be limited to, the specific guarantees of the first eight Amendments. The overwhelming historical evidence marshalled by Professor Fairman demonstrates, to me conclusively, that the Congressmen and state legislators who wrote, debated, and ratified the Fourteenth*

*Amendment did not think they were "incorporating" the Bill of Rights"* [71]

Any idea of incorporation was struck down numerous times when the 14th amendment was ratified as well as multiple cases afterward were clear the rights were not incorporated. The fact that states Bills of Rights were still changed and updated after the 14th amendment was ratified should be clear enough that the states did not believe the 14th intended to incorporate the Bill of Rights. It wasn't until the 20th century that the courts started passing judgment that the Bill of Rights were incorporated. There was not an act of Congress that said The Bill of Rights was now incorporated; it was politically appointed judges that decided to rule that way. First, under Klan member and New Dealer, Justice Hugo Black appointed by Franklin D Roosevelt and then later pushed by Justice James Earl Warren. Most people know his name from the "Warren Commission" that investigated the assassination of JFK. It was this period in the Supreme Court that truly set a precedent for incorporation.

> *"This is what the Incorporation Doctrine has given us: in place of reservation of these areas of law to state governments for regulation via legislative elections, we get seizure of control over them by unelected, unaccountable, politically connected lawyers (that is, federal judges) who purport to substitute reason for the (one infers) unreasonable regulations crafted by elected officials…"* -Kevin Gutzman [72]

We are only scratching the surface of this topic, Legal Scholar Raoul Berger's book "Government by Judiciary: The Transformation of the Fourteenth Amendment" from 1977 destroys the idea that the fourteenth amendment incorporated the bill of rights including selective incorporation. Read the entire work here:

https://oll.libertyfund.org/titles/berger-government-by-judiciary-the-transformation-of-the-fourteenth-amendment

## McDonald v Chicago 2010

Much like the preceding and more popular case in 2008 DC v Heller, McDonald v Chicago is again regarding restrictions placed on handguns. In this case, the city of Chicago banned possession of a handgun. Otis McDonald sued the city of Chicago and initially lost in District Court. The court ruled that the Heller case did not issue an opinion on whether the 2nd amendment applied to the states.

When this case made it to the Supreme Court, McDonald won, the opinion further solidified the idea that the 2nd amendment was incorporated and affirmed the Bill of Rights applied to the states. As we've already covered, incorporating the Bill of Rights was never the intention of the 14th amendment. Lew Rockwell explains:

> *"The purpose of the Bill of Rights was to state very clearly and plainly what the Federal Government may not do. That's why they were attached to the Constitution. The states, under the influence of skeptics of the Constitution's limits on the central power, insisted that the restrictions on the government be spelled out. The Bill of Rights did not provide a mandate for what the Federal Government may do. You can argue all you want about the 14th amendment and due process. But a reading that says it magically transforms the whole Bill of Rights to mean the exact opposite of its original intent is pure fantasy"* [73]

### Supremacy Clause

> *"The Union was formed by the voluntary agreement of the States; and these, in uniting together, have not forfeited their Nationality, nor have they been reduced to the condition of one and the same people. If one of the States chose to withdraw its name from the contract, it would be difficult to disprove its right of doing so."*
> *-Alexis de Tocqueville* [74]

I'll be honest I didn't know where to bring this up, I almost waited until we cover the 10th amendment but it seems every time I talk about the Bill of Rights not applying to the states someone brings up the Supremacy Clause.

So first, what is the Supremacy Clause?

> *"This Constitution, and the Laws of the United States which shall be made in Pursuance thereof; and all Treaties made, or which shall be made, under the Authority of the United States, shall be the supreme Law of the Land; and the Judges in every State shall be bound thereby, any Thing in the Constitution or Laws of any State to the Contrary notwithstanding" -Article VI, Clause 2* [75]

Did you catch it? For the longest time I didn't. "In Pursuance thereof," as Michael Maharrey explains:

> *'The federal government can only assert supremacy when it takes an action in pursuance of the Constitution – in other words, when it exercises a constitutionally delegated power. And since the Constitution delegates very few powers to the general government it isn't supreme very often."* [76]

Good time to quote James Madison in Federalist 45:

> *"The powers delegated by the proposed Constitution to the federal government are few and defined. Those which are to remain in the State governments are numerous and indefinite. The former will be exercised principally on external objects, as war, peace, negotiation, and foreign commerce; with which last the power of taxation will, for the most part, be connected. The powers reserved to the several States will extend to all the objects which, in the ordinary course of affairs, concern the lives, liberties, and properties of the people,*

*and the internal order, improvement, and prosperity of the State."* [77]

And perhaps more aptly to the topic, Alexander Hamilton Federalist 33:

> *"If a number of political societies enter into a larger political society, the laws which the latter may enact, pursuant to the powers entrusted to it by its constitution, must necessarily be supreme over those societies, and the individuals of whom they are composed. It would otherwise be a mere treaty, dependent on the good faith of the parties, and not a government, which is only another word for POLITICAL POWER AND SUPREMACY. But it will not follow from this doctrine that acts of the large society which are NOT PURSUANT to its constitutional powers, but which are invasions of the residuary authorities of the smaller societies, will become the supreme law of the land. These will be merely acts of usurpation and will deserve to be treated as such. Hence, we perceive that the clause which declares the supremacy of the laws of the Union, like the one we have just before considered, only declares a truth, which flows immediately and necessarily from the institution of a federal government. It will not, I presume, have escaped observation, that it EXPRESSLY confines this supremacy to laws made PURSUANT TO THE CONSTITUTION."* [78]

Lastly from James Madison again in the Virginia Resolutions:

> *"The states, then, being the parties to the constitutional compact, and in their sovereign capacity, it follows of necessity that there can be no tribunal, above their authority, to decide, in the last resort, whether the compact made by them be violated; and consequently, that, as the parties to it, they must themselves decide, in the last resort, such questions as may be of sufficient magnitude to require their interposition."* [79]

I suggest reading Michael Maharrey's book "Constitution Owner's Manual" as it covers this topic more in depth.

*https://www.michaelmaharrey.com/books-by-michael/*

---

# The Second Amendment

> *"The right of a citizen to keep and bear arms has justly been considered the palladium of the liberties of a republic, since it offers a strong moral check against the usurpation and arbitrary power of rulers, and will generally, even if these are successful in the first instance, enable the people to resist and triumph over them."*
> —*Joseph Story, 1833* [80]

## *Meaning*

To explain the 2nd amendment, we are going to break it down, look at it through two different lenses Textualism and Originalism. While they are often mixed up, they are two different ways to look at the law. Textualist, such as Scalia and Justice Hugo Black that we mentioned earlier, believe the Constitution should be viewed through the plain meaning of the text, as Scalia puts it "it is the law that governs, not the intent of the lawgiver." [81] The other view is that of Originalism, which focuses on the original intent of the text. Since Textualism seems to be the more common view, we will start with that first.

## *Grammar*

> *"A well-regulated Militia, being necessary to the security of a free State, the right of the people to keep and bear Arms, shall not be infringed."* [82]

Perhaps a problem right off the bat with Textualism is the issues one faces with the plain reading of the text. If we focused only on intent, a comma would possibly not matter. I, for one, am not a grammatical expert, and wading into the different arguments made is a daunting task. Luckily author J. Neil Schulman worked smarter and not harder by contacting an absolute expert Professor Roy Copperud, who is on the usage panel of the American Heritage Dictionary, and Merriam Webster's Usage Dictionary. Schulman broke down the discussion for the New Gun Week and the 2nd Amendment Foundation 17 years before DC v Heller. The discussion is numbered by question to reduce confusion:

> [Schulman:] "(1) Can the sentence be interpreted to grant the right to keep and bear arms solely to 'a well-regulated militia'?"
> [Copperud:] "(1) The sentence does not restrict the right to keep and bear arms, nor does it state or imply possession of the right elsewhere or by others than the people; it simply makes a positive statement with respect to a right of the people."

> [Schulman:] "(2) Is 'the right of the people to keep and bear arms' granted by the words of the Second Amendment, or does the Second Amendment assume a preexisting right of the people to keep and bear arms, and merely state that such right 'shall not be infringed'?"
> Copperud:] "(2) The right is not granted by the amendment; its existence is assumed. The thrust of the sentence is that the right shall be preserved inviolate for the sake of ensuring a militia."

> [Schulman:] "(3) Is the right of the people to keep and bear arms conditioned upon whether or not a well-regulated militia, is, in fact necessary to the security of a free State, and if that condition is not existing, is the statement 'the right of the people to keep and bear Arms, shall not be infringed' null and void?"

[Copperud:] "(3) No such condition is expressed or implied. The right to keep and bear arms is not said by the amendment to depend on the existence of a militia. No condition is stated or implied as to the relation of the right to keep and bear arms and to the necessity of a well-regulated militia as a requisite to the security of a free state. The right to keep and bear arms is deemed unconditional by the entire sentence."

[Schulman:] "(4) Does the clause 'A well-regulated Militia, being necessary to the security of a free State,' grant a right to the government to place conditions on the 'right of the people to keep and bear arms,' or is such right deemed unconditional by the meaning of the entire sentence?"
[Copperud:] "(4) The right is assumed to exist and to be unconditional, as previously stated. It is invoked here specifically for the sake of the militia."

[Schulman:] "(5) Which of the following does the phrase 'well-regulated militia' mean: 'well-equipped', 'well-organized,' 'well-drilled,' 'well-educated,' or 'subject to regulations of a superior authority'?"
[Copperud:] "(5) The phrase means 'subject to regulations of a superior authority;' this accords with the desire of the writers for civilian control over the military."

[Schulman:] "(6) (If at all possible, I would ask you to take account the changed meanings of words, or usage, since that sentence was written 200 years ago, but not take into account historical interpretations of the intents of the authors, unless those issues can be clearly separated."
[Copperud:] "(6) To the best of my knowledge, there has been no change in the meaning of words or in usage that would affect the meaning of the amendment. If it were written today, it might be put: "Since a well-

regulated militia is necessary to the security of a free state, the right of the people to keep and bear arms shall not be abridged.'

In the case DC v Heller, the Supreme Court in its majority opinion shared some of the same conclusions as Copperud in that the right to bear arms was not contingent on the militia:

> *"There are a few examples, all of which favor viewing the right to "keep Arms' as an individual right unconnected with militia service...'Keep arms' was simply a common way of referring to possessing arms, for militiamen and everyone else...*
> *Every late-19th-century legal scholar that we have read interpreted the Second Amendment to secure an individual right unconnected with militia service."* [84]

and that the right to bear arms preexisted the 2nd amendment:

> *"It is dubious to rely on [the drafting] history to interpret a text that was widely understood to codify a pre-existing right, rather than to fashion a new one."* [84]

The 2$^{nd}$ amendment meant self-defense:

> *"Putting all of these textual elements together, we find that they guarantee the individual right to possess and carry weapons in case of confrontation."* [84]

and it was not meant for hunting:

> *"If "bear arms' means, as the petitioners and the dissent think, the carrying of arms only for military purposes, one simply cannot add "for the purpose of*

> *killing game.' The right "to carry arms in the militia for the purpose of killing game' is worthy of the mad hatter."* [84]

Also:

> *"The prefatory clause does not suggest that preserving the militia was the only reason Americans valued the ancient right; most undoubtedly thought it even more important for self-defense and hunting."* [84]

## *DC v Heller 2008*

Since DC v Heller focuses predominantly on the text of the 2nd amendment, it makes sense to cover this case here. The summary of the DC v Heller is that the District of Columbia had a handgun law that made it illegal to carry an unregistered handgun, and the only way to carry a firearm was through a one-year license that was only approved by the chief. It also required guns within the home to be disassembled and unloaded or locked up.

Dick Anthony Heller sued the District of Columbia, stating it violated his 2nd amendment rights. He later won the case, and since then, this case has been applauded by the gun community.

Essentially the Heller case ruled that the 2nd Amendment was unconnected to service in the militia and protected the individual right to bear arms for lawful purposes such as self-defense, and correctly called those laws unconstitutional. It did, however, leave the door open to further gun control as it decided the right to bear arms was not unlimited. Scalia acknowledges the rights to bear arms precedes the Constitution and says the right to bear arms shall not be infringed. This seems somewhat inconsistent, that a right cannot be infringed yet it can be regulated (what an interesting notion!).

As Attorney Suzanne Sherman points out:

> *"To claim a right is so sacred that the government may not infringe upon it, but to then say the government has the authority to regulate the very same right is inherently contradictory."* [85]

The realities of the Heller decision produce many problems; the main one is that it leaves the door wide open to government intervention and regulations. Scalia still believes that the government possesses the right to regulate firearms even though in his 64-page opinion he quotes St George Tucker:

> *"when the right of the people to keep and bear arms is, under any color or pretext whatsoever, prohibited, liberty, if not already annihilated, is on the brink of destruction."* [85]

There are other issues with Scalia's interpretation as well for instance:

> *"The term (arms) was applied, then as now, to weapons that were not specifically designed for military use and were not employed in a military capacity."* [84]

That is a ridiculous conclusion that cannot even be blamed on textualism. It is just an attempt to legislate from the bench. Just look at what we know from our section on the history of bearing arms, and you will see "arms" mean military-style rifles, and frankly, you only had one type of firearm at that time, no such thing as a "military-style" or a "deer rifle." James Madison knew this would happen and makes the case to interpret the constitution as it was ratified:

> *"I entirely concur in the propriety of resorting to the sense in which the Constitution was accepted and ratified by the nation. In that sense alone it is the legitimate Constitution. And it that be not the guide in expounding it, there can be no security for a consistent and stable, more than for a faithful exercise of its powers. If the meaning of the text be sought in the*

*changeable meaning of the words composing it, it is
evident that the shape and attributes of the Government
must partake of the changes to which the words and
phrases of all living languages are constantly subject.
What a metamorphosis would be produced in the code of
law if all its ancient phraseology were to be taken in its
modern sense."* [86]

Continuing with Scalia's opinion:

*"Read in isolation, Miller's phrase "part of ordinary
military equipment' could mean that only those
weapons useful in warfare are protected. That would be
a startling reading of the opinion, since it would mean
that the National Firearms Act's restrictions on
machineguns (not challenged in Miller) might be
unconstitutional, machineguns being useful in warfare
in 1939."* [84]

I find this to be quite amusing because he is clearly choosing an
outcome and then making the text fit; he might as well say, "The
NFA might be unconstitutional, no way that could be; therefore,
we must need to read the Miller decision differently." The
Miller case was never actually argued, the decision in that case
that a short-barrel shotgun was not a weapon used in warfare
was false and possibly if a defense attorney was there to make
the case, he could have shown that it was indeed a weapon in
military service. Furthermore, reading a phrase in isolation is a
poor way to deduce the intent. The court's opinion was clear,
although I disagree with its reading as well, the Miller opinion
was still based on military-style weapons:

*"The Constitution as originally adopted granted to the
Congress power "to provide for calling forth the Militia
(etc.) ..." With obvious purpose to assure the
continuation and render possible the effectiveness of
such forces the declaration and guarantee of the 2nd*

*amendment were made. It must be interpreted and
applied with that end in view.*

*The signification attributed to the term "militia"
appears from the debates in the Convention, the history
and legislation of the colonies and states, and the
writings of approved commentators. These show plainly
enough that the militia comprised all males physically
capable of acting in concert for the common defense ...
and further, that ordinarily when called for service
these men were expected to appear bearing arms
supplied by themselves and of the kind in common use
at the time."* [84]

Scalia continues to put his foot in his mouth regarding the
Miller case:

*"We therefore read Miller to say only that the 2nd
amendment does not protect those weapons not typically
possessed by law-abiding citizens for lawful purposes,
such as short-barreled shotguns... The handgun ban
amounts to a prohibition of an entire class of "arms'
that is overwhelmingly chosen by American society for
that lawful purpose. The prohibition extends, moreover,
to the home, where the need for defense of self, family,
and property is most acute. Under any of the standards
of scrutiny that we have applied to enumerated
constitutional rights, banning from the home "the most
preferred firearm in the nation to "keep' and use for
protection of one's home and family,' would fail
constitutional muster."* [84]

Currently, there are more military-style rifles in the US than
there were handguns at the time of the Miller case, does that
mean they are now in common usage by lawful citizens? Some
estimates put the current amount of AR15s in civilian hands
alone at 15 million, which sounds like a rather common firearm
used for the protection of one's home.

> *"We also recognize another important limitation on the right to keep and carry arms. Miller said, as we have explained, that the sorts of weapons protected were those "in common use at the time.' 307 U. S., at 179. We think that limitation is fairly supported by the historical tradition of prohibiting the carrying of "dangerous and unusual weapons."* [84]

The historical tradition in the United States was local city and state ordinances; they were not federal laws. Many of those laws, as we explain in our section on historical gun laws, were also overturned.

> *"Although we do not undertake an exhaustive historical analysis today of the full scope of the 2nd amendment, nothing in our opinion should be taken to cast doubt on longstanding prohibitions on the possession of firearms by felons and the mentally ill, or laws forbidding the carrying of firearms in sensitive places such as schools and government buildings, or laws imposing conditions and qualifications on the commercial sale of arms."* [84]

Longstanding is a stretch as any of those laws were not in place for the majority of our country's history, most are only around 50 years old. Again, it appears he starts with a conclusion and then reads that version into the text.

### *Individual vs Collective*

> *"There is the matter of the sort of freedom for which America stands. It is a freedom of individual men. It is a freedom of individual responsibility and individual rights. It abhors the collective, effete "safeties" of older, tired nations in which the people must be "protected" from themselves."* -Karl Hess [87]

I didn't want to take it for granted and merely imply that this right is individual and collective, so even though I see this as an uncommon argument, I want to explain this further by looking at some of the other amendments.

1st Amendment:

> *"Congress shall make no law respecting an establishment of religion or prohibiting the free exercise thereof; or abridging the freedom of speech, or of the press; or the right of the people peaceably to assemble, and to petition the Government for a redress of grievances."* [88]

4th Amendment:

> *"The right of the people to be secure in their persons, houses, papers, and effects, against unreasonable searches and seizures, shall not be violated, and no Warrants shall issue, but upon probable cause, supported by Oath or affirmation, and particularly describing the place to be searched, and the persons or things to be seized."* [89]

Both the 1st and the 4th Amendment include the same phrase as the 2nd *"the right of the people."* All the first ten amendments reference individuals, whether they be owner, person, accused, or just merely implied. They may reference the collective, but they also all imply an individual. If we take the view that the 2nd is only collective, then are we to assume that the 1st Amendment only means we have free speech when we are assembled? Do we only have the right from unreasonable searches when we are in a group; this of course is not the case and saying the 2nd is the only Amendment that is purely collective is just plain wrong.

Legal scholar David Vandercoy explains from Blackstone's commentary:

*"Blackstone described the right to keep arms as absolute or belonging to the individual, but ascribed both public and private purposes to the right. The public purpose was resistance to restrain the violence of oppression; the private was self-preservation. Blackstone described this right as necessary to secure the actual enjoyment of other rights which would otherwise be in vain if protected only by the dead letter of the laws."* [90]

## *History of Bearing Arms*

To get at the real meaning of the 2nd amendment, we must look at the history of bearing arms. The right to bear arms predates governments, as we explain in our chapter on Natural Law, self-defense is a Natural Right. In this section, we are moving past Natural Rights and going into when the "right to bear arms" was added to constitutions, articles, charters, etc...You may be thinking that the right to bear arms is unique to the US, but it does predate the 2nd amendment by centuries.

In his work Politics, Aristotle wrote in the 4th century BC, that the ownership of weapons was necessary for true citizenship and participation in the political system [91]. In around 44 BC Marcus Tullius Cicero in De Officiis wrote his support of bearing arms for self-defense of the individual and public defense against tyranny [92]. Centuries later, however, in the English Assize of Arms, we see our first glimpse at what would become an example for the right to bear arms. It was written and signed into law by King Henry II in 1181 this law permitted the carrying of arms in self-defense [93]. Its other purpose was to enable the creation of a militia when needed quickly; this is similar to a Fyrd in Anglo-Saxon England from around 605, a Fyrd being a militia agreement where free men in tribes could be called on for military service [94]. These tribes believed carrying arms was a right and a duty of free men. They believed it so much the ceremony for giving freedom to a former slave was that they were presented the arms of a "freeman."

The Assize or Arms spells out what each freeman should have at a minimum according to his rank, for example:

> *"Let every holder of a knight's fee have a hauberk, a helmet, a shield and a lance. And let every knight have as many hauberks, helmets, shields and lances, as he has knight's fees in his demise."* [93]

This is not unlike the Militia Act of 1792 and other state laws that required:

> *"A good musket, or fire lock, a sufficient bayonet and belt, two spare flints, knapsack, a pouch, proper powder and ball."* [95]

King Henry III expanded the Assize of Arms in 1253 to include everyone between 15 and 60 years old. He also made it mandatory that all *"citizens, burgesses, free tenants, villeins and others"* [96] be armed. As David T Hardy writes:

> *"Even the poorest classes of these were required to have a halberd (a pole arm with an axe and spike head) and a knife, plus a bow if they owned lands worth over two pounds sterling."* [97]

Edward III continued the tradition, and he required that his countrymen practiced archery routinely and required every town to have a range. Also mandating:

> *"every Englishman or Irishman dwelling in England must have a bow of his own height."* [98]

A longbow at the time would have been considered one of, if not the deadliest weapon. The longbow was such a superior weapon that bans in the 16th century on crossbows and firearms were not because of fear of those items. This ban was because the longbow was considered a much deadlier weapon, a more efficient weapon on the battlefield. The king did not want them to get out of practice with the longbow.

Under Queen Elizabeth, in the 16th century, we first see "Militia" used to describe the concept of a universally armed people ready to stand in defense of the nation. But from James I in 1567 to James II in 1685, Great Britain struggled through disarmament, military rule under Oliver Cromwell, and the rise of standing armies and the erosion of rights. However, after James II fled the continent, the Glorious Revolution resulted in the Declaration of Rights and the return of the right to bear arms.

The Declaration of Rights laid out the abuses of James II, one of which was keeping up standing armies and disarming the populace. During the discussions in the House of Commons, members specifically mention the seizing of private arms in the 1662 militia act as just one of many of their grievances. The final version of their right to bear arms reads as:

> *"The subjects which are Protestant may have arms for their defense suitable to their conditions and as allowed by law."* [99]

They were not saying only Protestants could possess arms; it's that Catholics were not disarmed and were already in possession of arms.

Granville Sharpe the English abolitionist summarizes the English stance on the right to bear arms when he explains:

> *"No Englishman can be truly loyal who opposed the principles of English law whereby the people are required to have arms of defense and peace, for mutual as well as private defense...The laws of England always required the people to be armed, and not only armed, but to be expert in arms."* [100]

Early Colonist held to the same beliefs towards militias. Like Edward III 300 years prior, Virginia required weekly military musters following church services:

> *"All men that are fitting to bear arms, shall bring their pieces to church."* [101]

Other colonies had similar laws like:

> *"Every free man or other inhabitant of this Colony provide for himself and each under him able to bear arms, a sufficient musket and other serviceable piece for war"* [102]

Notice "arms" are considered "pieces of war"

By the time the 2nd amendment came around eight states had their own constitutions that included a "right to bear arms." It was common sense that they were able to possess arms

> *"There are other things so clearly out of the power of Congress, that the bare recital of them is sufficient. I mean "rights of conscience, or religious liberty, the rights of bearing arms for defense, or for killing game, the liberty of fowling, hunting, and fishing."*
> *-Winchester Gazette 1788 (Virginia)* [103]

Another one of the reasons each state had these amendments was because of their stance on standing armies and militias.

### *Standing Armies*

Throughout the history of the right to bear arms, we see the "militia" and "standing armies" brought up over and over. Although militias are a common topic when discussing the 2nd amendment, standing armies are not. The reason we don't see this presented much maybe because so many gun owners are also fans of our vast military. For some reason the same people who like to bring up the founders in many other instances are completely quiet about standing armies - even when these standing armies mean an immense debt which the founders also warned about. It is quite incredible that it gets left out so much when the 2nd amendment has so much to do with countering a standing army.

Understanding the founders' view on standing armies is what is truly lacking in the 2nd amendment debate, it is such a large motive for it. There are lots of shallow answers given referencing British confiscation and revolting against a tyrannical government, even quotes such as:

> *"We should not forget that the spark which ignited the American Revolution was caused by the British attempt to confiscate the firearms of the colonists"*

This quote is attributed to Patrick Henry, even though we have no evidence he said this. We like it, though, because that is our answer and belief, but again it is so much more than just that.

The 2nd Amendment is the answer to a standing army that the founders warned. It targets Article 1 of the Constitution explicitly. "A Maryland Farmer," wrote in his essay on 29 Feb 1788 regarding the first article of the Constitution.

> *"It will be asked how has England preserved her liberties, with at least an apparent standing army?--I answer, she did lose them; but as there was no standing army until lately, she regained them again:--She lost them under the Tudors, who broke the then oppressive power of the aristocracy, but the unparalleled avarice of Henry VIIth, the boundless extravagance of Henry VIIIth, the short reign of Edward VIth, (which was but the sickly blaze of a dying candle) the bigotry of that weak woman Mary, who had no other object than religious persecution, and lastly the parsimony of Elizabeth, who had no children of her own to provide for, and who hated her legal successor and his family-- all conspired to prevent their establishing a military standing force, sufficient to secure their usurpations; and the nation recovered from their paroxysm under the*

*Stuarts, who were too weak and too wicked to command even respect, notwithstanding their dignity.--On the revolution in 1688, the patriots of that day formed some glorious bulwarks, which seem as yet to have secured them from the evils and danger of their present standing army, though still in my opinion, they hold their remaining liberties by a very precarious tenure indeed, as the first enterprising and popular Prince will most probably convince them."* [104]

"Glorious Bulwarks" is referencing the Declaration of Rights that gave English citizens the right to bear arms. In this letter, it is clear that John Francis Mercer (the probable real name of the Maryland farmer, who was part of the constitutional convention and an anti-federalist) is explicitly calling out the power of the government to create permanent standing armies. As this was before the bill of rights, his argument is they had no protection like the Brits. He continues to say:

*"In England, by their bill of rights, a standing army is declared to be contrary to their constitution, and a militia the only natural and safe defense of a free people--This keeps the jealousy of the nation constantly awake and has proved the foundation of all the other checks.*

*In the American constitution, there is no such declaration, or check at all"* [104]

As were many of the founders, he was worried about a standing army. Like the rest of the anti-federalists, he pushed the need for a bill of rights linking the protection against a standing army to the right to bear arms using state constitutions as examples:

*"For this I appeal to the constitutions of the several States.*

*In the declaration of rights of Massachusetts, sect. 17. -- The people have a right to keep and to bear arms for the common defense. And as in time of peace, armies are dangerous to liberty, they ought not to be maintained without the consent of the legislature, and the military power shall always be held in exact subordination to the civil authority and be governed by it."*

*"Declaration of rights of Pennsylvania, sect. 13.--That the people have a right to bear arms for the defense of themselves and the State; and as standing armies in the time of peace, are dangerous to liberty, they ought not to be kept up: And that the military should be kept under strict subordination to, and governed by civil power."*

*"Declaration of rights of Maryland* (as well as Delaware)*, sect. 25. --That a well-regulated militia is the proper and natural defense of a free government. Sect. 26. That standing armies are dangerous to liberty and ought not to be raised or kept without consent of the legislature."*

*"Declaration of rights of North-Carolina, sect. 17.-- That the people have a right to bear arms for the defense of the State; and as standing armies in time of peace are dangerous to liberty, they ought not to be kept up; and that the military should be kept under strict subordination to, and governed by the civil power."*
[104]

States knew the power of standing armies and rightly protected themselves, they did that through armed militias.

Virginia's ratifying debates on Article 1 were like that of A Maryland Farmer. George Mason during these debates explains:

*"Give me leave to recur to the page of history, to warn you of your present danger. Recollect the history of most nations of the world. What havoc, desolation, and destruction, have been perpetrated by standing armies! An instance within the memory of some of this house*

*will show us how our militia may be destroyed. Forty years ago, when the resolution of enslaving America was formed in Great Britain, the British Parliament was advised by an artful man, who was governor of Pennsylvania, to disarm the people; that it was the best and most effectual way to enslave them; but that they should not do it openly, but weaken them, and let them sink gradually, by totally dis-using and neglecting the militia."* [105]

The founders were not ignorant or shy when it came to explain their fears of a powerful central government, debt, and standing armies. They also were not without plenty of examples. Mason and the others had just fought a war for independence, and saw France working on a similar revolution, they knew of the history of England's revolution a hundred years prior. Mason links the two central premises of the 2nd amendment, self-defense, and defense against standing armies.

*"By these amendments I would give necessary powers, but no unnecessary power. If the clause stands as it is now, it will take from the state legislatures what divine Providence has given to every individual--the means of self-defense. Unless it be moderated in some degree, it will ruin us, and introduce a standing army."* [106]

Patrick Henry also expressed his disdain for standing armies and warned of their threat:

*"I was heard to say, a few days ago, that the sword and purse were the two great instruments of government; and I professed great repugnance at parting with the purse, without any control, to the proposed system of government. And now, when we proceed in this formidable compact, and come to the national defense, the sword, I am persuaded we ought to be still more cautious and circumspect; for I feel still more reluctance to surrender this most valuable of rights."* [107]

In this same debate on ratification in Virginia Henry points out the reason for the wording in the 2nd amendment as the answer to Article 1 of the constitution:

> *"But, says the honorable member, Congress will keep the militia armed; or, in other words, they will do their duty. Pardon me if I am too jealous and suspicious to confide in this remote possibility."* [107]

They did not want the federal government to disarm the militia once armed:

> *"The great object is, that every man be armed. But can the people afford to pay for double sets of arms? Everyone who is able may have a gun. But we have learned, by experience, that, necessary as it is to have arms, and though our Assembly has, by a succession of laws for many years, endeavored to have the militia completely armed, it is still far from being the case. When this power is given up to Congress without limitation or bounds, how will your militia be armed? You trust to chance; for sure I am that that nation which shall trust its liberties in other hands cannot long exist. If gentlemen are serious when they suppose a concurrent power, where can be the impolicy to amend it? Or, in other words, to say that Congress shall not arm or discipline them, till the states shall have refused or neglected to do it? This is my object. I only wish to bring it to what they themselves say is implied. Implication is to be the foundation of our civil liberties; and when you speak of arming the militia by a concurrence of power, you use implication. But implication will not save you, when a strong army of veterans comes upon you. You would be laughed at by the whole world, for trusting your safety implicitly to implication."* [107]

In debates, letters, and newspapers, we see over and over that the 2ⁿᵈ amendment was for self-defense and an answer to standing armies that would be the destruction of liberties because of military power and the debt that comes with standing armies. James Madison, the author of the 2ⁿᵈ amendment, explained during the constitution convention 1787:

> *"A standing military force, with an overgrown Executive will not long be safe companions to liberty. The means of defense against. foreign danger have been always the instruments of tyranny at home. Among the Romans it was a standing maxim to excite a war, whenever a revolt was apprehended. Throughout all Europe, the armies kept up under the pretext of defending, have enslaved the people."* [108]

Then writing Federalist 46 in 1788:

> *"the greatest danger to liberty is from large standing armies, it is best to prevent them, by an effectual provision for a good militia."* [109]

Tench Coxe in Philadelphia Gazette writing under the pseudonym "A Pennsylvanian" in 1789:

> *"As civil rulers, not having their duty to the people duly before them, may attempt to tyrannize, and as the military forces which must be occasionally raised to defend our country, might pervert their power to the injury of their fellow citizens, the people are confirmed by the article in their right to keep and bear their private arms."* [110]

Later maintained this belief writing in "Political Observations" 1795:

> *"Of all the enemies to public liberty war is, perhaps, the most to be dreaded, because it comprises and develops the germ of every other. War is the parent of armies;*

*from these proceed debts and taxes; and armies, and debts, and taxes are the known instruments for bringing the many under the domination of the few. In war, too, the discretionary power of the Executive is extended; it's influence in dealing out offices, honors, and emoluments is multiplied; and all the means of seducing the minds, are added to those of subduing the force, of the people. The same malignant aspect in republicanism may be traced in the inequality of fortunes, and the opportunities of fraud, growing out of a state of war, and in the degeneracy of manners and of morals engendered by both. No nation could preserve its freedom in the midst of continual warfare."* [111]

Other pivotal leaders and authors maintained the same belief that standing armies were dangerous, and the people should retain their right to arms. George Tucker in Blackstone's Commentaries on the Laws of England written in 1768:

*"Wherever standing armies are kept up, and when the right of the people to keep and bear arms is, under any color or pretext whatsoever, prohibited, liberty, if not already annihilated, is on the brink of destruction."* [99]

Samuel Adams in 1776:

*"A standing Army, however necessary it may be at some times, is always dangerous to the Liberties of the People.... Such a Power should be watched with a jealous eye."* [112]

Noah Webster 1787:

*"Before a standing army can rule, the people must be disarmed as they are in almost every kingdom of Europe. The supreme power in America cannot enforce unjust laws by sword; because the whole body of the people are armed and constitute a force superior to any*

*bands of regular troops than can be, on any pretense, raised in the United States."* [113]

Brutus in 1788:

> *"The liberties of a people are in danger from a large standing army, not only because the rulers may employ them for the purposes of supporting themselves in any usurpations of power, which they may see proper to exercise, but there is great hazard, that an army will subvert the forms of the government, under whose authority, they are raised, and establish one, according to the pleasure of their leader."* [114]

Going further back in Nicholas Machiavelli's Art of War in 1532:

> *"That a prince who relies upon mercenaries must either remain embroiled in wars, or risk overthrow when the mercenaries became unemployed with the advent of peace."* [115]

George Nicholas didn't even believe the constitution would pass, a standing army was the only mode of defense and he debated over the best way to secure the country:

> *"One of three ways must be pursued for this purpose. We must either empower them to employ, and rely altogether on, a standing army; or depend altogether on militia; or else we must enable them to use the one or the other of these two ways, as may be found most expedient. The least reflection will satisfy us that the Convention has adopted the only proper method. If a standing army were alone to be employed, such an army must be kept up in time of peace as would be sufficient in war. The dangers of such an army are so striking that every man would oppose the adoption of this government, had it been proposed by it as the only mode*

*of defense. Would it be safe to depend on militia alone, without the agency of regular forces, even in time of war? Were we to be invaded by a powerful, disciplined army, should we be safe with militia? Could men unacquainted with the hardships, and unskilled in the discipline of war, --men only inured to the peaceable occupations of domestic life, --encounter with success the most skillful veterans, inured to the fatigues and toils of campaigns? Although some people are pleased with the theory of reliance on militia, as the sole defense of a nation, yet I think it will be found, in practice, to be by no means adequate."* [116]

One alternative to a standing army was a select militia.

### *National Guard*

Currently, the select militia is the National Guard. Many ASDM'ers like to say the National Guard removes the need for the 2nd amendment. The two problems with that idea are that the 2nd amendment is also a protection of an individual right not dependent on a militia clause and the National Guard doesn't replace anything except the militia act of 1792. The 1903 militia act distinguishes between two different militias.

> *"The militia shall consist of every able-bodied male citizen of the respective States, Territories, and the District of Columbia, and every able-bodied male of foreign birth who has declared his intention to become a citizen, who is more than eighteen and less than forty-five years of age, and shall be divided into two classes- the organized militia, to be known as the National Guard of the State, Territory, or District of Columbia, or by such other designations as may be given them by the laws of the respective States or Territories, and the remainder to be known as the Reserve Militia."* [117]

So, you have the organized militia, which is the National Guard and the unorganized militia, which is able-bodied men that are not in the National Guard. The founders warned about select militias as well, Richard Henry Lee in "Federal Farmer."

> *"First, the constitution ought to secure a genuine and guard against a select militia, by providing that the militia shall always be kept well organized, armed, and disciplined, and include, according to the past and general usage of the states, all men capable of bearing arms"* [118]

John Smiley also warned about a select militia during the Pennsylvania ratifying convention:

> *"Congress may give us a select militia which will, in fact, be a standing army.... When a select militia is formed, the people in general may be disarmed."* [119]

Smiley did not just imagine something that "could" happen; he is speaking of history. In the British militia act of 1662, the select militia was able to disarm anyone "judged dangerous to the peace of the kingdom." [120] Then In 1671, parliament strengthened their ability to disarm non-landowners with the Hunting Act. So, Smiley was pretty accurate.

But whether they are a select militia or just an extension of a standing army is really beside the point. What they are not, is much more important; they are not the militia as pointed out by the Senate Subcommittee on the Right to Bear Arms:

> *"These commentators contend instead that the amendment's preamble regarding the necessity of a "well regulated militia . . . to a free state" means that the right to keep and bear arms applies only to a National Guard. Such a reading fails to note that the Framers used the term "militia" to relate to every citizen capable of bearing arms, and that Congress has established the present National Guard under its power to raise armies, expressly stating that it was not doing so under its power to organize and arm the militia."* [121]

## Militia

So, who is the militia if not the National Guard? George Mason said:

> *"It is the whole people, except for few public officials"* [122]

Tenche Coxe posed it like this:

> *"Who are the militia? Are they not ourselves? Is it feared, then, that we shall turn our arms each man against his own bosom? Congress have no power to disarm the militia. Their swords, and every other terrible implement of the soldier, are the birthright of an American... The unlimited power of the sword is not in the hands of either the federal or state governments, but, where I trust in God it will ever remain, in the hands of the people."* [110]

Richard Henry Lee said the militia is:

> *"A militia, when properly formed, are in fact the people themselves...and include all men capable of bearing arms."* [118]

What is the militia for?

> *"It is to prevent the establishment of a standing army, the bane of liberty. ...Whenever Governments mean to invade the rights and liberties of the people, they always attempt to destroy the militia, in order to raise an army upon their ruins."*
> -Elbridge Gerry, Fifth Vice President of the United States [123]

*"The militia, sir, is our ultimate safety. We can have no security without it."*
-*Patrick Henry* [124]

The armed populace/ militia was the defense against a standing army:

> *"...that standing army can never be formidable to the liberties of the people, while there is a large body of citizens, little if at all inferior to them in the use of arms."* -*Alexander Hamilton, Federalist Paper #29* [125]

Some in the ASDM camp that try to argue against the militia by downplaying its power by using the words of George Washington:

> *"The militia was lazy, it would not obey orders, and it showed scant respect for its officers.* [126]

First off, as a prior NCO in the military, the standing army has plenty of lazy people that will not obey orders and do not show respect to officers, so not much of an argument. What Washington's real issue was with the militia is the great strength of the militia. The militia full of regular citizens did not want to participate in aggressive campaigns; they were not invaders; they were not looking to join in offensive battles of conquest. Cato's Letters reverses the argument against the militia and instead describes the weakness of standing armies and the strength of an armed populace:

> *"When a Tyrant's Army is beaten, his Country is conquered: He has no Resource; his Subjects having neither Arms...nor Reason to fight for him. And therefore, it is fit that Mankind should know...that his Majesty can be defended against them...without Standing Armies; which would make him formidable only to his People...*

*When the People are easy and satisfied, the whole Kingdom is the King's Army."* [127]

For decades most gun owners have tried to distance them from the term "militia" my assumption is that the distancing increased significantly after the Oklahoma City bombing. Militia groups themselves even try to distance themselves from the word; some even call themselves "home guards," which is a term for a volunteer force. I understand their reasoning and see how the media demonizes the word "militia." Even the federal government and the Department of Homeland defense have demonized the term, but we will cover that later. [128]

The point being is that we shouldn't have left the term behind or let it become taboo. We are all part of the militia. When we turned from that belief is when we saw the newest attacks against the 2nd amendment. Our abandonment and creating a taboo of the term is also why so many are confused as to its original intent.

Furthermore, what the founders' thought would be an issue, training the militia, is a non-issue. There are trainers in every state and ranges in most cities. The citizen militia is better trained and better equipped than it probably ever has been.

So now the question is, is this militia and the 2nd amendment still relevant?

## *2nd Amendment Still Relevant?*

To answer this, we can be boil it down into three sections: National defense, defense against tyranny, and self-defense.

### *National defense*

If we took the every-other country in the world and looked at their military budget, the US military would make up 37% of that figure. [129] We spend as much on our military as the next seven combined, and that's just the department of defense spending, not CIA and this does not include aid that goes to foreign armies, and it certainly isn't accounting for unfunded liabilities. [130] As of 2017, we have around 157 bombers, 637 drones, 3,476 tactical aircraft, 760 attack helicopters, 2,831 tanks, 93 cruisers and destroyers, ten aircraft carriers, 68 submarines, and last but not least almost 5,000 nukes. [131] When it comes to manpower, we are third after China and India, with 1.3 million troops. [132] Two hundred thousand of those troops are spread out in 170 countries spanning approximately 800 bases. [133]

Running through those figures, you may think there is no reason for a militia, well I disagree. All the people, bases, and equipment I just listed cost money, the money of which the US government is quickly racking up. Just think the pentagon has only been audited once in its entire history, it failed spectacularly [134]; by the way, the audit alone cost 400 million dollars. [135] It's no wonder Thomas Jefferson said:

> *"I sincerely believe... that banking establishments are more dangerous than standing armies. "* [136]

Eventually, the still never audited, Federal Reserve will have to stop printing money and stop manipulating interest rates. At that time, the military isn't going to be able to sustain itself; this is an apparent vulnerability that the militias are immune to since they would not be fighting for money they would be fighting for their freedom and existence. If it were me, I wouldn't want to disarm the last real line of defense against an invading force.

I know some use Isoroku Yamamoto, the Japanese Admiral during WWII as an example of the armed populace in America being a defense against invasion. Even Remington used it in their adds for the Remington 700:

> *"You cannot invade the mainland United States. There*
> *would be a rifle behind every blade of grass"*

And although there is no actual proof that he himself said it, the quote was from that era and rings true. After all William Pitt did say something similar to Isoroku's quote

> *"If I were and American as I am an Englishman, while*
> *a foreign troop was landed in my country, I never would*
> *lay down my arms, never, never, never! You cannot*
> *conquer America!"* [137]

## *Defense against tyranny*

> *"To be sure, it was the "idea" of freedom that inflamed*
> *the colonies against a foreign ruler. But it was the long*
> *rifle, lovingly bored at Pennsylvania forges,*
> *and skillfully carried into the central woodlands, that*
> *brought freedom to America...*
> *Freedom is never thought into existence. It is fought*
> *into existence"* -Karl Hess [87]

A good indicator that politicians are indeed fearful of an armed populace is the lack of large gun control bills passed. They seem to do this little by little, like they do everything else, except for spend money. It is the soft despotism Tocqueville wrote about:

> *"After having thus taken each individual one by one into*
> *its powerful hands, and having molded him as it pleases,*
> *the sovereign power extends its arms over the entire*
> *society; it covers the surface of society with a network of*
> *small, complicated, minute, and uniform rules, which the*
> *most original minds and the most vigorous souls cannot*
> *break through to go beyond the crowd; it does not break*
> *wills, but it softens them, bends them and directs them; it*
> *rarely forces action, but it constantly opposes your*
> *acting; it does not destroy, it prevents birth; it does not*
> *tyrannize, it hinders, it represses, it enervates, it*
> *extinguishes, it stupefies, and finally it reduces each*

*nation to being nothing more than a flock of timid and*
*industrious animals, of which the government is the*
*shepherd.*
*I have always believed that this sort of servitude,*
*regulated, mild and peaceful, of which I have just done*
*the portrait, could be combined better than we imagine*
*with some of the external forms of liberty, and that it*
*would not be impossible for it to be established in the*
*very shadow of the sovereignty of the people."* [138]

The political power brokers must always be worried that their
actions could spawn real rebellion. Just look at Hong Kong as I
write this in 2019, imagine if they had the guns. They even had
signs saying they want a 2nd amendment of their own. [139]
Imagine if they took to the streets armed with firearms instead
of with umbrellas, or look at France, imagine if they had
firearms to go with their yellow vests, they should've known
better than to let themselves be disarmed.

> *"If the representatives of the people betray their*
> *constituents, there is then no resource left but in the*
> *exertion of that original right of self-defense which is*
> *paramount to all positive forms of government, and*
> *which against the usurpations of the national rulers, may*
> *be exerted with infinitely better prospect of success than*
> *against those of the rulers of an individual state. In a*
> *single state, if the persons intrusted with supreme power*
> *become usurpers, the different parcels, subdivisions, or*
> *districts of which it consists, having no distinct*
> *government in each, can take no regular measures for*
> *defense. The citizens must rush tumultuously to arms,*
> *without concert, without system, without resource;*
> *except in their courage and despair."*
> *- Alexander Hamilton, Federalist No. 28* [140]

Now, look at America. The armed populace is rather quiet; they
show up to a few organized events and marches. My opinion as
to why there are not more people showing up to these marches

is that gun owners believe, that since it's their right and supposedly protected by the Constitution, they don't have to go out and fight for it. They think that if someone comes to their door to take their guns, then they will fight, not realizing they will be just a small blip in the local newspaper, and it won't rally anyone to help you.

That's not to say gun owners have never attempted to flex on the government. Shay's Rebellion, Whiskey Rebellion, Frie's Rebellion, even Jon Brown trying to arm and free slaves, one recent example is the Bundy Ranch standoff in 2014 that drew around 5,000 armed individuals and consisted of numerous militias. You can read more about what lead up to this elsewhere, but eventually, the government wasn't willing to replay Waco or Ruby Ridge and finally gave up the armed conflict. They then went after a few of those individuals using the courts, but few served jail time. Oddly enough, they could inspire 5,000 people to come from around the United States to protect this farmer and his cattle but couldn't get anyone to show up to protest these court hearings. Of course, the second "Bundy Standoff" at the Bureau of Land Management in Oregon went a little different at that time; no one showed up, and Lavoy Finicum was murdered by the FBI. [141]

A couple of interesting things from those court hearings are the charges that were presented. [142] Perhaps this is why no one wants to organize an armed standoff.

> -conspiracy to impede federal officers
> -interstate travel in aid of extortion

Before this in 2012, Schaeffer Cox of Alaska was shipped to Washington state for trial and then imprisoned in Indiana. Courts in Alaska would not prosecute the bogus charges levied against him and more than likely did not want to deal with the possibility of an armed uprising. [143]
What I am saying is that the government seemed to learn from the public relations nightmares that were Waco and Ruby Ridge and realized their better course of action is to take them and all

their friends to court. It is why Jury Nullification is such an important component and has been throughout the history of this country — Theophilus Parson's in the Massachusetts ratification debates in 1788:

> *"But, sir, the people themselves have it in their power effectually to resist usurpation, without being driven to an appeal of arms. An act of usurpation is not obligatory; it is not law; and any man may be justified in his resistance. Let him be considered as a criminal by the general government, yet only his fellow-citizens can convict him; they are his jury, and if they pronounce him innocent, not all the powers of Congress can hurt him; and innocent they certainly will pronounce him, if the supposed law he resisted was an act of usurpation."*
> [144]

Athens, Tennessee, is another example cited as the need for an armed civilian population. The battle of Athens in 1946 is an excellent example of civilians attempting to vote and work within the system but terrorized by local politicians and law enforcement. The result was the returning WWII veterans taking up arms against the local sheriff that, amongst other things, was rigging the election. The veterans armed themselves by breaking into a national guard armory and used dynamite along with Molotov cocktails. They eventually took over the jail; the local government was forced to disband and was replaced.

These are just some examples, the battle of Athens was a win, but both Bundy standoffs were somewhat of a mix. Neither, however, answer the statement on how a militia could stand up against a more advanced fighting force like the US military. The obvious answer to this is that we are almost at 20 years fighting in Afghanistan against basically a militia force, which at its height had 60,000 members. That fighting force is nothing numerically to the armed citizens in America.

Consider just a birds-eye view of the numbers. If an unrealistic 99% of gun owners disarmed and turned in 99% of their weapons, you'd still have 3.9 million firearms in the hands of 1.7 million civilians. [145] Compare that to around 1.3 million active-duty military members, [129] 120,000 federal agents, [146] and 750,000 local law enforcement officials. [147] Of course, they would never be able to get 99% of gun owners to comply especially when you look at compliance rates around the country. Only 3% of Californians registered their "assault weapons" [148] the NY safe act resulted in around 4% compliance. [149] When New Jersey banned 30 round magazines, and so far no one showed up to turn any in. [150]

Now look at the active-duty military and ask yourself how many are going to support attacking Americans? There are plenty that are ate-up and will blindly follow orders, but a lot of those military guys are the gun nuts, a conservative estimate is that you'd lose 10% right off the bat of military members switching sides. Then imagine all the military members who only serve in a support capacity, I doubt dental or protocol will be showing up on the front line.

This fight isn't Afghanistan or Iraq, where the military can call in airstrikes on civilians. It isn't a far-off place where you are generally safe on base, and your family is safe thousands of miles away. You can't go out, kill some gun owners, and then casually go back to base and expect to live normally. As Larry Correia puts it:

> "The confiscators don't live on base. They live in apartment complexes and houses in the suburbs next door to the people you expect them to murder. Every time they go out to kick in some redneck's door, their convoy is moving through an area with lots of angry people who shoot small animals from far away for fun, and the only thing they remember about chemistry is the formula for Tannerite." [151]

The fight isn't the civil war where there was a distinct line; this would be government officials attacking neighbors. You will quickly lose the support of even the anti-gun crowd when you drag innocent people out of their homes because they won't give in, and you will only strengthen the resolve of the resistance. So no, the military is not so powerful that it renders the 2$^{nd}$ amendment obsolete.

The real issue is not a military force or door to door confiscation; the real problem is the slow decay; this is why I keep referring to Soft Despotism the term coined by Alex de Tocqueville. A common analogy for this is the boiling frog metaphor; the idea is that if you put a frog into boiling water, he will immediately fight and attempt to jump out, but if you put that frog in lukewarm water and gradually increase the heat, the frog will not perceive the threat until it is too late. I like how Dodge Watterson puts it

> *"It seems we have the ability and the tendency to suffer infringements on rights so long as the suffering can be made comfortable."*

Soft despotism is what the real threat to gun rights and other liberties are, the slow change. It would be rather easy to gain support or come together when there is a sizeable immediate threat, but now imagine the scenario that Child Protective Services threatens to take your kids away. In the media, it will be "Children Removed from Right-Wing Extremist Home" it will be played down like you were dangerous, so other gun guys will accept it was a one-off, or maybe it needed to happen, perhaps you were dangerous. While you can make an excellent argument to shoot other armed individuals attempting to steal your property, how will it look if you attack a "lowly CPS agent just trying to do her job?" We see this propaganda play out all the time on atrocities played in favor of the government by the corporate press.

This part tends to get conspiratorial, but we know the NSA collects data through google, Facebook, and Instagram, [152] they may have a more detailed inventory of your firearms than you do.

What happens when they don't go through the pain of collecting firearms from gun owners and instead freeze your accounts somewhat like what they attempted to do through Operation Chokepoint. [153] What if they destroy your credit like the Social Credit system they are implementing in China? [154] Will it just be that you are denied homeowner's insurance or health insurance if you do not comply?

Just look at civil asset forfeiture [155], will they take everything they can from you? Think about this, the department of justice demanded the release of everyone who downloaded American Technologies Network (ATN) gun scope app because they said they were investigating possible breaches of weapon export regulations. [156]

To summarize, the Militia could take on a sizeable imposing force, but a community that is not united and believes that what happens to others in that same community will not affect them cannot stand; this section may sound extremist but in the words of Barry Goldwater

> *"I would remind you that extremism in the defense of liberty is no vice! And let me remind you also that moderation in the pursuit of justice is no virtue!* [157]

For more information:
- The Bear Went Over the Mountain: Soviet Combat Tactics in Afghanistan - the Soviet viewpoint
- The Other Side of the Mountain: Mujahideen Tactics in the Soviet-Afghan War - the CIA and Afghan viewpoint
- Victory Has a Thousand Fathers: Sources of Success in Counterinsurgency https://www.rand.org/content/dam/rand/pubs/monographs/2010/RAND_MG964.pdf
- The Sling and the Stone
- David Kilcullen also has a million books on the topic.

## Self defense

Possibly the main argument against the individual right to own firearms is that it is no longer needed because we have the police, we cover this in length later. Instead, let's look at groups that had to take up arms because no one else was or is protecting them.

The Deacons for Defense and Justice (DDJ) [158] was an African American group that founded in 1964, just two years before the Black Panthers. The Deacons intended to provide armed protection for civil rights activists and their families. These were people in places like Alabama, Mississippi, and Louisiana that could not go to the police as many of them participated in Klan activities. Even the FBI targeted and harassed groups like the DDJ.

As I said, the DDJ was founded just a few years before Huey P Newton, and Bobby Seale formed the Black Panther Party, originally named "the Black Panther Party for Self-Defense." [159]

While Marxism greatly influenced Huey and Seale's ideas, their idea to protect other African Americans from police brutality by arming themselves and following cop cars on their patrol was innovative for the time. I'm sure some will read this and think they were just black extremists, but groups in rural Alaska and places like Montana have implemented the "liberty bell" system which is similar to what the panthers were doing.

One last thing to mention about the Black Panthers, and that is the bipartisan effort to expand gun control when blacks are involved. In the case of the Black Panthers, it was specifically Republican (Governor at the time) Ronald Reagan who called for gun control after the panthers staged a protest [160]. I bring this up because so many want to point the finger at one party when in reality it has been both parties that have pushed and passed gun control.

Fast forward to 1992, much like what spawned the formation of the DDJ and Panthers, Los Angeles erupts in violence following the Acquittal of several police officers in the beating of Rodney King. It's almost as if this has been a trend since Crispus Attucks. This time the group that stood up together was who we now refer to as "Rooftop Koreans." The LA riots resulted in widespread rioting that killed more than 50 people, injured more than 1,000 and caused around $1 billion in damage, much of that damage was sustained by Korean owned businesses

While the rioting, looting, and arson happened right in front of them, they were helpless, and as many recalled, they didn't see any police in the area for days. The law enforcement they saw on the television were merely containing the violence to their city, a small barricade, or wall. Their only option was to take up arms and protect their families and what they could of their businesses.

Retired Army infantry Colonel and attorney Kurt Schlichter who deployed as part of his National Guard unit explains the reality:

> *"See, the dirty little secret of civilization is that it's designed to maintain order when 99.9% of folks are orderly. But, say, if just 2% of folks stop playing by the rules...uh oh. Say LA's population was 15 million in 1992...that's 300,000 bad guys. There were maybe 20,000 cops in all the area agencies then, plus 20,000 National Guard soldiers and airman, plus another 10,000 active soldiers and Marines the feds brought in. Law enforcement is based on the concept that most people will behave and that the crooks will be overwhelmed by sheer numbers of officers."* [161]

Schlichter points out the obvious, cops cannot, and sometimes will not be there to help you. The "Rooftop Koreans" knew this instantly and took responsibility for their families and businesses.

It doesn't end there with groups like this. Google search for "armed citizen patrols" will give you numerous examples of citizens policing their neighborhoods.

When we get down to individual self-defense, the stories become overwhelming 12yr olds defending their homes with ARs, single moms, dads, grandmas, grandpas, and everyone in between. It happens all the time, of course, the ASDM downplay this which is so fascinating to me that you can point to statistics that show guns are used in self-defense more often than used in a murder and yet they don't want to hear it, almost like they have an agenda.

Gifford's ASDM group will say the numbers have been debunked, of course, they say that arguing from their own debunked studies. So, the hard part is figuring out how often they are used in self-defense. The numbers range from 65,000 to 2.5 million, quite a spread I'd say, but take the lower amount 65,000 that's a ton of self-defense cases surely that's enough to prove our point. If someone says that small figure is still too much, then cut that in half, would 32,500 be enough. That's 32,500 people who couldn't wait for the police, that's 32,500 would be assaults, rapes, murders, robberies.

What I am confused about is a group (the ASDM) that is continually arguing for legislation after mass shootings, which in 2019 have killed 517 people, but are against 32,500 people defending themselves with firearms. Even in a pragmatic or utilitarian view the 32,500 seems like a greater number than 517.

Since some have claimed that armed self-defense is uncommon and much less than the number I presented previously, we look to the CDC. In 2013 the CDC and the National Academies' Institute of Medicine and National Research Council concluded:

> "defensive gun used by crime victims is a common occurrence" [162]

Further saying:

> *Almost all national survey estimates indicate that defensive gun uses by victims are at least as common as offensive uses by criminals, with estimates of annual uses ranging from about 500,000 to more than 3 million, in the context of about 300,000 violent crimes involving firearms in 2008.* [162]

It's a joke to say, "God made man, Sam Colt made them equal," but it's one of those where you say, "funny because it's true." The kid standing up to multiple burglars had no chance. The people who had been beaten numerous times by their partners and couldn't defend themselves with their own hands, or the 125lb chick walking to her car in a dark parking garage, they do not have a chance without an equalizer or a force multiplier. We use adages like "don't bring a knife to a gunfight" for the obvious reason that a knife doesn't beat a gun. In the same way, don't bring 125lbs to a 300lb fight.

So no, the 2nd amendment is not obsolete in any way, shape, or form. The right the 2nd amendment intends on protecting is timeless; its faults have come from its underutilization.

# Regulation

> *"They (the general government) cannot interfere with the opening of rivers and canals; the making or regulation of roads, except post roads; building bridges; erecting ferries; establishment of state seminaries of learning libraries; literary, religious, trading or manufacturing societies; erecting or regulating the police of cities, towns or boroughs; creating new state offices, building light houses, public wharves, county jails, markets, or other public buildings making sale of state lands, and other state property; receiving or appropriating the incomes of state buildings, and*

*property; executing the state laws; altering the criminal law; nor can they do any other matter or thing appertaining to the internal affairs of any state, whether legislative, executive or judicial, civil or ecclesiastical."*
*-James Madison Federalist 45* [163]

Currently firearms are regulated in this country under the idea that is falls under interstate commerce, and in the case of firearms interstate commerce is regulated by the ATF.

### *Interstate Commerce*

As with every topic, it would seem that a backstory or a caveat has to be added before we can move on. Since we are covering the ATF, we need first briefly to cover the commerce clause and interstate commerce.

> *Article I, Section 8, Clause 3 of the Constitution:*
> *"To regulate Commerce with foreign Nations, and among the several States, and with the Indian Tribes."*
> [164]

Does this mean Congress can regulate every activity? If graphite for pencils mined in Montana and the wood is harvested in Oregon and then sold in New York, would that give Congress the power to regulate writing utensils? Of course not, and Justice Clarence Thomas in his opinion in United States v. Lopez argued that commerce power jurisprudence had:

> *"drifted far from the original understanding of the Commerce Clause"* [165]

Similarly, in Gonzales v. Raisch, a medical Marijuana case he stated:

> *"If the Federal Government can regulate growing a half-dozen cannabis plants for personal consumption (not because it is interstate commerce, but because it is inextricably bound up with interstate commerce), then*

*Congress' Article I powers – as expanded by the
Necessary and Proper Clause – have no meaningful
limits. Whether Congress aims at the possession of
drugs, guns, or any number of other items, it may
continue to "appropriate state police powers under the
guise of regulating commerce."* [166]

Thomas is exactly right, after all US v. Lopez held that:

*"possession of a handgun near school is not an
economic activity nor has a substantial effect on
interstate commerce, and therefore cannot be regulated
by Congress."* [165]

If possessing a handgun near a school fell under interstate
commerce, then you could easily interpret congress has the
power to do whatever it wants, and the constitution be damned.

Now look deeper at Gonzales v. Raich, a case 12 years after
Lopez. Angel Raich suffered from numerous ailments and
severe pain; she was also allergic and had many other
sensitivities to medication. Her physician suggested she tried
medicinal marijuana, stating:

*"Angel has no reasonable legal alternative to cannabis
for the effective treatment or alleviation of her medical
conditions or symptoms associated with the medical
conditions because she has tried essentially all other
legal alternatives to cannabis and the alternatives have
been ineffective or result in intolerable side effects.
Angel will suffer imminent harm without access to
cannabis. Angel needs to medicate every two waking
hours. After a certain number of medications have been
tried, it would be malpractice to subject the patient to
further unnecessary harm." Angel's medical records
show she runs a very real risk of malnutrition and
starvation without the use of medical cannabis."* [167]

California, at the time, allowed the use of medicinal marijuana, Raich grew her marijuana in her own home. No commerce was involved, certainly not interstate commerce. Yet this case the court ruled that Congress may ban the use of cannabis even if states approve its use for medicinal purposes.

Justice O'Conner in her dissenting opinion:

> *"We enforce the "outer limits" of Congress' Commerce Clause authority not for their own sake, but to protect historic spheres of state sovereignty from excessive federal encroachment and thereby to maintain the distribution of power fundamental to our federalist system of government... One of federalism's chief virtues, of course, is that it promotes innovation by allowing for the possibility that "a single courageous State may, if its citizens choose, serve as a laboratory; and try novel social and economic experiments without risk to the rest of the country." [168]*

Cases like Raich and Lopez are great examples because they are two hot button issues that still divide the country weed and guns. They work great because the best place to argue with someone is on their side, fight the right from the right and the left from the left as Scott Horton says. Marijuana advocates should use gun arguments when arguing with the right, and gun advocates should argue using marijuana advocates talking points. Of course, some gun guys will say "weed isn't in the Constitution" that misses the whole point of the Constitution and bill of rights as it is not a list of enumerated rights.

Since these cases we see more and more states legalizing weed for recreational use, the result is that without the state's assistance, the DEA is helpless in enforcing federal laws. Now, can we see why this is important when it comes to firearms legislation?

The ninth circuit has since used the Raich case in United States v Stewart. US v. Stewart wrongly held that the Commerce

Clause had the power to criminalize the possession of homemade machine guns, just as it could criminalize homegrown marijuana. [169]

Reading opinions like that makes me want to bring up more of Thomas in Gonzales v. Raich:

> *"If the majority is to be taken seriously, the Federal Government may now regulate quilting bees, clothes drives, and potluck suppers throughout the 50 States. This makes a mockery of Madison's assurance to the people of New York that the "powers delegated" to the Federal Government are "few and defined", while those of the States are "numerous and indefinite." [166]*

Again, I circle back, if congress has the power to regulate homegrown marijuana under the commerce clause then it has the power to regulate homemade firearms. The answer is they shouldn't be able to do either, but inch by inch their power grows from seemingly innocent legislation.

But what is the commerce clause as it was originally intended? It was simply a way to promote trade and exchange between states. It in no way was meant to be a backdoor to regulate activities. The interstate commerce act of 1887 was essentially aimed towards railroads. The states attempted to regulate this industry, but it was considered unconstitutional for the states to regulate interstate commerce themselves as it was up to congress regulate commerce between the states. Again, this should be a lesson in how seemingly (emphasis on seemingly) common sense legislation can be twisted into something much worse.

### *National Reciprocity*

National Reciprocity is said by the NRA to be their "highest legislative priority." It was made abundantly clear in Wayne LaPierre and Chris Cox's joint statement following the Vegas shooting, where they also endorsed bump-stock bans and agreed with additional regulations on firearms.

> *"the NRA remains focused on our mission: strengthening Americans' 2nd amendment freedom to defend themselves, their families and their communities. To that end, on behalf of our five million members across the country, we urge Congress to pass National Right-to-Carry reciprocity"* [170]

I saw it all over on social media, people saying "who cares about bump stocks we want national Reciprocity." Many were repeating what they heard gun celebs, many of which have lost their jobs as Wayne rides that organization from scandal to scandal in overpriced suits. [171]

It is such a talking point that I'm sure many of you are wondering why I am seemingly negative on this topic; well the answer is National Reciprocity is unconstitutional. To explain, we must rewind a bit and start when National Reciprocity began to gain traction in the gun community. In 2015 the Supreme Court decided in Obergefell v. Hodges that states were required to recognize same-sex marriages. The justices based their decision on the due process clause of the 14th amendment. Gun owners subsequently started saying that their "right to carry" should also be held to that same standard, and a concealed pistol license (CPL) in one state should be suitable for all states.

If you've read this far, you may see the issue with this, if not let me explain. Federal control over firearms means you get the good and the bad. Sure, you get the legal protection to carry to a state you previously could not, but you also open the door to more options of federal gun control such as Assault Weapon Bans. You open that door a crack, and the federal government will kick the door open (and shoot your dog.) The door leads to a federal CPL process that certainly leads to a national registry of gun owners.

It is also a much easier way to get this through than federal gun control; it's easier for the states to work together, which is how the current system works. For instance, my CPL issued in Michigan is good in 39 states, these agreements didn't happen under some federal power, but because the individual states worked together. It makes much more sense for the states to work together to agree rather than getting the federal government on board.

## *ATF*

> *"Congress have no power to disarm the militia. Their swords, and every other terrible implement of the soldier, are the birth-right of an American… The unlimited power of the sword is not in the hands of either the federal or state governments, but, where I trust in God it will ever remain, in the hands of the people." Tench Coxe, Pennsylvania Gazette, Feb. 20, 1788. [110]*

Alcohol, Tobacco, and Firearms better known as the ATF, although technically the Bureau of Alcohol, Tobacco, Firearms, and Explosives (BATFE) can trace its roots as far back as 1792 when the US government set out to collect taxes on alcohol to pay off war debts. In 1862 when congress created the Internal Revenue Service, they hired three detectives which was the actual start of what we now know as the ATF.

It wasn't until Prohibition in 1919 that they grew in scale, and they were called the Bureau of Prohibition. They remained under the IRS until 1930 when they were moved under the Department of Justice. Where they were renamed the Alcohol Tax Unit, however after the National Firearms Act of 34 and gun control act of 38 the government decided it needed to appoint people to handle the enforcement of those acts. This is when they take on their role in firearms.

Due to the restrictions and requirements in the gun control act of 1968 the government renamed them again, this time the Alcohol and Tobacco Tax Division. In 1972 they finally become their own bureau, doubling in size and labeled as the ATF. Before that only 8.3% of its arrests were firearm related. In the 1970's sugar prices soared which lead to many moonshiners going out of business. To put it in perspective in 1956 15,000 distilleries were raided, in 1976 only 609. Now the ATF had to justify itself, so they started focusing more heavily on firearm regulations. Because of their tactics, complaints made their way to numerous congressional committees. [172]

Some of those complaints were from states that said they were unable to get the ATF to accept cases against felons, which was the point of the gun control act of 1968. The Bureau's own statistics reflect this with felons making up only 10% of their firearm cases. 55% were no felony convictions and another third had no priors. [172]

The subcommittee found that agents to inflate their quotas targeted collectors and other gun owners to get them on technicalities. They specifically targeted gun collectors and ignored others based on the values of the collections. According to the subcommittee report:

> "75 percent of BATF gun prosecutions were aimed at ordinary citizens who had neither criminal intent nor knowledge, but were enticed by agents into unknowing technical violations. (In one case, in fact, the individual was being prosecuted for an act which the Bureau's acting director had stated was perfectly lawful.) In those hearings, moreover, BATF conceded that in fact only 9.8 percent of their firearm arrests were brought on felons in illicit possession charges; the average value of guns seized was $116, whereas BATF had claimed that "crime guns" were priced at less than half that figure; in the months following the announcement of their new "priorities", the percentage of gun prosecutions aimed at felons had in fact fallen by a third, and the value of confiscated guns had risen. All this indicates that the Bureau's vague claims, both of

*focus upon gun-using criminals and of recent reforms, are empty words."* [172]

These findings by the committees lead to the Firearm Owners Protection Act (FOPA) of 1985, which we cover later. We should also note that the ATF was targeting these collectors and dealers while ignoring felons during the '80s, which was when gun crime had reached an all-time high.

While that legislation was badly needed, a repeal of NFA 34 and GCA 68 would've been better; there were high profile cases afterward that seemed to prove they didn't learn their lesson when it came to entrapment. One such example was Ruby Ridge.

Like most veterans after his enlistment from the Army, Randy Weaver enrolled in college to study criminal justice, he intended to become an FBI agent, but he could not afford the tuition. Holding apocalyptic views, he and his wife Vicki decided to take their family of four children to Idaho and begin a homesteading lifestyle.

The FBI and Secret Service began investigating the Weavers in 1985, yes, the same year as FOPA. They believed them to be members of the Aryan nation. This led to an ATF informant attempting to get Randy to shorten the barrels on two shotguns illegally. The story is mixed on the length the barrels were cut, Randy said they were legal length when he gave them to the informant, and the investigation seems to point to that as the truth. The whole intent was to get Randy scared enough for him to become an informant himself, which he would not do. Later the ATF tried again to get him to infiltrate the Aryan nation threatening him with the shotguns. Again, Randy would not do it and was arrested.

Things turned worse when the court changed the date of the hearing and sent him a completely different time; this led Randy to believe he was being set up and had no chance at a fair trial, resulting in the infamous events. Randy's son Sammy was shot dead, and Randy shot in the back. His wife was shot in the back of the head while she held their ten-month-old by FBI sniper Lon Horiuchi. Randy Weaver was eventually cleared of all charges based on self-defense, except for his failure to appear in court. The later civil suit against the government resulted in the government paying a million dollars to each of his daughters. And $100,000 to himself, later $380,000 to his friend that was also in his house.

In 1997 Boundary County Idaho charged Lon Horiuchi with murder but was removed based on the supremacy clause, argued by Donald Trump's Attorney General William Barr. [173] But Ruby Ridge wasn't the end of Lon or the ATF.

Perhaps better well known than Ruby Ridge was the events of the Waco Siege. Like Ruby Ridge, my intent is not to give you an in-depth look at these events. Whenever you bring up Waco, you get people who want to talk say it was about a cult-like Jim Jones or it was about Koresh molesting kids. First off, it's not the ATF's job to determine cults or regulate their religious practices that are not harming anyone. Branch Davidians are a break off group of Seventh Day Adventists, which depending on what protestant denomination you ask, is also a cult. The fact of the matter is there are many subsets and spinoffs of mainline denominations that are considered cults. It's a weak argument to say that the reason they should have been raided was that they were a cult.

Regarding allegations of molestation and rapes by Koresh. It goes without saying that if that was the case, then Koresh should be thrown in prison. The thing is the Davidians, along with Koresh, were investigated. Child Protective Services were unable to turn up any evidence. As far as marrying 14-year-olds, well, you can legally marry at 14 in the state of Texas. That isn't to justify Koresh's actions or Davidian members, the point is they were investigated, and no evidence was found of any illegal activity, and more importantly for this situation is the ATF doesn't investigate polygamy.

So why was the ATF out there? It was reported that they were dealing in illegal weapons and grenades. The ATF was contacted after the post office had a box rip open to reveal inert grenades. These grenades are common items that are sold at every gun show, which is what the Branch Davidians did for extra money for the compound. The ATF contacted Koresh's gun dealer, Koresh tried to speak with the ATF, but they did not want to talk to him. He also offered to let the ATF come out and inspect it anytime.

February 28th, 1993, the ATF attempts to execute the search warrant on the Mt. Carmel compound, what happened next is disputed. Like Han Solo, everyone still argues who shot first. Did the shots start from the inside of the compound or the outside? It's hard to know because it centers around the main door of the building, which was lost, yes, a whole door that was evidence was lost.

Word of the siege reached Paul Fatta; the Davidian's gun dealer who had taken a large portion of the gun inventory to a gun show in Austin. Fatta contacted the ATF to tell them he was at the gun show and asked if they wanted him to come back with the firearms, and they told him no. So was this about the guns or not?

After this initial debacle the FBI took over the scene, in what turned into a 51-day standoff that ended in a ball of fire that resulted in the deaths of 76 men, women, and children. While some of the Waco residents were charged on multiple accounts, all were released by 2007.

My intention wasn't to give an in-depth recount of the events at Mt. Carmel, so many tidbits and conflicting stories that it's hard to dive into too much detail without going down numerous rabbit holes. For more info, two documentaries that can be pulled up on YouTube are "Waco: The Rules of Engagement" and "Waco: A New Revelation." These include the congressional hearing on the events of Waco.

Back to my point about Waco, this all happened because of the possibility of Koresh modifying weapons. Koresh even said during negotiations, "you could have picked me up any time" while he was running or while he was at Walmart.

The most straightforward summary of Waco is that 80 individuals were murdered, 76 died horrible deaths from burning alive. All because the ATF wanted to make sure no one was drilling holes in lower receivers without paying the tax.

In 2006 a house oversight committee convened to investigate the ATF once again, this time, it was their gun show operation. One gun show operator testified there were 45 agents and law enforcement officers under ATF direction. What were they doing there? In his words:

> "People were approached and discouraged from purchasing guns, before attempting to purchase they were interrogated and accused of being in the gun business without a license, detained in police vehicles, and gun buyer's homes visited by police and much more." [174]

Between 2006 and 2011 ATF begins one of its most controversial projects to date: Fast and Furious, no not the overdone movie series but ATF's Gun-Walking scandal. Fast and Furious is where the ATF allowed licensed firearm dealers to sell weapons as straw purchases. The intent being that they would track where these firearms ended up inside Mexican cartels. Around 2,000 firearms sold, and less than half have been returned.

The program gained national attention when border patrol agent Brian Terry was killed with one of these firearms. What was not as widely spread was more than 150 Mexicans have been killed or injured with the weapons that were sold by the ATF, and no cartels were taken down or even disturbed by this operation. Many documents regarding this operation have not been made public and were restricted by Eric Holder and then-President

Obama. You would think that if they can't keep track of 2,000 firearms, how do they expect to keep track of a couple hundred million? [175] [176]

We could also go on into the huge illegal gun sale racket; it involved guns coming up missing from ATF evidence lockers. Or the "off the books" cigarette racket that funneled millions into the ATF for undercover work. [177] Or the numerous fake gun stores the ATF setup that increased violence in every neighborhood they set up in. [178] [179] But instead of mentioning those we can take the words of Rep. Jim Sensenbrenner from Wisconsin, who proposed the ATF Elimination Act.

> "The ATF is a scandal-ridden, largely duplicative agency that lacks a clear mission. Its 'Framework' is an affront to the 2nd amendment and yet another reason why Congress should pass the ATF Elimination Act," [180]

I do agree with this statement from Sensenbrenner. However, I don't think it means that you take the majority of their functions and give them to the FBI and DEA. When you remove a tumor, you don't replace it with different cancer.

It seems that whenever I talk about law enforcement, I get the replies that not all are bad, they won't take your guns, and my friend/uncle/dad/cousin is a cop and would never (fill in the blank). But that's not the point, and it's not the point when I bring up the ATF either. As a gun dealer, I've talked with the ATF via phone, email, and in-person multiple times. I have zero bad things to say about my personal experiences; they were more than helpful if something is incorrect the agents, I've dealt with, assisted me on how to do it correctly in the future and weren't out to get me. They have even stopped an attempted break in of my store.

But again, that's not my point; my point is the power those people have that can wreck your life, kill your dog, and walk away with a paid vacation and full pension. No official or office should have that much power; fighting in court costs hundreds of thousands of dollars, and the cards are stacked against you as the judge is on the same team as law enforcement. No one could seriously think this is justice.

## *Anti-Commandeering Doctrine*

> *"It's a surprise tool that will help us later" -Mickey Mouse*

The anti-commandeering doctrine may be an idea you're not familiar with; not many people talk about it. Yet multiple court cases have been won on this idea, even the Brady Bill, as it was first drafted was struck down by this. It may seem like this is out of place being right after the ATF, but this is precisely where it is needed.

The Anti-Commandeering doctrine according to SCOTUS blog:

> *"the federal government cannot require states or state officials to adopt or enforce federal law."* [181]

Justice Alito in the 2018 case Murphy v. NCAA:

> *"The anticommandeering doctrine may sound arcane, but it is simply the expression of a fundamental structural decision incorporated into the Constitution, i.e., the decision to withhold from Congress the power to issue orders directly to the States ... Conspicuously absent from the list of powers given to Congress is the power to issue direct orders to the governments of the States. The anticommandeering doctrine simply represents the recognition of this limit on congressional authority."* [182]

This is also in line with what the National Association of Governors has stated:

> *"States are partners with the federal government in implementing most federal programs."* [183]

Looking at the Supreme Court cases we start in 1842 with Prigg v. Pennsylvania, which argued over the 1793 fugitive slave act. The courts ruled that states were not required to enforce Federal Laws. In justice Joseph Story's court opinion:

> *"The clause is found in the national Constitution, and not in that of any state. It does not point out any state functionaries, or any state action to carry its provisions into effect. The states cannot, therefore, be compelled to enforce them; and it might well be deemed an unconstitutional exercise of the power of interpretation, to insist that the states are bound to provide means to carry into effect the duties of the national government, nowhere delegated or entrusted to them by the Constitution."* [184]

In 1992 New York sued the US government over the low-level radioactive waste policy amendment act of 1985, claiming the US government violated the 10th amendment. The Supreme Court agreed:

> *"the Act's take title provision offers the States a 'choice' between the two unconstitutionally coercive alternatives–either accepting ownership of waste or regulating according to Congress' instructions–the provision lies outside Congress' enumerated powers and is inconsistent with the Tenth Amendment."* [185]

An important opinion comes from Sandra Day O'Conner:

> *"Congress may not simply "commandeer" the legislative processes of the States by directly compelling them to enact and enforce a federal regulatory program...While Congress has substantial powers to*

*govern the Nation directly, including in areas of intimate concern to the States, the Constitution has never been understood to confer upon Congress the ability to require the States to govern according to Congress' instructions."* [186]

In 1997 congress was again handed a defeat in Printz v. United States regarding the Brady gun bill. Supreme Court ruled the law unconstitutional, Scalia in his majority opinion wrote:

> *"We held in New York that Congress cannot compel the States to enact or enforce a federal regulatory program. Today we hold that Congress cannot circumvent that prohibition by conscripting the States' officers directly. The Federal Government may neither issue directives requiring the States to address particular problems, nor command the States' officers, or those of their political subdivisions, to administer or enforce a federal regulatory program. It matters not whether policymaking is involved, and no case-by-case weighing of the burdens or benefits is necessary; such commands are fundamentally incompatible with our constitutional system of dual sovereignty."* [187]

Also promising is that the Supreme Court ruled the US government cannot withhold funds from a state that refuses to enforce federal laws. Justice Roberts explains in Independent business v. Sebelius 2012:

> *"The legitimacy of Congress's exercise of the spending power "thus rests on whether the State voluntarily and knowingly accepts the terms of the 'contract.' " Pennhurst, supra, at 17. Respecting this limitation is critical to ensuring that Spending Clause legislation does not undermine the status of the States as independent sovereigns in our federal system. That system "rests on what might at first seem a counterintuitive insight, that 'freedom is enhanced by*

*the creation of two governments, not one.' " Bond, 564
U. S., at ___ (slip op., at 8) (quoting Alden v. Maine,
527 U. S. 706, 758 (1999)). For this reason, "the
Constitution has never been understood to confer upon
Congress the ability to require the States to govern
according to Congress' instructions." New York, supra,
at 162. Otherwise the two-government system
established by the Framers would give way to a system
that vests power in one central government, and
individual liberty would suffer."* [188]

So why did I say that the anti-commandeering doctrine fits good
after covering the ATF? The ATF has around 2,600 special
agents; or 52 agents per state on average, simply put, there are
not enough agents to enforce all federal gun laws. The ATF
relies heavily on local law enforcement to do the enforcing.

Like the DEA and marijuana legalization, the DEA cannot
operate without the local state government's help. If a state were
to choose to legalize weed, or in our case, decide the federal
government is no longer going to dictate gun laws in their state,
the federal control is significantly weakened. As we discuss
throughout this book, states can nullify federal laws, and should.
The 10th amendment and the anti-commandeering doctrine are
some of the greatest tools and yet are mostly unknown or
misunderstood.

## Putting it All Together

The writer and cartoonist Scott Adams has explained the many
ways that someone can come to know the truth; he lists off all of
the usual sources but also describes their shortcomings.
However, he says the key is consistency. My goal in laying out
this chapter has been to show consistency. For example, if the
founders just fought a revolution and were suspicious of
governments, would it make sense that they would put the

power to regulate arms that they just used to fight tyranny in the hands of another government? If states had their own Bill of Rights and fought so long and debated so much before ratifying the Constitution making sure they would not be giving up power, does it make sense they'd hand over all the power to a national government as well as the ability to resist?

If the point of the National Firearms Act was to tax firearms that met the government criteria to discourage the use of those weapons, then isn't that an infringement? If taxing rights is unconstitutional, then isn't taxing any firearm or accessory an infringement. And if that's true, then why does the ATF exist?

# Section 3: Gun Control

Chances are what you believe now is what you will believe by the end of this section on gun control. The gun debate is not unlike other highly contested arguments, and the likelihood of me persuading you to move off your presupposition is slim. Therefore, this section is more of an explanation and defense, almost a gun owner's manifesto on gun control arguments. I want to make a few things clear.

-I am not minimizing even one loss of life or being light on any murder, whether it be inner-city Chicago on a weekend or a suburban elementary school. There are some good and honest people on both sides that are attempting to end gun violence. The method to end the violence is the argument. I disagree entirely that disarming will prevent murders, and I regard someone wanting to disarm me as an act of violent aggression. While some may scoff that I say there are good people on the gun control side, I do believe that I think they have been grossly misinformed by shoddy research and tons of propaganda (I am sure they feel the same way about me/us)

-When I bring up party affiliation such as Democrat or Republican, these are merely titles, and I am not saying their arguments or positions are valid or invalid based solely on party lines. You will see, most gun laws had bipartisan support. Example: every gun law Bill Clinton signed into law; Reagan endorsed. It is an issue that has divided these parties mainly just over the last 30 or so years. Before that, gun rights were not specific to one party.

-Not all reports and statistics are created equal, just because an article is published in a prominent peer-reviewed journal, or a statistic is mentioned on the news does not mean the information is correct or unbiased, this is on both sides of this argument.

-Gun Control is an issue where everyone has an opinion, and everyone has a bias one way or another, to say otherwise would be a lie. My attempt in this is to explain the gun owners' position clearly. And to give a defense, while being honest and transparent.

-Throughout this section, I will reference John R Lott Jr; oddly enough, I never really read Lott before this. Granted, it would seem every pro-gun argument from a statistical point of view can be traced back to Lott, so in that way, I was well aware of him. I had not read him for a couple of reasons; one I don't want to regurgitate inaccurate info, and I've seen many in the gun community espouse information that was incorrect to support their beliefs. Secondly, if you read anti-gun materials, you will see people continuously bash Lott, or at least try. So, this kind of supported my initial feeling the information is biased and perhaps not the most upstanding scholarship. The question then becomes, "why did you add him if you felt this way?" Because I finally read him, I picked up his book "More Guns, Less Crime" from the library, and at about twenty pages in, I went to eBay and bought every one of his books. I then watched every lecture he's given on YouTube, news programs, interviews, and debates. He is brilliant, and it is clear to see that his work is solid. The attacks levied against him have been personal, or they are claims made about motives. Those who criticize the work he did seem to have never read his papers, his books are thorough, his methods are precise, and his sources are well documented and freely available. While many researchers have gathered small data sets, his research extends to thousands of counties across the country. He also keeps his research up to date with sources on his website crimresearch.org. Initially, I added more stats from Lott in this section, but I feel that his work is better read in full, and you should read his books if you are interested in the data as he explains his methods much better than I could. [189]

# Pre 20<sup>th</sup> Century Arms-Control

What about common-sense sword control? Arms control before the founding of America is undoubtedly beyond the scope of this writing. Controlling the people's means to resist tyranny has always been a goal of many a man who rises to power, but again the full history before 1776 is not the intention of this writing. Our intent in this section is to educate gun owners who thought gun control began in 1934 with the National Firearms Act. This section shows gun control laws that were in place before, during, and after the initial writing of the constitution and ratification. As we go through, you will see the difference in gun control and the deterioration of the original intent.

A lot of these laws have been presented by Saul Cornell in his attempt to prove early gun control, if you would like to read what he wrote follow the link in the bibliography [190]

### *Registration*

We begin with registration; some ASDM's believe that the founders favored gun control measures such as registration. The proof given is the numerous colonies that had laws requiring registration. What I find misleading, perhaps unintentionally, is the proof. The primary evidence presented are the few local laws that required men to have a firearm in working order along with sufficient ammunition such as The Public Laws of the State of Rhode-Island and Providence Plantations. [191]

This is a unique way to make a case for firearm registration when the law referenced was to make sure you <u>had</u> a firearm along with the rest of your gear. After all modern-day registration is meant to know who has a gun with the possibility of taking that firearm away, this law was that you would be reprimanded for not having the firearm, absolutely nothing to do with control due to fear of firearms. Also, if the guns being "registered" were being checked by the Brigade Inspector at a Battalion meeting of the militia, then it would stand to reason that those firearms in possession were military-style then weren't they, and not just arms for hunting. This act is clearly for the militia, considering the section of law referenced from Rhode Island is titled "An Act to Organize the Militia of the State." [191] This did not imply that all firearms had to be listed, again it was only to ensure you had the minimum amount to serve in the militia.

We already know from Section 1 that the right to bear arms is not contingent on service in a militia but to review. What is the militia? Well, it is every able-bodied man, or to borrow from the same source:

> "That each and every free able-bodied white male citizen of the respective state, who is over eighteen but not over forty-five." [191]

Note again at what is being "registered." The firearms and gear that are being checked are the ones required by the state, not personal firearms per sei. As the same document states, the state shall provide:

> "a good musket, or fire lock, a sufficient bayonet and belt, two spare flints, knapsack, a pouch, proper powder, and ball." [191]

Anyone who has ever served in the military would look at this and think, "yeah, that's just a standard readiness inspection." In short, no, the founders did not favor anything like the registration that is pushed in current gun-control measures. This is like a person in the future looking at a requirement for an open ranks inspection in the military and declaring that the government in 2020 required all people to have polished shoes and fresh haircuts.

One last note regarding this document referenced, when referencing the militia, it says

> *"Where as by the constitution of the United States, the congress have power to provide for organizing, arming and disciplining the militia, and for governing such part of them as may be employed in service to the United States; reserving to the States respectively the appointment of officers, and the authority of training the militia according to the discipline prescribed by congress."* [191]

This is an example of a "well-regulated militia" they are organizing, training, disciplining. As the Cambridge dictionary defines, regulate:

> *"adjust something to a desired level or standard."* [192]

Or to stick with the theme of militia, the law further stipulates how the militia will be divided and organized, such as battalions. A battalion is generally part of a "Regiment." Regiment and Regulate have the same root, to rule, govern, organize. Alexander Hamilton, in Federalist number 29, describes "well-regulated."

> *"To oblige the great body of the yeomanry, and of the other classes of the citizens, to be under arms for the purpose of going through military exercises and evolutions, as often as might be necessary to acquire the degree of perfection which would entitle them to the character of a well-regulated militia"* [193]

A well organized, well equipped, well trained, regimented militia. The ASDM hate this version and disbelieve this meaning of regulate, however it is clear, and it is crucial to see that these laws listed are laws governing the actions of a military force (militia).

### *Firearm and Ammunition Storage*

Another stretch is in regard to ammunition and firearm storage laws. Cities did have ammunition and firearm storage laws;

these laws, however, were not intended to regulate firearm use. They were enacted because of the explosive power of black powder at the time. To clarify, black powder is an explosive, smokeless gun powder that we use now is a "propellant," gun powder as we use today was not invented until the 1880's.

These laws stated the amount a person could own in town; conversely, they did allow for a person to own as much as they wanted. The catch was it needed to be placed outside of town or in a public magazine. Clearly, the intent was fire protection as they also had laws regarding black powder on a ship and how it needed to be unloaded quickly. They included regulations regarding the amount of tar, pitch, and hemp that could be in your dwelling. These instances again are clearly from a fire protection standpoint and nothing to do with "gun laws" as we see them today.

Numerous cities had laws like this; here is one example from Pennsylvania.

> *"(Section I, P.L.) Whereas by an act, entitled "An act for the better securing the city of Philadelphia from danger of gunpowder," passed in the year one thousand seven hundred and twenty-four, and a supplement thereto, passed in the year one thousand seven hundred and forty-seven, continuing the said act in force until altered by a future assembly, it was directed that all gun-powder brought into the port of Philadelphia should be deposited in a certain powder house therein described, under the penalty of ten pounds for every offense: And Whereas another powder house or magazine hath been erected in the said city in the public square on the south side of Vine street, between the Sixth and Seventh streets from Delaware at the public expense: And whereas the said penalty of ten pounds is not deemed sufficient to deter persons from storing large quantities of gunpowder in private houses and stores, to the great danger of the inhabitants: [Section I.] (Section II, P.L) Be it therefore enacted and it is hereby enacted by the*

*Representatives of the Freemen of the Commonwealth of Pennsylvania in General Assembly met, and by the authority of the same, That no person whatsoever, within the precincts of Philadelphia, nor within two miles thereof, shall, from and after the passing of this act, presume to keep in any house, shop or cellar, store or place whatsoever, in the said city, nor within two miles thereof, other than in the said public magazine, any more or greater quantity at any one time than thirty pounds weight of gun-powder, under the penalty of forfeiture of the whole quantity so over and above stored, together with a fine of twenty pounds for every such offense. (An Act for the better securing the city of Philadelphia)* [194]

This was a Massachusetts version of the law; I chose it because it looked the shortest and didn't need an example that spans two pages. There are however numerous laws that include more details that the Gun control crowd laws fail to mention, this is one of those gems.

*"That all cannon, swivels, mortars, howitzers, cohorns, fire arms, bombs, grenades, and iron shells of any kind, that shall be found in any dwelling-house, out-house, stable, barn, store, ware-house, shop, or other building, charged with, or having in them any gun-powder, shall be liable to be seized by either of the Firewards of the said Town: And upon complaint made by the said Firewards to the Court of Common Pleas, of such cannon, swivels, mortar, or howitzers, being so found, the Court shall proceed to try the merits of such complaint by a jury; and if the jury shall find such complaint supported, such cannon, swivel, mortar, or howitzer, shall be adjudged forfeit, and be sold at public auction." (1783 Mass. Acts 37)* [195]

These storage laws were based on fire hazards and the volatility of black powder. What this shows is that the public was allowed things such as cannons, howitzers, mortars, swivels, coehorns (all of these are artillery pieces) bombs, grenades, firearms, etc. Meaning the public could own military-grade weapons.

One other thing that is peculiar about the wording of these storage laws is the term "fire arm," they just listed; howitzers, swivels, cannons, which are all basically cannons. Coehorns and mortars are mostly the same things, and that is mortars. So why say "fire arms" instead of saying; pistols, carbines, blunderbusses, muskets, fusee, wall piece, hand gun, fire lock? I bring this up because in the laws we bring up later regarding oaths of allegiance, they list these all of them out by name. In other words, they do not say "fire arms" to indicate a category but rather a specific item and not a general term as we use today. Given the list of weapons in the law above, it is more fitting that a "fire arm" is referencing perhaps a hand cannon, signal cannon, or hand mortar that were all available at that time and not the storage of a firearm such as a handgun or a rifle. It doesn't change the meaning, and other laws in Massachusetts say:

> "depositing of loaded arms in the houses of the town of Boston, is dangerous to the lives of those who are disposed to exert themselves when a fire happens to break out in said town." (The Charter and Ordinances of the City of Boston) [196]

In that I would say it's clear they mean all firearms.

The real point of gun control advocates in presenting ammo storage laws is to prove the point that an aspect of firearms could be regulated. As I said, earlier this is a stretch to connect these to proof of early gun control as they were meant only for fire safety and not to keep firearms out of the hands of anyone. More importantly, these were local ordinances; they were not federal; these citizens were able to store as much as they wanted outside of town.

To reiterate these laws explain how weapons that had no hunting purpose whatsoever were available to the public and further destroys the gun control argument that the founders did not mean "military-grade."

## ***Stand Your Ground***

Stand your ground is yet another example cited as proof of early gun control. Stand your ground laws and castle doctrine laws have received constant negative press since the case of Trayvon Martin. This chapter is not an essay on the Trayvon Martin case; however, if George Zimmerman engaged Trayvon after the threat was gone, then that is not "stand your ground," your ego being harmed is not covered by that law. And if Trayvon was attacking Zimmerman, then Zimmerman had the right to defend himself.

It has been said numerous times throughout this writing and will continue to be stressed; you have a natural right of self-defense. Stand your ground is a natural right further implied under the constitution and was covered in section 1, also in cases such as Bliss v. Commonwealth that I've also mentioned.

Furthermore, past laws used as proof as gun control, like laws regarding brandishing, also prove self-defense is a Natural Right. A quick note on brandishing, brandishing is not open carrying a weapon; brandishing is using that weapon in a threatening manner, such as pulling a knife or pointing a gun at someone in a situation other than self-defense. Typically, when a pro-gun person argues against brandishing, it was because they were charged on an issue that was, in fact, not brandishing. Holstering a weapon in a parking lot when getting out of your car, or open carrying a firearm in a store is not generally considered brandishing. Again, historic laws back this up:

> *"Crimes, Misdemeanors and Criminal Prosecution, §
> 55. If any person having or carrying any dirk, dirk knife,
> Bowie knife, sword, sword cane, or other deadly
> weapon, shall, in the presence of three or more persons,
> exhibit the same in a rude, angry and threatening
> manner, <u>not in necessary self-defense</u>" (The Statutes of*

*the State of Mississippi of a Public and General Nature)*
[197]

Also dueling was legal for most of our country's history, and laws forbidding the practice were not fully enforced until the early twentieth century. In the mid-19th century, only half the states had laws on dueling, so to say they believed in a "duty to retreat" is easily falsifiable. [198]

## *Loyalty Oaths*

Loyalty oaths for better or worse have always been a part of America, oaths of office are part of the constitution; politicians, armed forces, law enforcement, even government workers during WW1 and WW2 have all been required to take oaths. Loyalty oaths are currently on a Form 4473, the paperwork you fill out to purchase a handgun. The question is presently "have you renounced your citizenship," This may seem somewhat odd as you can sell to a non-US-citizen who has the proper paperwork. But the manner of question is more in line with have you denounced the US as in are you an enemy of the state? So, what about these oaths though, first they are not all as they seem. Example:

> *"...[T]he colonel or next officer in command of every battalion of militia in this state is hereby authorized, empowered and required to collect, receive and take all the arms in his district or township nearest to such officer which are in the hands of non-associators in the most expeditious and effectual manner in his power, and shall give to the owners receipts for such arms (1776 Pa. Laws 11, An Ordinance Respecting The Arms Of Non-Associators, § 1)* [199]

If we look closer at these laws, we see that there was more to them. The point of loyalty oaths at the time was to take the firearms from "non-associators." Those who would not swear allegiance and give those firearms to men who did not have a firearm. They were given a receipt and were paid for these weapons. Furthermore, if the guns were not needed by the army, then they were returned to the owner.

Now, this wasn't always the case, Pennsylvania law in 1779:

> *§ 4. And whereas it is very improper and dangerous that persons disaffected to the liberty and independence of this state shall possess or have in their own keeping, or elsewhere, any firearms, or <u>other weapons used in war</u>, or any gun powder. § 5. ... That from and after the passing of this act, the lieutenant or any sub lieutenant of the militia of any county or place within this state, shall be, and is hereby empowered to disarm any person or persons who shall not have taken any oath or affirmation of allegiance to this or any other state and against whom information on oath shall be given before any justice of the peace, that such person is suspected to be disaffected to the independence of this state, and shall take from every such person any cannon, mortar, or other piece of ordinance, or any <u>blunderbuss, wall piece, musket, fusee, carbine or pistols, or other fire arms, or any hand gun; and any sword, cutlass, bayonet, pike or other warlike weapon</u>, out of any building, house or place belonging to such person. (1779 Pa. Laws 193)* [200]

Again, I point to this place being an active war zone, and they were removing weapons from the enemy. This law is an excellent example of the futility of gun control laws; after all, what was to stop these people from just pledging their allegiance and keeping their firearms? Should also note from these laws the list of the available military weapons that the public was able to own. Lastly, these laws were state laws not federal.

Arguments like these are meant to dissuade from the fact that firearms are meant as a protection against tyranny. Not wanting your enemy to have means to fight you is common sense, this is precisely what gun owners have been arguing. Gun control through history has been the government taking firearms from its citizens, so the populace has no way to fight back. Mention gun control, and inevitably you will hear how Hitler, Mao, or many other commies and socialist dictators like in Venezuela took away firearms before they murdered countless.

## *Carrying Firearms*

Public carrying of firearms, was regulated in the 18th and 19th centuries. Old West towns, such as Tombstone, had laws against carrying in town as well as other states such as Tennessee and Ohio had laws against the carrying of concealed firearms:

> *"Each and every person so degrading himself, by carrying a dirk, sword cane, French knife, Spanish stiletto, belt or pocket pistols . . . shall pay a fine of five dollars for every such offence."* [201]

Nunn v. Georgia references the 2nd amendment protected the Natural Right of self-defense and that forbidding the open carry of firearms was unconstitutional.

> *"Nor is the right involved in this discussion less comprehensive or valuable: "The right of the people to bear arms shall not be infringed." The right of the whole people, old and young, men, women and boys, and not militia only, to keep and bear arms of every description, not such merely as are used by the militia, shall not be infringed, curtailed, or broken in upon, in the smallest degree; and all this for the important end to be attained: the rearing up and qualifying a well-regulated militia, so vitally necessary to the security of a free State. Our opinion is, that any law, State or Federal, is repugnant to the Constitution, and void, which contravenes this right, originally belonging to our forefathers, trampled underfoot by Charles I. and his two wicked sons and successors, reestablished by the revolution of 1688, conveyed to this land of liberty by the colonists, and*

*finally incorporated conspicuously in our own Magna Charta!* [202]

The ruling seems rather clear, but the court also ruled that concealed carry could be restricted and would be within the realm of the 2nd amendment. Nunn could not be proven to be carrying concealed, so his charges were reversed.

Nunn v Georgia is not the oldest case to argue the 2nd amendment. Years earlier, in 1822 Bliss v. Commonwealth the case was over concealed carry; The Bliss court invalidated the law as a diminution of the Kentucky constitution which provided:

> *"that the right of the citizens to bear arms in defense of themselves and the State shall not be questioned."* [203]

The court reasoned that the right as defined has no limits and:

> *"in fact, consists of nothing else but the liberty."*

Any restriction on the right, including the prohibition of concealed carry, was a violation of the right.

> *"Let your gun therefore be the constant companion of your walks"* -Thomas Jefferson (From Thomas Jefferson to Peter Carr, 19 August 1785) [204]

## *Civil War*

Maybe one of the greatest traits of politicians is the ability to screw stuff up or to exasperate a problem; healthcare, federal reserve, taxation, defense, etc. From the moment many of them take an oath of office, their ego or "grand ideas" start to wreak havoc. The civil war is no exception, and neither was Lincoln who limited the press, ordered voter intimidation, overturned habeas corpus and ordered gun confiscation; it's easy to say that by our 16th president, the Constitution was heavily ignored. For more information on this topic, I urge you to read Thomas DiLorenzo's book "The Real Lincoln."

> *"Lincoln was a typical example of the humanitarian with the guillotine: a familiar modern 'reform liberal' type whose heart bleeds for and yearns to 'uplift' remote mankind, while he lies to and treats abominably actual people whom he knew." ---Murray Rothbard* [205]

There was gun confiscation and laws that came about during and as a result of the Civil War, these were unconstitutional. Using them to argue that we had gun control before the 20th century is a moot point as we would agree that those laws were infringements.

## *Age Restrictions*

Age restrictions are another point that is often mentioned in pre-twentieth-century gun control. One law states gun powder could not be sold to a minor under fifteen without authority from his parents, but this still shows that they could purchase it if the parent was aware, and not necessarily with them. It also was not saying the minor could not buy a firearm or possess the ammunition. A Tennessee law seems to be counter the gun control narrative as it stated that you could not sell a firearm or loan a firearm to a minor unless it was for hunting or for defense. So, the minor can purchase the firearm if they use it for hunting or defense? Which doesn't sound like much of a restriction. Interesting as well is that many of these laws are not just for minors; they were also for freed slaves, which we are covering next. [206]

## *Racist Roots*

We know that early gun laws were racist, and we know many of the gun laws on the books now are also racist. [206] [207]

For more on the racist roots of gun control I urge you to check out Clayton Cramer "The Racist Roots of Gun Control," he's already done all the work on this topic: [208]

## *Summary: Pre-20<sup>th</sup> Century Arms Control*

To summarize this, yes, there were variances of gun laws, all of which were city or state laws and not federal. These laws are a stretch to compare them to the gun-control laws as we see them today. The story they tell is much more in favor of the gun community as they show the public in possession of military arms and that even minors could possess weapons for self-defense. While I always believed the intent the founders had for the 2<sup>nd</sup> amendment was that these firearms would be military in nature, I was surprised to see it in such a clear way as the laws listed here. Those were legitimate artillery pieces that had no use whatsoever in hunting.

Lastly, in 1982, a subcommittee was formed, and a subsequent report was written titled "The Right to Keep and Bear Arms Report of the Subcommittee on the Constitution of the Committee on the Judiciary United States Senate Ninety Seventh Congress." In this, they make the following statement that is pertinent to this our section on the pre-twentieth century. [209]

> *"In the colonies, availability of hunting and need for defense led to armament statues comparable to those of the early Saxon times. In 1623, Virginia forbade its colonists to travel unless they were "well armed"; in 1631 it required colonists to engage in target practice on Sunday and to "bring their pieces to church." In 1658 it required every householder to have a functioning firearm within his house and in 1673 its laws provided that a citizen who claimed he was too poor to purchase a firearm would have one purchased for him by the government, which would then require him to pay a reasonable price when able to do so. In Massachusetts, the first session of the legislature*

*ordered that not only freemen, but also indentured
servants own firearms and in 1644 it
imposed a stern 6 shilling fine upon any citizen who was
not armed."*

*"William Rawle's "View of the Constitution" published
in Philadelphia in 1825 noted that under the 2nd
amendment: "The prohibition is general. No clause in
the Constitution could by a rule of construction be
conceived to give to Congress a power to disarm the
people. Such a flagitious attempt could only be made
under some general pretense by a state legislature. But
if in blind pursuit of inordinate power, either should
attempt it, this amendment may be appealed to as a
restraint on both." The Jefferson papers in the Library
of Congress show that both Tucker and Rawle were
friends of, and corresponded with, Thomas Jefferson.
Their views are those of contemporaries of Jefferson,
Madison and others, and are entitled to special weight.
A few years later, Joseph Story in his "Commentaries on
the Constitution" considered the right to keep and bear
arms as "the palladium of the liberties of the republic",
which deterred tyranny and enabled the citizenry at
large to overthrow it should it come to pass."*

---

# NFA 1934 HR 9006

*"The National Firearms Act fit in perfectly with the
systematic creation of government programs and deficit
spending that Franklin Roosevelt immediately began to
institute the instant he took office. The NFA was a
model vehicle for the continued expansion of
government power: It was arbitrary; it gave the
government sweeping authority over something very
common; it focused on inanimate objects rather than
criminal behavior; it levied draconian taxes on these*

*objects; and most certainly, it created millions of criminals with the stroke of a pen, just as prohibition had."*
*-John Ross* [210]

Perhaps the first gun control legislation enacted that we are still feeling today is the National Firearms Act of 1934. To this day, almost ninety years later, gun shops, online forums, and social media posts are still a buzz at what falls under the NFA and what they need to do to stay out of jail or be heavily fined.

Although a lot of gun owners understand the high-level overview of what the NFA entails; Short barrel rifles (SBR) and short-barrel shotguns (SBS), suppressors, machine guns, destructive devices, and any other weapons (AOW), few know the origins of this juggernaut. So, we will begin there with how it started.

To give context as to the time and events around the NFA prohibition had ended the year before in 1933; they were in the middle of the Great Depression, and of course, gangsters were running wild, this was perhaps the most violent this country has ever been even in comparison with the 1980s. Gang violence was the driving factor of the bill, however other things had happened in the country that perhaps furthered unrest. Two years prior, in 1932, there was civil unrest when the Bonus Army marched in Washington, DC. There was the less well-known Business Plot to overthrow Franklin Delano Roosevelt and a separate assassination attempt on FDR that same year in 1933.

On April 16, 1934, Attorney General Homer Cummings brought H.R. 9006 to the committee on Ways and Means. Homer's intent was primarily to use congress's power of taxation and its ability to regulate interstate commerce to better fight gangsters of the era. His claim was that the underworld had two to three times more people than that of the Navy and Army. He may have been right; the primordial soup of disaster had been brewing. As mentioned, prohibition began in 1920, creating an enormous black market, the fascist Benito Mussolini took power in 1922 spurring on immigration of waves of Sicilian Mafia members into the United States. Also, the stock market crash hit in 1929. Yes, there were a lot of gangsters, Homer's guess was around 500,000 members in the underworld.

What Homer had in mind was to enact legislation to charge gangsters with crimes of having unregistered machine guns. They were having issues getting evidence to charge these gangsters with crimes and were also limited on a federal level in what they were able to do, and their solution was to make these crimes federal. So, their answer was to come up with an all-new crime. An example given in Homer's disposition is the famous case of Al Capone. Law enforcement had been unable to charge him with anything of substance, but they were able to get him for tax evasion. Homer also took cues from the Harrison Narcotics Act of 1914 [211], where the government used a special tax to regulate drugs. Hence this idea of using taxes on firearms to combat crime.

Asst Attorney General Keenan:

> *"We are fully alive to the grave possibility that we will not keep the criminal from getting firearms, but we do hope to make it a simple matter, when we do apprehend the criminals with firearms, that they will not be able to put up vague alibis and the usual ruses, but that it will be a simple method to put them behind the bars when they violate these regulations."* [212]

And later:

> *"We have recognized that from the beginning. We do not believe that this bill will disarm the hardened gangster, nor do we believe that it will prevent him from obtaining firearms. We do believe that it will permit effective and adequate prosecution, and take that man out of circulation when he does not comply."* [212]

The bill initially was much harsher, and Homer was open to presenting quite a few other additions. Such as registration of all firearms, including magazines, handguns, semiautomatics. Also, registration and outlawing bulletproof vests. In his words:

> *"A sawed-off shotgun is one of the most dangerous and deadly weapons. A machine gun, of course, ought never to be in the hands of any private individual. There is not the slightest excuse for it, not the least in the world."* [212]

At least someone asked the question in the committee hearing, congressman James McClintic of Oklahoma:

> *"I would like to ask just one question. I am very much interested in this subject. What in your opinion would be the constitutionality of a provision added to this bill which would require registration, on the part of those who now own the type or class of weapons that are included in this bill?*
>
> > *ATTORNEY GENERAL CUMMINGS. We were afraid of that, sir.*
> > *MR. MCCLINTIC. Afraid it would conflict with State laws?*
> > *ATTORNEY GENERAL CUMMINGS. 1 am afraid it would be unconstitutional"* [212]

Side note on Homer Cummings, Homer was a long-time supporter of FDR, he argued for some of the worst of FDRs programs including the Gold Clause [213], National Industrial Recovery Act [214], and the Agricultural Adjustment Act [215]. He also was part of one of FDR's most significant scandal of his day "court-packing plan" which was an attempt to add judges to the Supreme Court to get the new deals passed. [216] I say this to point out his less than constitutional dealings. The committee on Ways and Means seemed to be inept on the constitution and was taking Homer's word for it time and time again. The most telling line from Cummings on how gun control was implemented and how it has been done ever since is how he maneuvers around the Constitution:

> *"MR. LEWIS. I hope the courts will find no doubt on a subject like this, General; but I was curious to know how we escaped that provision in the Constitution.*
> *ATTORNEY GENERAL CUMMINGS. Oh, we do not attempt to escape it. We are dealing with another power, namely, the power of taxation, and of regulation under the interstate commerce clause. You see, if we made a statute absolutely forbidding any human being to have a machine gun, you might say there is some constitutional question involved. But when you say "We will tax the machine gun" and when you say that "the absence of a license showing payment of the tax has been made indicates that a crime has been perpetrated", you are easily within the law."* [212]

Despite the few harsher items, the bill that passed was very close to the way it was originally presented. Most specifically was the dollar amount that was suggested to Homer by FDR, and that was a 100% tax. The cost of a machine gun at the time was $200, so the tax stamp on a machine gun was $200. Later, when covering the Gun Control Act of 1968, we will see some of his proposals pop back up. The hearings oddly never mention why a suppressor was included, not even once, or as they listed it "silencer or muffler," was added to the bill.

Now it is common to say the National Rifle Association (NRA) backed this bill at the time; I have even said it. That is correct on its surface; they did end up supporting the act as passed. However, they are the reason it is much less restrictive than the government initially wanted. For example, the definition of a machine gun, before they entered the discussion would have included all semi-automatics; and the dollar amount for dealers and dollar amount for manufactures became substantially less with the NRA's suggestions.

If it weren't for the NRA, specifically Frederick and General Reckord, congress would have certainly included all handguns in the NFA. I have seen numerous blurbs about what was said by Frederick during the NFA hearing. In the past, I was utterly annoyed; however, after reading the four days of transcripts from the hearings, it isn't as damning to me as I previously thought. I concede that while reading, you want them to say certain things differently, but frankly, we are seeing it through the eyes of eighty-five years of gun control. We fully understand the "slippery slope" and ineffectiveness of gun control now.

> *MR. FREDERICK. You have put your finger on it. My general objections to most of the regulatory provisions are proposed with that in view. I am just as much against the gangster as any man. I am just as much interested in seeing him suppressed, but I do not believe that we should burn down the barn in order to destroy the rats. I am in favor of some more skillful method of getting the rats without destroying the barn. In my opinion, most of the proposals the regulation of firearms, although ostensibly and properly aimed at the crook, do not reach the crook at all, but they do reach the honest man. In my opinion, the forces which are opposed to crime consist of two general bodies; one is the organized police and the second is the unorganized victims, the great mass of unorganized law-abiding citizens, and if you destroy the effective opposition of either one of those, you are inevitably going to increase crime, because as you destroy the forces of resistance in the human body to disease, you are going to increase disease. So, by destroying the resistance of anybody which is opposed to crime, you are going to increase crime. I think we should be careful in considering the actual operation of regulatory measures to make sure that they do not hamstring the law-abiding citizen in his opposition to the crook. [212]*

Frederick goes on to explain what we have all been saying for years and what has been said for centuries, criminals don't obey laws:

> *MR. FREDERICK. I think that is the opinion of any person who has knowledge of the subject. In most instances, the guns are stolen. They are not gotten through legitimate channels. Dillinger stole his guns. I have a half-dozen cases where guns have been used in prisons to effect a break; we have had that in New York, and all over the country. If you cannot keep guns out of the hands of criminals in jails, I do not see how you can keep them out of the hands of criminals walking about on the public highways. [212]*

Fredrick further goes on to explain civilians stopping crimes to which congress was completely stumped by, they had never heard of a case of defensive gun use. This case set a precedent that I believe no one was ready for, least of all the NRA who was barely if at all a lobbying arm at the time. That is clear given that Frederick had to explain who the NRA was to congress, even though Congress had appropriated around $500,000 to the NRA previously for firearm training.

## 1939 Miller

Fast forward a few years, and this new law is tried in court based on the merits of the 2ⁿᵈ amendment. Jack Miller and Frank Layton were indicted in 1938 for taking an unregistered short barrel shotgun across state lines. From what I've read, you can tell what side of the gun debate the author of the article is on by if they mention that Jack Miller and Frank Layton were moonshiners and bank robbers. The general rule if they say, bank robbers, then the point of the article will be that guns are bad. I haven't seen them listed as bank robbers or moonshiners in any pro-gun article. I don't know if that is showing a bias, as in I don't believe the author is trying to hide information, they just are coming from the angle that it has nothing to do with the case at hand. I do not want it to seem like I am sidestepping the issue, which is why I mention it.

Jack Miller and Frank Layton have little to do with the case; what we are looking at is what was debated in court. Jack Miller was part of the O'Malley gang and had been indicted for robbing multiple banks; he snitched on his friends to get out of serving time. What amped up Miller's need for a self-defense weapon was that the four other gang members escaped. Two of them were later captured, and two were killed by police as I said this case as far as gun rights have nothing to do with Jack Miller's character and everything to do with the court cases that transpired because of him. To set the record straight, they weren't "suspected" they were bank robbers, both were criminals.

January 3, 1939, the duo's lawyer Paul Gutensolan argued that the National Firearms Act was a violation of the 2nd amendment. The US district court of western Arkansas agreed and declared the NFA to be unconstitutional. However, the federal government wasn't having it, and US Attorney General Clinton Barry appealed to the US Supreme Court.

The case was set for March 30, 1939, two days prior the duo's lawyer telegrams the court advising that he will not be taking the case as his defendants are unable to pay him. The case that went to the Supreme Court had no representation from Miller or Layton, not even those two were able to make the trip from Arkansas. Layton was unable to afford to travel to Washington, DC. Miller was unable to make the trip as the court was hundreds of miles away, and more inhibiting was that he was dead. That moron held up a bar for $80 and was later shot numerous times with a 38 special by more than likely his accomplice in the hold-up.

It is hard to call this a case that proved the constitutionality of the NFA; after all, there was no counter position argued. No briefs offered, no oral arguments, and the lower District court that ruled it violated the 2nd amendment did not provide any explanation as to why they believed it to infringe on the right to bear arms. Therefore, the justices unanimously held up the constitutionality of the NFA, Justice James Clark McReynolds opinion:

> *"In the absence of any evidence tending to show that possession or use of a "shotgun having a barrel of less than eighteen inches in length" at this time has some reasonable relationship to the preservation or efficiency of a well-regulated militia, we cannot say that the 2nd amendment guarantees the right to keep and bear such an instrument. Certainly it is not within judicial notice that this weapon is any part of the ordinary military equipment, or that its use could contribute to the common defense."* [217]

Looking at the court's opinion, it seems that any defense could have changed the case. The Justice stated they have no evidence the shotgun could be linked to the militia, however that is not true. Shotguns under 18" were used by members of the military/militia, example the Naval Blunderbuss was 16 inches, and the average length of a blunderbuss is around 14.5 inches. [218] [219]

Like the hearings on the NFA five years prior, the constitutionality and pure meaning of the 2nd amendment had not been tried in this high of a court. In our history of gun control section, we cover a few lower courts, but Miller was the first time it found its way to the Supreme Court.

While Justice McReynolds had several character flaws, I wouldn't say his actual opinions were devious or malicious. As mentioned earlier, Attorney General Homer Cummings, who initially presented the NFA, was part of the plot to get judges out that did not back FDR. McReynolds was one of those judges; I would reason that if McReynolds's attitude was applied to cases, then this would have been overturned as FDR pushed for the NFA. Point being, he seemed to be levelheaded when it came to cases he heard and not vindictive. It was said of him by the Christian Science Monitor:

> *"the last and lone champion on the Supreme Bench battling the steady encroachment of Federal powers on State and individual rights."* [220]

I do not believe you can glean much from his opinion as the case was not tried, no defense was ever given. What we can look at in this case is the prosecution. The prosecution noted that the right to bear arms was a right that preceded the Constitution. In other words, it was not contingent on the Constitution, it pre-existed:

> *"The 2nd amendment does not confer upon the people the right to keep and bear arms; it is one of the provisions of the Constitution which, recognizing the prior existence of a certain right, declares that it shall not be infringed by Congress. Thus, the right to keep and bear arms is not a right granted by the Constitution and therefore is not dependent upon that instrument for its source."* -United States v. Cruikshank, 92 U. S. 542, 543; Presser v. Illinois, 116 U. S. 252, 265; Robertson v. Baldwin, 165 U. S. 275, 281. [217]

However, they then state:

> *"Accordingly, in determining the nature and extent of the right referred to in the 2nd amendment, we must look to the common law on the subject as it existed at the time of the adoption of the Amendment."* [217]

This is where I believe the case could have been argued. Common law is not the sole basis for gun rights nor the sole basis for the 2nd amendment. Just look at the Amendment before the right to bear arms and the Amendment after, these amendments were seemingly there to combat specific problems the ratifiers had with English rule, and it would seem that the prosecution partially agreed:

> *"Thus, it would seem that the early English law did not guarantee an unrestricted right to bear arms. Such recognition as existed of a right in the people to keep and bear arms appears to have resulted from oppression by rulers who disarmed their political opponents and who organized large standing armies which were obnoxious and burdensome to the people. (Cooley's Constitutional Limitations (8th ed.) Vol. 1, p. 729; 28 Harvard Law Review 473.)*
>
> *This right, however, it is clear, gave sanction only to the arming of the people as a body to defend their rights against tyrannical and unprincipled rulers. It did not permit the keeping of arms for purposes of private defense."* [217]

To repeat; the right to bear arms is a Natural Right of self-defense. The founders did not create an enumerated list of rights. Looking to the English bill of rights to determine context is excellent. However, it is not a full picture as we should be looking at how we adopted it and the differences in what we wrote, which we covered earlier.

> *"In this country, as in England, it has been almost universally recognized that the right to keep and bear arms, guaranteed in both the Federal and State Constitutions, had its origin in the attachment of the people to the utilization as a protective force of a well-regulated militia as contrasted with a standing army which might possibly be used to oppress them"* [217]

One has to see the glaring problem of a group like the founders and ratifiers, believing firearms are a right that is needed to defend against tyranny and then writing that the government, the same possible source of oppression, would be the ones to regulate those weapons.

To summarize, no defense was ever argued, and the NFA has not been challenged since. Perhaps the point of the militia and the verbiage of the 2nd amendment could have been argued, or the defense could have pointed to case Simpson v. The State of Tennessee where it was stated:

> *"But suppose it to be assumed on any ground, that our ancestors adopted and brought over with them this English statute, [the statute of Northampton,] or portion of the common law, our constitution has completely abrogated it; it says, 'that the freemen of this State have a right to keep and bear arms for their common defense.' Article II, sec. 26.* **By this clause of the constitution, an express power is given and secured to all the free citizens of the State to keep and bear arms for their defense, without any qualification whatever as to their kind or nature;** *and it is conceived, that it would be going much too far, to impair by construction or abridgment a constitutional privilege, which is so declared; neither, after so solemn an instrument hath said the people may carry arms, can we be permitted to impute to the acts thus licensed, such a necessarily consequent operation as terror to the people to be incurred thereby; we must attribute to the framers of it, the absence of such a view." Simpson v. State, 13 Tenn. 356, at 359-60 (1833).* [221]

## *What it is Now: (as of 2019)*

26 U.S. Code Chapter 53- Machine Guns, Destructive Devices, and Certain other firearms. [222]

Comparable to Civil Asset Forfeiture, which like the NFA, began as a simple law to catch mobsters. Civil Asset Forfeiture grew into billions of dollars of assets seized from citizens that have never been found guilty. [223] The NFA, as initially written, took all of six pages. Now the document is fifty-one pages and turns law-abiding citizens into criminals.

Most important section is probably the definition section.

> *(a) Firearm. The term 'firearm' means (1) a shotgun having a barrel or barrels of less than 18 inches in length; (2) a weapon made from a shotgun if such weapon as modified has an overall length of less than 26 inches or a barrel or barrels of less than 18 inches in length; (3) a rifle having a barrel or barrels of less than 16 inches in length; (4) a weapon made from a rifle if such weapon as modified has an overall length of less than 26 inches or a barrel or barrels of less than 16 inches in length; (5) any other weapon, as defined in subsection (e); (6) a machinegun; (7) any silencer (as defined in section 921 of title 18, United States Code); and (8) a destructive device. The term 'firearm' shall not include an antique firearm or any device (other than a machinegun or destructive device) which, although designed as a weapon, the Secretary finds by reason of the date of its manufacture, value, design, and other characteristics is primarily a collector's item and is not likely to be used as a weapon.*

> *(b) Machinegun. The term 'machinegun' means any weapon which shoots, is designed to shoot, or can be readily restored to shoot, automatically more than one shot, without manual reloading, by a single 95 function of the trigger. The term shall also include the frame or receiver of any such weapon, any part designed and intended solely and exclusively, or combination of parts designed and intended, for use in converting a weapon into a machinegun, and any combination of parts from which a machinegun can be assembled if such parts are in the possession or under the control of a person.*

> *(c) Rifle. The term 'rifle' means a weapon designed or redesigned, made or remade, and intended to be fired*

from the shoulder and designed or redesigned and made or remade to use the energy of the explosive in a fixed cartridge to fire only a single projectile through a rifled bore for each single pull of the trigger, and shall include any such weapon which may be readily restored to fire a fixed cartridge.

(d) Shotgun. The term 'shotgun' means a weapon designed or redesigned, made or remade, and intended to be fired from the shoulder and designed or redesigned and made or remade to use the energy of the explosive in a fixed shotgun shell to fire through a smooth bore either a number of projectiles (ball shot) or a single projectile for each pull of the trigger, and shall include any such weapon which may be readily restored to fire a fixed shotgun shell.

(e) Any other weapon. The term 'any other weapon' means any weapon or device capable of being concealed on the person from which a shot can be discharged through the energy of an explosive, a pistol or revolver having a barrel with a smooth bore designed or redesigned to fire a fixed shotgun shell, weapons with combination shotgun and rifle barrels 12 inches or more, less than 18 inches in length, from which only a single discharge can be made from either barrel without manual reloading, and shall include any such weapon which may be readily restored to fire. Such term shall not include a pistol or a revolver having a rifled bore, or rifled bores, or weapons designed, made, or intended to be fired from the shoulder and not capable of firing fixed ammunition.

(f) Destructive device. The term 'destructive device' means (1) any explosive, incendiary, or poison gas (A) bomb, (8) grenade, (C) rocket having a propellant charge of more than four ounces, (0) missile having an explosive or incendiary charge of more than one-quarter ounce, (E) mine, or (F) similar device; (2) any type of *weapon by whatever name known which will, or which may be readily converted to, expel a projectile by the action of an explosive or other propellant, the barrel or barrels of which have a bore of more than one-half inch in diameter, except a shotgun or shotgun shell which the Secretary finds is generally recognized as particularly suitable for sporting purposes; and (3) any combination of parts either designed or intended for use in converting any device into a destructive device as defined in subparagraphs (1) and (2) and from which a destructive device may be readily assembled. The term 'destructive device' shall not include any device which is neither designed nor redesigned for use as a weapon; any device, although originally designed for use as a weapon, which is redesigned for use as a signaling, pyrotechnic, line throwing, safety, or similar device; surplus ordnance sold, loaned, or given by the Secretary of the Army pursuant to the provisions of section 4684(2), 4685, or 4686 of title 10 of the United States Code; or any other device which the Secretary finds is not likely to be used as a weapon, or is an antique or is a rifle which the owner intends to use solely for sporting purposes.*

If you didn't read all that, I don't blame you; It's a confusing mess that hems up many a gun owner who doesn't realize that by improperly accessorizing his firearm could land then in prison and a hefty fine. Of course, the ATF has a book explaining these laws with a length of 220 pages. We will cover what you need to know to get a tax stamp at the end of this section.

As I said earlier, the NFA hearings never stated why "silencers and mufflers" were included, there was no mention of them in the Congressional hearing. Originally called silencers or mufflers, for this book, we will use the common name "suppressor." The first suppressors became commercially available in 1902 by Hiram Maxim, the son of the inventor of the Maxim machine gun. A suppressor intends to reduce the noise to a more comfortable level, just like a muffler on an automobile. Movies have fictionalized the sound reduction while in real numbers it reduces the sound by 40db or less. That is a significant improvement but not exactly the "Assassin" level from Silvester Stallone and Antonio Banderas movie. Many people probably do not realize the decibel level is still at a point where hearing protection is advised even while using a suppressor. The fearmongering of suppressors in the corporate press and by ASDM politicians is outlandish and proof they have never heard the difference in real life.

Suppressors have many advantages besides noise reduction, such as felt recoil reduction and the flinch that shooters get when they are startled by the sound. This is especially true for hunters that prefer not to wear ear protection in the woods. Contrary to myths, they are also not a common implement used in crime; from 1995 to 2005, there were only 153 crimes involving suppressors. [224] The majority of those "crimes" were merely for illegal possession of a suppressor.

The "Hearing Protection Act" has been introduced multiple times in an attempt to remove suppressors from the NFA. But as of this writing has not gotten through. To learn more about this legislation and legislation regarding suppressors take a look at the American Suppressor Association at americansuppressorassociation.com

### *How to buy a Suppressor, SBR, SBS, MG, and AOW*

*These laws change all the time, so the best source is your local class II/III dealer*

First are they legal in your state, list below show states that the item is illegal (current as of 2019).
- Suppressors: CA, DE, HI, IL, MA, NJ, NY, and RI.
- Short Barrel Rifles: AL, HI, IL, NJ, NY, RI, WA.
- Short Barrel Shotgun: AL, HI, IL, IN, KS, MA, NJ, NY, RI, and WA
- Machine Gun: DE, HI, IL, KS, NY, RI, and WA.

- AOW: HI, MA,

You can look at this list and see that lawmakers do not understand the laws. For example, in Illinois, a short barrel shotgun is illegal, but an AOW is not illegal. Therefore, you can purchase an item such as a Serbu shorty, which is just a short barrel shotgun with a vertical foregrip; the vertical front grip makes it an AOW. To add insult to injury, that configuration AOW is only $5 to transfer instead of the usual $200 to transfer a short barrel shotgun.

The next step is deciding how you want to register the thing. May sound bizarre, but the item doesn't have to be registered in your name, it can be registered to a trust or corporation. NFA trusts have gained popularity for several reasons. A common one is for estate planning of all your firearms, adding family members allows them to "own" the same NFA item, so there is not an additional transfer fee. If a member of your trusts borrows the item, you are all covered. Both of you can possess the NFA item. Also, the items stay with the trust when you die.

Third, you will need to find a dealer that is licensed to sell NFA items — usually listed as class 2 or 3 dealer. Then choose the NFA item you want. In some cases, you can order online and have them shipped directly to that dealer to do the paperwork. The dealer will hold on to the item, which I call purgatory, while the paperwork is processed.

Next comes the forms, all will need to be in duplicate:
- Registration form 4
- Responsible party questionnaire form 5330.20 Fingerprints on form FD-258 these can be obtained by numerous places online.
- Passport photos taken.
- (one) Check for $200, or the $5 for an AOW

Your dealer should be able to walk you through these steps. Silencershop.com has streamlined this process and reduced the uncertainty significantly. Silencer Shop's system is not reserved for suppressors only. They handle it all and can even set you up with a Trust.

Now wait, the waiting period can be as little as a few weeks or I have seen the process take eight months and longer. Once approved, the dealer will sell the item like any other gun through a form 4473.

# 1938 Federal Firearms Act (FFA)

The Federal Firearms Act of 1938 is a little-known gun control measure that is not as notable because it's big brother "Gun Control Act of 1968" replaced it.

Herein lies another example of what the pro-gun community deems as a slippery slope. In 1934 we had gun control enacted using Congress's position that they had the power to tax and regulate interstate commerce. In 1938 the torch was passed, and we have new laws. The powers they use again is interstate commerce.

The FFA regulates the sale of firearms and ammunition. It banned anyone who is known or believed to be under indictment, a fugitive, or a person who has been charged with the crime of violence. It sets up the license requirement of Dealers, Importers, and Manufacturers. The Act also requires record-keeping of firearms and ammunition.

Gun control advocates like to say that the Act prohibited felons, but that's not the case. The Act prohibited persons charged with "crime of violence." There are numerous felonies on the books today that are non-violent. To say that it prohibited felons is misleading.

An interesting note about the FFA is that 22 caliber rifles were exempt from many of the provisions. That may explain why there are so many old 22s to this day and why Sears, JC Penny, and Montgomery Ward, for example, all had a line of 22s.

This bill is rarely mentioned in the long line of Gun Control policies because it was ineffective. You were still able to buy a gun through the mail, and there was no background check system in place to prove it a person was a "prohibited person." The Act was fluff, thirty years later however these seemingly meaningless laws would get teeth.

# 1968 Gun Control Act (GCA)

Three decades had gone by for the legislature to brew on more gun control measures. Federal gun laws were quiet throughout the '40s then a few updates to the Federal Firearms Act in the late '50s, but the 60's as we will see change that. While the NFA is mentioned all the time because it restricts specific weapons, the Gun Control Act (GCA) strengthens that bill and forms gun control as we know it today. Federal gun control legislation such as the Hughes amendment and the Brady bill all build on the GCA.

An easy way to stay ahead of the arguments that ASDM will use in the future is to look at what measures have been proposed in the past. You can see this as we go through; for example, magazine bans were first proposed in 1934, now they are law in a few states. Import bans on military surplus are the same way.

In 1958 perhaps in a moment of premonition, the then-Senator John F Kennedy proposed a ban on surplus rifles, although not all is as it seems when it comes to JFK's motive. The NRA member, was a Senator from Massachusetts which is home to; Smith & Wesson, Springfield Armory, Savage Arms, and Auto Ordinance, may have had something besides public safety in mind. You see, in 1955, domestic production was 556,000 rifles, and only 15,000 imported. In 1958 the number of imports rose to 200,00, and domestic production dropped to 405,000. Handguns were also imported in high numbers, 1955, almost 67,000, 1959 that number had about doubled to 130,000, in 1966 practically quadrupled to 500,000. By 1968 over one million handguns imported. [225]

This rise in imports may be the reason another senator from a major gun manufacturing state looked at the issue. If the Godfather of gun control is Attorney General Homer Cummings, then Senator Thomas Dodd of Connecticut is the Godson. A former FBI agent who attempted to capture John Dillinger and a onetime assistant to Attorney General Homer Cummings.

It should go without saying, albeit sadly, that the legislation and actions pushed and passed by representatives are not always constitutional. It seems that the Constitution is usually referenced only to exploit a loophole to gain more control, other times it is just disregarded entirely. Dodd was the poster child of corrupt politicians who ignore their oath to the Constitution and the American people. For example, he attempted to have Martin Luther King Jr arrested for violation of the Logan Act. MLK's crime? Being anti-war, encouraging men to be "conscientious objectors." So, already its clear he wasn't a fan of the 1st Amendment.

Another example that he may not exactly be operating in the best interests of Americans was that while a congressman he was hired by Guatemala for legal advice at $50,000 a year (about $460,000 in today's money) [226] when he then became a senator, he successfully lobbied to send Guatemala fifteen million dollars. [227] Again, I don't say this as an argument against gun control; what I am pointing out is that more than likely, his motives were not pure. The Constitution and public safety were not his main concerns.

Dodd was later censured for funneling campaign funds to his personal accounts, he also double-billed his travel expenses and pocketed that money. The Senate voted 92-5 to censure Dodd;

of course, Dodd was one of the nays. In the twentieth century, there were only six representatives censured. The democrats would go on to not endorse him for reelection in 1970; then, he lost in his run as an independent.

Let us rewind to the beginning though, Dodd was elected as Senator in 1959, two years later in his role as chairman of the juvenile justice subcommittee he had his staff conduct a study on mail-order firearms. Dodd presented numerous gun control bills following the studies collusion. There are some stories of his staffers who were working on the case, getting in criminal trouble with concealed firearms, and stories they manipulated the data. The hearings focused on mail-order firearms, juveniles, felons, and what was termed "the cheap products that are so frequently sold mail-order" translation of that term would be "imports," as in the ones we mentioned earlier that were driving sales. These cheap firearms were also called "Saturday Night Specials." Did I mention yet the NRA supported these "Dodd" bills in 1963, 1965, and 1968?

The hearings on juvenile delinquency were a way to get the public's attention on these issues, and the committee hearings take up thousands of pages. These committees were not limited to guns as Dodd had them investigating narcotics such as LSD, pornography, and the effects of violence on television.

Five days after the assassination of JFK (1963), Dodd added shotguns and rifles to his bill, but that died in the commerce committee. It wasn't the end though, he made it more restrictive and introduced it two months later, this time with the push of the Johnson Administration. While this bill was not enacted either, the gun control debate was officially started.

Ultimately the bill would come in 1968 the day after Robert F. Kennedy was assassinated as part of the Omnibus crime bill and later strengthened further. The main components of the law were:

- Raising the minimum age requirements

- o Handguns 21
- o Rifles 18
- Increasing the fees for registration as a dealer and manufacturer.
  - o They explicitly did this to keep the number down so they would have an easier time regulating.
- Later on that year the bill would get larger and add in a ban of interstate sales of handguns and rifles.
- Licensees were prohibited from selling firearms to out-of-state residents, minors, felons, persons under indictment for felonies, fugitives and certain other categories of persons and required to maintain records of all sales.
- The addition of "destructive devices" was added, which mean a firearm with a bore of over 1 1/2 inches in diameter. To put it simply, anything over a 50 caliber.
- Manufacturers and importers had to begin identifying every firearm by stamping the name of the manufacturer or importer and a serial number on the receiver. Firearms not suitable for sporting purposes and surplus military firearms were restricted from importation.

As with all the other gun control legislation, the pieces build on each other. What is said to be "just one more law" compounds, and the phrase "if we just...." becomes more frequent. The hearings regarding the NFA and the GCA are foreshadowing.

### *More Tyranny from GCA 1968*

While you may have never heard of this scandal, the gun rights advocacy group "Jews For the Preservation of Firearm Ownership" (JFPO) made sure every Congressman, Senator, and Supreme Court Justice were aware twenty years ago. They sent a copy of Aaron Zelman's book "Gateway to Tyranny" to all of them. Gateway to Tyranny shows how GCA 1968 was a copy of The Nazi Weapon Law of 1938. The book includes the correspondence from Senator Thomas Dodd, with the Library of Congress, who translated the Nazi law:

*" ... we are enclosing herewith a translation of the Law on Weapons of March 18, 1938, prepared by Dr. William Solyom-Fekete of [the European Law Division - ed.] as well as the Xerox of the original German text which you supplied" (Subcommittee Hearings, p. 489) this was the "Reichsgesetzblatt" which was all of their firearm laws. [228]*

Examples of Nazi firearm Laws:
- Addition of the requirement "Hunting weapons/ sporting purpose" to firearms
- Handgun registration (that lead to confiscation)
- Firearm ownership relegated to party members only
- Removal of all weapons from Jews including clubs and knives

Sen Dodd held hearings on:
- Requiring registration (s.3604)
- Disarm lawless persons (s.3634)
- National firearm registry (s.3637)

This is not a new allegation either; the first allegation was made in 1967, saying the GCA was based on Nazi Weapon Laws. During the hearings one representative John Dingell (D-MI) said:

*"Are you inferring that our system here, gun registration or licensing, would in any way be comparable to the Nazi regime in Germany, where they had a secret police, and a complete takeover?"*

Dingell went on to say in this exchange:

*"...they (Nazis) started out with a very modest figure, and they never got around really to confiscating them. They just kept raising the registration fee, until finally it*

*got to the point where it simple was not economical for*
*a citizen to have a gun around the house."* [229]

What I find more concerning is that while I think the evidence is clear he used the text to help them write GCA, and perhaps we could write that off if someone wasn't acutely aware of the holocaust and what was able to take place due to these firearm laws. However, we cannot give Dodd that excuse, he spent fifteen months in Germany as one of the lawyers during the Nuremberg trials.

## 1983 The Right to Keep and Bear Arms: *report of the Subcommittee on the Constitution of the Committee on the Judiciary, United States Senate, Ninety-seventh Congress.* [230]

I found these items to be significant to the argument over the Firearm Owners Protection Act, but more so I think it is important to note what was going on and how federal agents were targeting innocent individuals. People throughout history want to say, "it won't happen" or "it couldn't happen here" then a few years pass, and we find out the truth. Then the following generation repeats and they say, "it won't happen" or "it couldn't happen here" and the cycle continues.

> *"Based upon these hearings, it is apparent that enforcement tactics made possible by current **federal firearms laws are constitutionally, legally, and practically reprehensible.** Although Congress adopted the Gun Control Act with the primary object of limiting access of felons and high-risk groups to firearms, the overbreadth of the law has led to neglect of precisely this area of enforcement. For example the Subcommittee on the Constitution received correspondence from two members of the Illinois*

*Judiciary, dated in 1980, indicating that they had been totally unable to persuade BATF to accept cases against felons who were in possession of (pg.21) firearms including sawed-off shotguns. The Bureau's own figures demonstrate that in recent years the percentage of its arrests devoted to felons in possession and persons knowingly selling to them have dropped from 14 percent down to 10 percent of their firearms cases. To be sure, genuine criminals are sometimes prosecuted under other sections of the law. Yet, subsequent to these hearings,* **BATF stated that 55 percent of its gun law prosecutions overall involve persons with no record of a felony conviction, and a third involve citizens with no prior police contact at all."**

*"This, of course, has given the enforcing agency enormous bargaining power in refusing to return confiscated firearms. Evidence received by the Subcommittee on the Constitution demonstrated that* **Bureau agents have tended to concentrate upon collector's items rather than "criminal street guns".** *One witness appearing before the Subcommittee related the confiscation of a shotgun valued at $7,000. Even the Bureau's own valuations indicate that the value of firearms confiscated by their agents is over twice the value which the Bureau has claimed is typical of "street guns" used in crime. In recent months,* **the average value has increased rather than decreased, indicating that the reforms announced by the Bureau have not in fact redirected their agents away from collector's items and toward guns used in crime."**

*"BATF had informed dealers that an adult purchaser could legally buy for a minor, barred by his age from purchasing a gun on his own. BATF made no effort to suggest that this was applicable only where the barrier was one of age. Rather than informing the dealers of this distinction,* **Bureau agents set out to produce mass arrests upon these "straw man" sale charges, sending**

*out undercover agents to entice dealers into transfers of this type. The first major use of these charges, in South Carolina in 1975, led to 37 dealers being driven from business, many convicted on felony charges."*

*"These practices, amply documented in hearings before this Subcommittee, leave little doubt that the Bureau (ATF) has disregarded rights guaranteed by the constitution and laws of the United States. It has trampled upon the 2nd amendment by chilling exercise of the right to keep and bear arms by law-abiding citizens. It has offended the Fourth Amendment by unreasonably searching and seizing private property. It has ignored the Fifth Amendment by taking private property without just compensation and by entrapping honest citizens without regard for their right to due process of law."*

*"In hearings before BATF's Appropriations Subcommittee, however, expert evidence was submitted establishing that approximately 75 percent of BATF gun prosecutions were aimed at ordinary citizens who had neither criminal intent nor knowledge, but were enticed by agents into unknowing technical violations. (In one case, in fact, the individual was being prosecuted for an act which the Bureau's acting director had stated was perfectly lawful.) In those hearings, moreover, BATF conceded that in fact (1) only 9.8 percent of their firearm arrests were brought on felons in illicit possession charges; (2) the average value of guns seized was $116, whereas BATF had claimed that "crime guns" were priced at less than half that figure; (3) in the months following the announcement of their new "priorities", the percentage of gun prosecutions aimed at felons had in fact fallen by a third, and the value of confiscated guns had risen. All this indicates that the Bureau's vague claims, both of*

## 1986 Firearm Owners Protection Act and HUGHES Amendment (FOPA)

*"While I oppose most gun control proposals, there is one group of Americans I do believe should be disarmed: Federal Agents." -Ron Paul*

Reviewing the reason this bill was fought should be considered a win for all Americans, the innocent people that were destroyed by the government was a disgusting display of jackbooted thugs. I urge any ASDM person to look at what was passed through FOPA and show me how the 1986 legislation made it easier for criminals to get guns or somehow resulted in even one death.

Reading the articles posted by ASDM makes me wonder if they read any part of the bill. It's like they picked words out without looking at complete sentences. I wanted to list out their arguments to counter them, but my explanations would have just been "that's not what happened" and "no, it doesn't do that." Frankly, they don't see a gun dealer, manufacturer, or gun-owning law-abiding citizen as innocent, so they cannot understand the gravity of what was going on since the GCA. Any competent person could see that what was going on was wrong, no matter what side of the argument you land on. A few examples that were given:

- A dealer was charged with 115 felonies, the charges you ask? Cities were listed on the transfer forms but not the counties.
- Licensed dealer David Moorhead: ATF agents attempted to purchase a firearm illegally but were unsuccessful. Moorhead called the ATF to report the possible crime, not knowing the buyers were agents. When the illegal purchase

did not work, they noticed an M14 on the wall, while this was a semi-automatic version the ATF decided since the type of weapon had been initially intended for full auto, they would charge him with illegal possession of a machine gun. They seized his entire gun inventory. The case was dismissed with the judge apologizing to Moorhead, but the damage was done. His license was revoked, and since there was no appeal process for licenses, his business folded because of the case.

- There were numerous cases given as evidence where the ATF had seized collections and damaged them before they were proven innocent, no monies paid to the dealers for lost inventory.
- Other times the ATF seized entire gun collections when defendants were found not guilty the ATF kept the firearms saying that it only means the case was not proven beyond a reasonable doubt, but since civil asset forfeiture does not require this proof, they kept the firearms.

As for the bill, it is not something that the average gun owner is impacted by, most of this applies to dealers.

- Dealers can sell a long arm to a non-resident, handguns are still banned from being sold out of state, which is nonsense and antiquated as the original motives were to catch bank robbers and kidnappers crossing state lines.
- Updated prohibited persons, under the GCA even a pardoned felon or a felon who had his rights restored could still be charged for felony possession
- FOPA allowed gun dealers to sell at gun shows. So ASDM is mad you can buy a gun from a private seller at a gun show and were also mad that gun dealers could sell at gun shows.

### *The Epic Failure of FOPA: The Hughes Amendment*

> *"If they make a law which the Constitution does not authorize it is void"* -Oliver Ellsworth (Jan 1788 Connecticut Ratifying Convention) [231]

The Hughes Amendment may be the most unconstitutional federal gun bill ever passed. If we look at all the other laws we've talked about, ASDM could argue, and do, that these do not violate the 2nd amendment because you can still own and purchase the item, saying that inconvenience is not infringing. However, they can't use that argument with the Hughes Amendment.

The Hughes amendment limited the sale of fully automatic firearms to those already existing; no new machine guns can be built for the private sector. So, you can imagine now after thirty-three years these are not easy to find. If you do find one, you will pay a massive premium for the opportunity. For example, a nontransferable machine gun, which is one made after 1986 for law enforcement or military, would cost around $500. Take the same type of firearm but made before 1986 and that gun will now cost you over $3,000 and could be $40,000 easily. Of course, as the years go by, that dollar amount only increases, and less will come available for sale.

The 1986 FOPA was a bill that took seven years of arguing to get passed. It's easy for us to look at it three decades later and insert how we think this Hughes amendment should have been handled at the time, but the fact of the matter is that if you look up the footage available on YouTube the amendment never had a chance to be debated and if you really look at it, the amendment did not pass in time and should have never been enacted. [232]

The NRA supported the FOPA at the time and accepted the Hughes amendment because they believed the good of the FOPA outweighed the bad of the Hughes.

We can't hold the NRA solely responsible for fighting for our rights now, and we can't hold them solely responsible back then. The US has at least a hundred million-gun owners, and the NRA makes up only 5% of that. I may disagree with the NRA, but I'm more annoyed at the 95% who stay quiet when our rights are on the line.

While the NRA says they did not want to argue against the Hughes for risk of messing up the FOPA, I find this to be misleading. Because since the FOPA passed they have not once tried to repeal the Hughes Amendment and they have in fact said they support legislation that restricts access to automatic weapons:

> *"The NRA believes that devices designed to allow semi-automatic rifles to function like fully-automatic rifles should be subject to additional regulations."* [170]

## 1988 Undetectable Firearms Act

The Undetectable Firearms Act (UFA) was signed by Ronald Reagan in 1988. ASDM congressmen were happy to support the bill because it gave them the opportunity to act tough on guns. So called "pro-gun" advocates supported the bill partially because they believed into the false narrative that polymer firearms [233], Glocks, could pass through metal detectors. The other reason they supported the bill was because it was backed by the NRA. Much like how the gun lobby tried to attack import guns in the 60s on behalf of American gun manufacturers, they were at it again here. Glock was quickly gaining a great reputation around the world for being a quality lightweight firearm and this threatened established US manufacturers.

I thought about skipping this topic, it isn't incredibly important since even now an undetectable firearm is a bit of a novelty. The reason I brought it up is because it is an example of Republicans and the NRA supporting gun control. Also, this has become more relevant as 3D printed firearms become more common.

NRA statement:

> *"Many anti-gun politicians and members of the media have wrongly claimed that 3-D printing technology will allow for the production and widespread proliferation of undetectable plastic firearms. Regardless of what a person may be able to publish on the Internet, undetectable plastic guns have been illegal for 30 years. Federal law passed in 1988, crafted with the NRA's support, makes it unlawful to manufacture, import, sell, ship, deliver, possess, transfer, or receive an undetectable firearm."* [234]

As it sits right now there are very few firearms that could be 3D printed that would be considered undetectable. It is just the same fake fear they tried to cause in 1988 with the Glocks. Generally, now a 3D printed firearm will need metal components, for instance; a 3D printed Glock would still need a metal slide, barrel, and slide rails (along with a few small components).

# 1989 Firearm Import Ban the 1993 Assault Weapon Ban.

> *"We cannot be secure in our property, if, without our consent, other may take it away."* John Dickinson the *"Penman of the Revolution"* [235]

The assault weapon ban (AWB) is possibly the most sought after policy by ASDM, like a sound cloud rapper it samples from all other bills grabbing the previously discarded and unapproved portions to create this Frankenpolicy. This monster is also the bill that has been pushed on many states. It is brought up every time a mass shooting occurs. We are going to break this down into what spawned the bill, the key elements, and cover the effect.

Republicans would prefer to put the AWB on Bill Clinton, but that isn't the full story. George H.W. Bush set the precedent in

1989. In January of 1989, five children lost their lives in a school shooting in Stockton, California; the shooter was armed with an AK-47. Bush subsequently banned the import of semiautomatic rifles in March of 1989, then made it permanent a few months later in July. [236]

This is nothing more than a legislative placebo, banning imports are protectionist policies and crony-capitalism in practice, as any of these firearms can just as easily be built here in the United States. What Bush did was blame an inanimate object; if imports are dangerous, then why wouldn't you ban them all? Well, of course, that's what happened in 1993 authored by career politician and ASDM Sen. Diane Feinstein, supported by former President's Gerald Ford, Jimmy Carter, and Ronald Reagan, then signed by Bill Clinton.

In typical newspeak fashion, the AWB was named "Public Safety and Recreational Firearms Use Protection Act." I wonder if they laughed when they said they put "Firearm Use PROTECTION Act" in the title. Essentially what the AWB did was create a class of weapons that are now called Assault Weapons. Its reason is clearly for propaganda purposes, after all the term has always been used to generate fear.

As the common telling of the story goes, we get the term "Assault Weapon" from none other than Nazi Germany; the lore is that Hitler wanted to strike fear in the enemy with the weapon they referred to as the Sturmgewehr which translates into Storm Rifle or "Assault Rifle."

The official term in the bill is "Semiautomatic Assault Rifle," which is just a made-up classification to demonize a weapon. The Air Force, on their recent bid request, does not refer to them as "Assault Rifles." The Air Force calls them "Aircrew Self-Defense Weapons." [237] Homeland Defense does not call them Assault Weapons either; they call them "Personal Defense Weapons." [238] According to the ATF Deputy Director Ronald Turk, the term "Assault Rifle" is a "politically contrived term with no real meaning." [239]

But obviously, the propaganda has worked as many do not think twice about the completely arbitrary definition. The description is as follows in AWB of 93 [240]:

*The term 'semiautomatic assault weapon' means—*
> *"(A) any of the firearms, or copies or duplicates of the firearms, known as—*
>> *"(i) Norinco, Mitchell, and Poly Technologies Avtomat Kalashnikovs (all models);*
>> *"(ii) Action Arms Israeli Military Indus- tries UZI and Galil;*
>> *"(iii) Beretta Ar70 (SC–70);*
>> *"(iv) Colt AR–15;*
>> *"(v) Fabrique National FN/FAL, FN/ LAR, and FNC;*
>> *"(vi) SWD M–10, M–11, M–11/9, and M–12*
>> *"(vii) Steyr AUG;*
>> *"(viii) INTRATEC TEC–9, TEC–DC9 and TEC–22; and*
>> *"(ix) revolving cylinder shotguns, such as (or similar to) the Street Sweeper and Striker 12;*
>
> *"(B) a semiautomatic rifle that has an ability to accept a detachable magazine and has at least 2 of—*
>> *"(i) a folding or telescoping stock;*
>> *"(ii) a pistol grip that protrudes conspicuously beneath the action of the weapon;*
>> *"(iii) a bayonet mount;*
>> *"(iv) a flash suppressor or threaded barrel designed to accommodate a flash suppressor; and*
>> *"(v) a grenade launcher;*
> *"(C) a semiautomatic pistol that has an ability to accept a detachable magazine and has at least 2 of—*
>> *"(i) an ammunition magazine that attaches to the pistol outside of the pistol grip;*

"(ii) a threaded barrel capable of accepting a barrel extender, flash suppressor, forward handgrip, or silencer;

"(iii) a shroud that is attached to, or partially or completely encircles, the barrel and that permits the shooter to hold the firearm with the nontrigger hand without being burned;

"(iv) a manufactured weight of 50 ounces or more when the pistol is unloaded; and

"(v) a semiautomatic version of an automatic firearm; and

"(D) a semiautomatic shotgun that has at least 2 of—

"(i) a folding or telescoping stock;

"(ii) a pistol grip that protrudes conspicuously beneath the action of the weapon;

"(iii) a fixed magazine capacity in excess of 5 rounds; and

"(iv) an ability to accept a detachable magazine.".

FEEDING DEVICE.—Section 921(a) of such title, as amended by section 2(b) of this Act, is amended by adding at the end the following:

"(31) The term 'large capacity ammunition feeding device only

"(A) means—

"(i) a magazine, belt, drum, feed strip, or similar device that has a capacity of, or that can be readily restored or converted to accept, more than 10 rounds of ammunition; and

"(ii) any combination of parts from which a device described in clause (i) can be assembled; but

"(B) does not include an attached tubular designed to accept, and capable of operating with, .22 caliber rimfire ammunition.".

Any gun guy will look at this description and think to themselves (well many will say it out loud adding a few expletives…) "who thought up this garbage?!?" So, let's explain each item that they consider part of an "Assault Rifle."

-**Folding or Telescoping Stock:** this takes a firearm from 34 inches down to a whopping 31 inches (based on a 16.5 barrel to fall under the rules of a rifle.) Telescoping or Collapsing and folding stocks are used for storage, which makes sense since the first military contract of AR-platform rifles were for aircrew in small quarters. Another reason for the collapsible stock is because these stocks allow for quick and easy adjustment. On traditional rifle stocks, the firearm had to be made custom if a gun owner wanted to change the length of pull.

"Length of pull" is the distance from the middle of your trigger finger to the end of a gunstock. To put it simply, Kevin Hart cannot shoot a gun custom made for Shaq; therefore, the stock is adjustable.

If the only idea were concealment, it wouldn't have six positions. Also, the same person may want to change the length depending on how they are equipped; for example, you may want to shorten the length if you are wearing body armor. Or you may want to change it if you are shooting prone versus standing. Ultimately though, if the purpose was solely concealment, what grand scheme is someone plotting when they think a 31 inches rifle is concealable but not 34 inches? Again, rifles aren't easy to conceal. If you think they are then you aren't thinking of a rifle, that would be either a pistol, which a fixed or collapsible stock is illegal or a short barrel rifle which does not fall under the AWB it falls under the NFA.

-**Pistol Grip:** A grip that protrudes conspicuously beneath the action of the weapon. The "deadliness" of a firearm does not change when your hand moves from 90 degrees to 45 degrees. The idea it's used to control a gun when fired from a hip or "spraying bullets" is stupid from the shooter's perspective, you will be more efficient if you shoulder the gun. For some reason the ASDM like to say these rifles are unwieldy, too powerful, and hard to control, then they say they can't have pistol grips because that makes them too controllable.

-**Bayonet Mount:** I agree this can make a gun deadlier if you're taking on ze Germans in trench warfare, and you're low on ammo and K-rations. The government wants the nation to perceive they understand the gun issue and are speaking with experts, and one of the items they suggest is the part that turns this scary gun into basically a spear? More obnoxious is it is not the weapon-mounted bayonet that is illegal; it is the mount itself that is regulated, a T-shaped piece of metal that is the scary part, not the blade.

-**Flash Suppressor or Threaded Barrel:** Have you ever checked a flashlight by looking right at it? Stupid, and it is blinding for a second, right? That is the reason for the flash suppressor; in low light conditions, you do not want to be temporarily blinded by a tiny flashbang. I do not know if they think it just looks scary or if they are concerned with the other benefit of a flash suppressor. Are they worried people won't know where the bullets are coming from? Who in that situation is looking around for a flash of light? Note, they list "flash suppressor," not a muzzle brake or compensator.

If you were designing a firearm for home self-defense, you would probably want a barrel at 16" or shorter. Unfortunately, the shorter the barrel, the less powder is burned up in the barrel, and the larger the flash. So again, you want a flash suppressor in your home, so you're not also blinded if you must fire your weapon in low light. Nothing sinister about wanting to see.

**-Grenade Launcher:** Grenades are regulated under the NFA. These are glorified flare launchers, it's a prop, a novelty. You can buy flare launchers at almost any marina or place where they sell boating supplies.

**-Ammunition Magazine that attaches to the pistol outside of the pistol grip**: This law must be based on what they saw and thought looked scary, like a Tec9, Mac10, or MP5. It makes no sense.

**-(Pistol) Threaded Barrel capable of accepting a barrel extender, flash suppressor, forward handgrip, or silencer:** My guess again is they looked at the Mac10 or Tec9 barrel extension and considered it an attribute of dangerous and scary guns. Take their logic further; if a collapsible stock is dangerous because it makes the firearm shorter and "concealable," then wouldn't extending the barrel make it less "concealable" and, therefore, less dangerous?

**-Shroud that is attached to, or partially or completely encircles, the barrel and that permits the shooter to hold the firearm with the non-trigger hand without being burned:** This particular one annoys me that it was added and proves how stupid this whole fiasco is. In later state bills, they have changed this to say "heat-shields/ barrel shrouds." But what danger does a shroud bring? It is a safety device for the firearm. I believe they're thinking that people who use these, fire from the hip or something. Their ideas are based on movies and not real life.

**-Manufactured weight of 50 ounces or more when the pistol is unloaded:** My guess is they weighed all the firearms they thought were scary and took the lowest weight to come up with this arbitrary standard. I

can't fathom why the weight was a factor. In response
to this, during the AWB, Olympic Arms sold a
skeletonized version of their AR to get around the
weight requirement.

**-Semi-automatic Version of an Automatic Firearm:**
nonsense.

The 2004 Christopher Koper study of the original ban reinforces
what I have said:

> *"The gun ban provision targets a relatively small
> number of weapons based on outward features or
> accessories that have little to do with the weapons'
> operation."* [241]

While the AWB expired in 2004, that doesn't mean there aren't
numerous AWB variants across the country, such as CA, CT,
HI, MD, MA, NJ, NY, and Cook County, IL. States like CO,
FL, OR, and WA have been in constant battles with clueless
lawmakers pushing this unconstitutional and ineffective bill.

Unconstitutional is a common way to describe gun laws in this
country, although I'm pretty sure constitutionality is only an
argument the pro-gun side uses. But let's be honest, if the
ASDM could somehow prove gun control was Constitutional,
would it matter to us? Nope. So, let's look at some stats
regarding the AWB.

> -National Research Council (2005): *"A recent
> evaluation of the short-term effects of the 1994 federal
> assault weapons ban did not reveal any clear
> impacts on gun violence outcomes."* [242]

> -National Institute of Justice (2004): *"There has been no
> discernible reduction in the lethality and injuriousness
> of gun violence, based on indicators like the percentage
> of gun crimes resulting in death or the share of gunfire
> incidents resulting in injury."* [242]

-Rand Corporation: *"We found no qualifying studies showing that bans on the sale of assault weapons and high-capacity magazines decreased any of the eight outcomes we investigated."*

> *-Evidence for the effect of assault weapon bans on total homicides and firearm homicides is inconclusive.*
> *-Evidence for the effect of assault weapon bans on mass shootings is inconclusive.* [243]

-Bloomberg School of Public Health: *"did not find an independent association between assault weapon bans and the incidence of fatal mass shootings after controlling for the effects of bans on large-capacity magazines"* [244]

Numerous studies produce conflicting or inconclusive results. The issue is there are too many variables to conclude that any decrease was due to the assault weapon ban, as numerous other laws have taken place simultaneously. Furthermore, when studying the 1993 AWB, you will see that firearm-related homicides were decreasing before the bill. [245]

# Brady Bill

Here's the story of a man named Brady. So, what does the NFA, FFA, GCA, and Jodi Foster have in common? Why do ASDM gun grabbers say gun owners support this legislation?

In 1981 John Hinckley Jr pulled the ultimate simp move to impress Jodi Foster and attempted to assassinate Ronald Reagan. In his attempt he also shot Thomas Delahanty and James Brady. The three were wounded, but Brady was shot right above the eye. This gunshot left him confined to a wheelchair and with speech problems for the remainder of his life.

Thomas Delahanty, the wounded DC police officer, later attempted to sue Rohm RG, the manufacturer of the .22 caliber pistol used in the assassination attempt. His argument was that small, cheap guns have no purpose except for crime, and thus that the company should be held responsible.

Not to get off on a tangent as we will cover this later, but to this day, people claim there should be excessive taxes on firearms or minimum prices. This stance is vile as it attacks the more impoverished communities disproportionately. Violent crime is highest among these areas, and yet the ASDM believes that removing these weapons will protect people. So, which is a more effective way to prevent crime by defending yourself or by being attacked and then filing a police report two hours later? Out of 1,000 rapes, 995 of the rapist will walk free. Out of 1,000 robberies, 22 will end in conviction. Violent assaults, only 41 out of 1,000, will end in a felony conviction. If you were a criminal, then I'd say your odds of success are pretty good. Out of all those crimes, how many of those criminals do you think needed firearms to conduct their crimes? How many could they have stopped? A cheap gun is better than an operator on the phone. [246]

James and, his wife Sarah went on a crusade for gun control, which included pushing for waiting periods and background checks. These were two things they felt would have stopped the shooting based on the would-be assassin's (who was released from prison in 2016) psychiatric history. More than likely, it would have just prevented him from carrying out that particular plot in that specific way.

The first Brady bill called for a five-day waiting period and the development of the NICS system. It was signed into law as part of a more massive crime bill, by Bill Clinton and endorsed by Ronald Reagan. [247]

Let me give you an example of how gun control in the form of paperwork and background checks work. I used to think the problem with welfare programs was that the requirements were not strict enough, that we needed more paperwork, more interviews, and better enforcement. Then you begin to look at the problem and see no, that's not the problem. The real issue is that entitlement programs are almost hereditary and get passed down like diabetes. The people who need assistance are bogged down in paperwork they don't understand and are disapproved on clerical errors, while others have their doctorate in getting handouts, they fill out that paperwork with ease. Gun Control is similar in that you do not dissuade criminals; you stop the honest people who are just trying to purchase a firearm and carry for protection. Meanwhile, career criminals know where and how to buy or obtain these weapons through other legal and illegal channels.

The Brady Bill, including waiting periods and other gun control measures, are like New York City crosswalk buttons, there are around 3,250 crosswalk buttons in NYC, and more than 2,500 of the buttons haven't worked since the 1980s. Yet, people push them thinking they are doing something. But don't take my word for it:

> *"I think any working policeman will tell you that the crooks already have guns. If a criminal fills out an application and sends his application... he's the biggest, dumbest crook I've ever seen."* -Willis Ross of the Florida Police Chiefs Association [248]

> *"Criminals acquire guns by theft, by trade or by using legal surrogate buyers. Drug dealers do not purchase their guns over the counter."* -Kansas City's chief of police [248]

> "Criminals do not buy guns through normal channels, but instead *"find ways of circumventing the screening system entirely... There has been no convincing proof that a police check on handgun buyers reduces violent crime rates."* -Philip Cook, Duke University [249]

More studies:

-Georgetown University and one from Duke University that was published in the Journal of the American Medical Association in 2000 examined the Brady Handgun Violence Prevention Act. The study concluded that the law's waiting period was associated with reductions in the firearm suicide rate for people age 55 and older, but not associated with reductions in homicide rates or overall suicide rates. [250]

Firearm Injury Center at the Medical College of Wisconsin said a Wisconsin study found a "sharp increase" in the risk of suicide within one week of a gun purchase. [251]

U.S. Centers for Disease Control and Prevention that reviewed studies on the effects of waiting periods on violence found that some studies indicated a decrease in violent outcomes associated with the delay, while others indicated an increase. [252]

One researcher from the University of Cincinnati and another from Arizona State University found no statistical effects from waiting periods on gun crimes. [253]

RAND Corporation
        -Evidence for the effect of waiting periods on mass shootings is inconclusive.
        -Evidence for the effect of waiting periods on violent crime and intimate partner homicide is inconclusive [254]

The Supreme Court also ruled on the original Brady Bill in 1997 stating that it was unconstitutional.

*"The federal government may neither issue directives requiring the states to address particular problems, nor*

*command the states' officers, or those of their political
subdivisions, to administer or enforce a federal
regulatory program," Justice Scalia* [255]

## Background Checks

The moment the FFA was signed in 1938, background checks
were bound to happen based on the trajectory of the country.
Once the government started regulating firearms, the checks
were inevitable. While I have some hope that one day
suppressors and possibly short barrel firearms will be moved off
the NFA and I am hopeful we will allow military surplus
firearms in this country and maybe even the repeal of the
Hughes Amendment. I have no hope whatsoever that
background checks and Brady bill will ever be overturned; the
government doesn't like to relinquish power once it obtains it.

Background checks and the National Instant Criminal
Background Check System (NICS) were another part of the
Brady Bill implemented in 1998. This level of gun control is
probably the one most accepted by gun owners, calling this gun
control "common sense." I believe with all the noise about the
evils of firearms, gun owners who are attempting to appease the
ASDM crowd bought into background checks as being a
necessary evil. Out of all the gun control laws proposed, this one
docs make the most sense, at least on the surface. But not all is
as it seems this isn't just a simple background check, and
background checks affect many more categories of gun control
that the gun owners who support this, are not thinking of.

First off, the background checks are unconstitutional, as Judge
Andrew Napolitano has said:

> *"Violation of the First Amendment, because it compels
> people to speak, provide information about
> themselves...At the same time, [the background check*

*system] could be seen as a violation of the right against self-incrimination under the Fifth Amendment because you have to provide evidence against yourself in order to require a gun. also the Tenth Amendment, because the requirement to provide this information ... is not something that is explicitly stated as a power of the federal government in the US constitution."* [256]

Second, it is ineffective. Consider this data from 2010; 6,037,394 background checks were run. How many of those six million do you think resulted in actual convictions? Do you think 20% or higher? Or do you think lower like 10% or even as low as 5%? Well, the answer is 13. You might be saying to yourself, "13%, that's a lot, but it's not great." But that's not what I said. I said 13, as in 13 out of six million checks a mere .0002%. [257]

One may argue, "yeah, but how many people were denied because of the background check system?" Again, using the data from 2010, out of the over six million checks, 72,659 were denied. That is just 1.2%. Now here is the real kicker, out of those 72,659 denials, an incredible 95% of them were "false positives." So, the real number of actual denials was just .06%. Also, it doesn't mean that .06% were justifiably denied, and do you think if one of that .06 % intended on committing a crime with a firearm that a simple denial stopped them? [258]

Next, think about this, the NICS system costs, on average, around $60 million annually. The recent "fix NICS" improvement act cost $1.3 billion. In 2008 George W. Bush signed a bill authorizing 1 billion dollars for improved record-keeping for NICS at the state level. Oddly enough, most of the money from fix NICS and Bush's authorization was never spent; they never even used it.

It does not work and will never work. How well is that drug war of ours going? Heroin is illegal, yet supposedly we have an epidemic. Prohibition was illegal, and it created one of the largest black markets ever. We can't even keep drugs and weapons out of prisons. Why would a background check stop anything?

Worst of all, the background check system can be misused, for example, the VA as early in as early as 1998 began reporting Veterans who were experiencing financial trouble to NICS as "mentally incompetent." Thousands of veterans were added to secret lists for not being able to manage their money. [259] This practice doesn't stop with veterans though, Social Security recipients were also at risk, [260] and here in lies one of the big problems with "common-sense gun laws" and the "slightly inconvenient" background checks. These checks become a great way to enforce behavior and deny people rights without due process. Luckily for Social Security recipients, this practice was undone in 2017.

Issues such as these are even more worrisome when you find out that all of the FBI agents NICS appeal examiners were reassigned off appeal cases to work on their backlog of background checks while Obama was in office. [261]

To reiterate one more time, it will not work; no one is going to accept the measures that would be needed for a system like this to actually "work." I put it in quotations because I don't mean work as in solving the problem, it will not reduce violence, robbery, suicide, rape, etc. It may work at reducing the number of those things done <u>with</u> firearms, but that is not a success. The goal should be to reduce violence, robbery, suicides, and rapes, no matter how those acts are achieved. It doesn't matter if a woman was attacked by an assailant with an ice pick or she was attacked with a gun, the point is, or at least should be, that she was attacked. Furthermore, if that person was attacked or threatened, they should not be at the mercy of the attacker; they should have the ability to defend themselves with equal or greater force. Remove all firearms, and you've created a "self-defense gap" with nothing to fill it.

What do I mean by "what would have to be done for it to work?" For a system like this, you must forgo all manner of privacy. All records would need to be in an accessible database. This would include all medical records, of course. But for many ASDM folks my question is isn't this precisely the reason the courts ruled in favor of Norma McCorvey in Roe v. Wade? The Court ruled that it is a violation of the fundamental right of privacy.

I'm confused by a generation that applauded Snowden and his revelation that the government was spying on all of us in a way that would make the Stasi jealous, yet simultaneously wants a system capable of supporting a background system like this.

For the gun owners who tout background checks are just common sense, I hope you realize that private sales would also have to banned completely. You cannot think they will stop at background checks and not move on to all private sales, which is what they are looking at with Universal Background checks.

I know career politicians have no understanding of what it takes to produce something, but they might be surprised to find you can make a gun rather easily. 3D printers, CNC machines, hell you can make numerous firearms from sheet metal or visiting the plumbing section at your local DIY store. Of course, you can impose fines for building, but that only drives product prices of black-market items up. The possible payout will offset the risk for black market entrepreneurs.

This one will be tough, but for background checks to work you'll have to stop all firearm theft, that is going to be a problem. Three hundred ninety million firearms in private hands, not to mention all the armories that have been robbed. As I write this, even the ATF headquarters just lost a bunch of guns... I assume the thieves (employees [262]) did not fill out the proper paperwork. Given its 10,000-year history, I don't think you will be able to solve the problem of theft. So, I guess we are circling back to the adage "when guns are outlawed only outlaws have guns" or put better by Thomas Jefferson:

*"Laws that forbid the carrying of arms ... disarm only those who are neither inclined nor determined to commit crimes. Such laws make things worse for the assaulted and better for the assailants; they serve rather to encourage than prevent homicides, for an unarmed man may be attacked with greater confidence than an armed one."* [263]

Then once you've cured firearm theft, banned private sales, regulated CNC machines, required background checks for plumbing fixtures, the ASDM will then argue about common sense knife control and wonder why arsons, rape, robbery, and bombings have skyrocketed. Just look at the peace and tranquility Londoners go through every day in their firearm free utopia. [264] You aren't getting rid of murder; you're just promoting another item to fill a void. If you think guns are the only item that can result in the carnage, then you certainly don't understand how easy it is for someone to make a pipe bomb or rent a moving truck.

In short, background checks are a Pandora's box of problems. A case where the cure is worse than the disease. A lot of us do not want to live in a surveillance state, or a nanny state, or be monitored constantly and directed as to what we can do and can't do. You're not solving the problem; you're merely creating a new one.

## Ongoing Backdoor Gun Control

Shopify, Salesforce, PayPal, Amazon, eBay, Square, YouTube, Facebook, Instagram, and Google are just a few of the companies that actively restrict the gun industry. Sure, these are private companies, and they can do what they want with their product, but that's not where this story ends. For some of these companies such as Shopify, they told people specifically that they could host their firearm sales webpage. [265] Some firearm companies spent tens of thousands, if not hundreds of thousands of dollars customizing and promoting their website on this platform.

Social media companies were fine with gun companies when they were trying to grow their so-called "free speech" platforms, but they were quick to limit, block, ban, and demonetize them once they served their purpose. The argument that these platforms being solely private isn't exactly right either; we know companies like Facebook have worked with other governments one example being the leaked transmission between Facebook CEO Mark Zuckerberg and German chancellor Merkel in 2015:

> *"The Facebook CEO was overheard responding that "we need to do some work" on curtailing anti-immigrant posts about the refugee crisis. "Are you working on this?" Merkel asked in English, to which Zuckerberg replied in the affirmative before the transmission was disrupted."* [266]

We do not know and may never know how much the limiting of gun pages came from political pressure. I do not believe it is the government's job to regulate these industries, but I also don't believe the idea that they are just a private company with no political agenda.

Then there was Operation Choke Point; the more popular firearm scandal of the Obama presidency was, of course, Fast and Furious, where his administration ran guns to drug cartels that were part of numerous murders, including a border patrol agent. Operation Choke Point, however, seemed not to get as much press in the firearm community, perhaps because it was an issue for dealers and manufacturers more than the end-user. A good summary comes from the Community Financial Services Association of America,

*"Newly-unsealed court documents released today show evidence of the federal government's illegal Operation Choke Point program in which top government officials and federal agencies pressured banks to cut all ties with lawful businesses. More than 100 records expose depositions and damaging emails of government officials, most notably at the Federal Deposit Insurance Corporation (FDIC), who executed a secretive campaign against lawful businesses it disfavored while ignoring due process and subverting the legal and regulatory process. This illegal campaign included threats from senior government officials that agency staff would be fired, and bank officials could be subject to criminal prosecution. The key findings disclosed in the filing indicate that this campaign was instituted at the very highest levels of the FDIC and has been ruthlessly and enthusiastically implemented in the field."* [267]

Norbert J. Michel of The Heritage Foundation:

*"For those unfamiliar, Choke Point consisted of bureaucrats in several independent federal agencies taking it upon themselves to shut legal businesses – such as payday lenders and firearms dealers – out of the banking system. Given the nature of the U.S. regulatory framework, this operation was easy to pull off."* [268]

There were numerous legitimate businesses targeted, in fact the FDIC listed 30 high risk categories which included Firearm sales and Ammunition sales:

*"After a year of mounting pressure from Congress and outside organizations like the National Shooting Sports Foundation, top officials from the Federal Deposit Insurance Corporation finally acknowledged their involvement and wrongdoing in Operation Choke Point. While I am very pleased the FDIC will put in place new polices and change the culture at the agency, there is*

*still work to be done, specifically with the Department of Justice. I am pleased the National Shooting Sports Foundation supports my legislation, the Financial Institution Customer Protection Act, and I have no doubt the foundation will remain steadfast in educating its members and continuing the fight in ending Operation Choke Point once and for all." -Rep Blaine Luetkemeyer* [269]

Even though Operation Choke Point has ended, and the Customer Protection Act is in place, that doesn't mean the banks didn't decide to do something on their own. Now companies like Citigroup, JP Morgan Chase, and Bank of America have enacted policies to not work with companies in the firearm industry. As I said these are their businesses, they can act how they want, the question becomes what or who is pushing these companies into making these decisions? Is this just "woke-capitalism" pandering to the new SJW or is it pressure from elsewhere?

## Summary: History of Gun Control

One thing I did not dive into that much in this section was the history of gun control at the state level. I may include it in a later edition, but for now, I keep thinking of more and more things that I want to add, and yet I want to complete this, so at some point, I have to stop making changes. The good news and a huge reason why I did not end up adding more history was that Sam Jacobs at the Libertarian Institute has already done a great rundown of these laws in his post "State Gun Control in America." If you're interested in that, please search for it at the Libertarian Institute or click on the link in the reference. [270]

# Gun Control Proposals and Their Arguments

*The supposed quietude of a good man allures the ruffian; while on the other hand, arms, like law, discourage and keep the invader and the plunderer in awe, and preserve order in the world as well as property. The balance of power is the scale of peace. The same balance would be preserved were all the world destitute of arms, for all would be alike; but since some will not, others dare not lay them aside. And while a single nation refuses to lay them down, it is proper that all should keep them up. Horrid mischief would ensue were one-half the world deprived of the use of them; for while avarice and ambition have a place in the heart of man, the weak will become a prey to the strong. The history of every age and nation establishes these truths, and facts need but little arguments when they prove themselves." -Thomas Paine, "Thoughts on Defensive War" in Pennsylvania Magazine, July 1775* [271]

*"You cannot make men good by law" -C.S. Lewis*

This section is meant to cover a large variety of questions and statements that are most commonly posed. I find that even when people come up with new arguments, they are just rewordings of the old arguments. Some of these topics I go into more depth and others not so much, I do this for a few reasons. For one, I am trying not to make this book 800 pages; second, some of these topics have been covered by others, and they do a much better job and to fully grasp the concept they need to be read in their entirety. So, I attempt to cover those topics briefly here but urge you to go and read further.

## *Private Sales and The Gun Show Loophole*

*"But at too many guns shows, a different, dangerous trend is emerging. Some of these gun shows have*

*become illegal arms bazaars for criminals and gun traffickers to buy and sell guns on a cash-and-carry, no-questions-asked basis...I believe this should be the law of the land: no background check, no gun, no exceptions,"* [272]

Bill Clinton (apparently, he wasn't aware that 2 years prior the National Institute of Justice found only 2% of criminal guns came from gun shows) [273]

I mention this a little bit in the previous section covering background checks. Gun control has been aimed at private sales for quite some time, basically since the NFA in 1934. The ASDM would have you believe that private sales, or at least most of them, are somehow malicious. They are not that at all, many of it is good old-fashioned horse-trading. For some, it's selling an item that they are bored with; others sell to buy their next toy or an item they feel fits better in their collection. Others it is that thrill of the hunt, finding a collectible piece at a great price, possibly making a buck off it or trading it for an even better item down the road. What I've come across most are just people who have come through a rough patch and need a few extra bucks. I also admit that some buy private simply because they despise the government being involved in the process, these are ordinary people who don't like being monitored.

The small percentage of private buys conducted to get around background checks will happen whether the law is in place. All that will happen with stricter restrictions is incentivizing people by raising the price due to increased risks. You've created a more massive black market and more incentive for people to steal firearms based on the reward. [274] You've created more crime and removed an innocent hobby for countless gun owners.

The "Gun Show Loophole" is mostly a myth; I say "mostly" because it depends on who you're talking to; there are people like Bernie Sanders who use the term "gun-show loophole," who are saying that to encompass "private gun sales" which of course is no loophole at all and perfectly legal.

Then there is the other view of the talking heads and social media personalities with blue checkmarks that think gun shows are an oasis of back-alley gun deals where background checks are not conducted; this view is false. In the latter sense, there is no such thing as a gun show loophole. A dealer always must do a background check or meet the requirement no matter where they sell; according to the ATF, the gun show is merely an extension of the firearm dealers' business.

Private gun sales also are not void of any background checks either. Many states have different requirements depending on the item purchased. For instance, in Michigan, a private seller cannot sell a handgun to another private individual unless a form is completed by law enforcement. Or they can take it to a dealer at a gun show and have them facilitate the purchase, meaning the licensed dealer conducts a background check.

Further stats from gunfacts.info

- *Only 0.7% of convicts bought their firearms at gun shows. 39.2% obtained them from illegal street dealers.*
- *Fewer than 1% of "crime guns" were obtained at gun shows. This is a reduction from a 1997 study that found 2% of guns used in criminal offenses were purchased at gun shows.*
- *The FBI concluded in one study that no firearms acquired at gun shows were used to kill police. "In contrast to media myth, none of the firearms in the study were obtained from gun shows."*
- *Only 5% of metropolitan police departments believe gun shows are a problem.*
- *Only 3.5% of youthful offenders reported that they obtained their last handgun at a gun show.*
- *93% of guns used in crimes are obtained illegally (i.e., not at gun stores or gun shows).*

- At most, 14% of all firearms traced in investigations were purchased at gun shows. But this includes all firearms that the police traced, whether or not they were used in crimes, which overstates the acquisition rate.
- Gun dealers are federally licensed. They are bound to stringent rules for sales that apply equally whether they are selling firearms from a storefront or a gun show.
- Most crime guns are either bought off the street from illegal sources (39.2%) or through strawman purchases by family members or friends (39.6%).

### 3 Day "Charleston loophole"

While completing a background check through the NICS system, you get three options; proceed, denied, delayed. The delayed can be for several reasons; usually I find that if someone does not want to provide their social security number for a background check, then it's a good chance the person gets delayed. Sometimes it is just delayed because the NICS system cannot handle all the applications at that time. The rule is that after three business days, the gun can be transferred if the status has not been updated. This helps prevent backdoor gun control where they leave you in limbo, wondering why you can't get a gun.

This three-day delay started being referred to as the "Charleston Loophole" after Dylann Roof murdered nine people in a Charleston church. Roof had a marijuana possession charge that would have disqualified him from purchasing under current guidelines, but the record was not up to date. Three days after no reply he was able to buy his handgun. The FBI called the gun dealer two months later, telling the dealer to deny the transaction. A big oof for the FBI was that this call was twelve days after the shooting. The FBI Director at the time, James Comey, blamed the shooting on the three-day delay. Makes you wonder if the FBI called the gun dealer as a CYA or if they were that ignorant to current events.

## No Fly, No Buy (Terror Loophole)

This was a popular bill; it has since moved from the limelight but is brought up whenever, in the words of Ilhan Omar, "some people do some things." The essence of this bill is also brought up in other arguments, so it makes sense that we would still cover it.

No-fly no buy seems simple enough; if you're on the terrorist watchlist, you are unable to fly, the ASDM wanted to extend this to not being able to buy a gun. You may be thinking, "obviously, we don't want terrorists to own guns," and you'd be mostly right, but who defines the word "terrorist," and who controls this list? One guy who wanted to know was Rep Tom McClintock from California. The reason he wanted to know was that he was labeled as a member of the IRA. Even though McClintock was an elected representative, he was on the no-fly list. Worst of all, it took him several months for the FBI to remove him from the list, now imagine how hard it would be for an average citizen to get off that list, or how much money it would cost. [275]

> "If your fundamental constitutional rights can be withdrawn at a bureaucrat's whim, then the Bill of Rights means nothing." -Tom McClintock. [275]

Of course, the media took to the case to demonize the NRA, but what they like to leave out was that the NRA had an unlikely ally, the ACLU:

> "(no fly, no buy) uses vague and overbroad criteria and secret evidence to place individuals on blacklists without a meaningful process to correct government error and clear their names," [276]

The idea to bring this No-fly list to firearms came after Omar Mateen murdered 49 people in an Orlando nightclub. Mateen had been on the terror watchlist twice and was removed both times. Oddly enough, they used this as an excuse for the "no-fly no buy" even though he was off the list at the time he made his purchases. Senator Harry Reid used Omar as part of his rhetoric and said we must close this "terror loophole." This is rather odd in this scenario as again, Mateen wasn't on the list at the time, it wouldn't have stopped him. Also, there is no evidence any other shooter was on this list. What is the "loophole, Harry?" What did they expect to gain from this except more control?

The answer could be in the ever-expanding definition of terrorist or extremist. An example is from this Homeland Security assessment from 2009 titled "Right-Wing Extremism." The 10-page assessment warns of the rise of militia groups. It's fair to say that this definition was one reason the activist and would-be politician Schaeffer Cox was arrested and currently serving 26 years as a political prisoner in "Little Gitmo" more specifically the "Communication Management Unit" in Indiana. In FBI memos concerning Cox, it was said that interest grew after a speech Cox gave in Montana, the same year of the Homeland Security assessment in 2009, where he stated he was head of a Militia in Alaska numbering 3,500. If you don't want to read the whole assessment by DHS, bear in mind just one footnote, to which the DHS later apologized for including, (not that the apology is worth anything.)

> "Rightwing Extremism: Current Economic and Political Climate Fueling Resurgence in Radicalization and Recruitment," said that while there is no specific information that domestic right-wing terrorists are planning acts of violence, such acts could come from unnamed "rightwing extremists" concerned about illegal immigration, abortion, increasing federal power and restrictions on firearms -- and singled out returning war veterans as susceptible to recruitment." [277]

Look at some of the other names on the no-fly list such as Cat Stevens, Sen John Lewis, Sen Ted Kennedy (well maybe Ted should've been on it), an 18-month-old, several actors, journalists, etc. It's hard to say how many people are on the list, I've seen numbers ranging from 21,000 to a million. Point being

we do not know who is all on the list, and that is
unconstitutional.

### *Red flag laws (ERPO)*

A lot of this is going to sound repetitive from what we discussed
regarding background checks and the "no-fly, no buy" bill that
was attempted. I would say all the legal arguments that were put
forth against a secret list, can just as easily be placed on Red
flag laws. Red flag laws have been regarded as Kafkaesque and
even compared to the movie Minority Report as they are also
referred to as predictive policing.

As with other proposed gun control legislation, this is another
reactionary idea because they found a scenario that it may have
stopped a shooting. I am referring to the mass shooting in
Parkland, FL. The Parkland shooter was called on 45 times,
[278] the school and the sheriff department had a policy not to
arrest kids so they could keep their crime figures down, [279]
for more information on that case read "Why Meadow Died" by
Parkland parent Andrew Pollack and Max Eden.

Red Flag Laws like other bills are touted as "common sense,"
these bills work by disarming people who allegedly present a
danger to themselves or others around them. While many say
this violates due process, I agree, but I doubt the argument will
get very far, considering how the Supreme Court and 9th district
courts have both ruled on previous cases such as US v. Valdes-
Vega and US v. Arvizu. Both cases the courts ruled that
searches were legal based on a preponderance of the evidence.
In other words, if they determine a list of suspicious traits and a
person exhibits those actions, then that would be enough
evidence. Furthermore, we don't have the benefit of a case that
was used to fight against the "No Fly List," in Latif v. Holder,
the courts ruled the way they did because the people were not
informed that they were actually on a list.
With Red flag laws, you would actually be informed, probably
in the form of a no-knock raid and a dead dog, but they would
call this "notified."

If you read earlier the abuses that resulted in the Firearm Owners Protection Act, you can see how an act like ERPO can turn into a free for all. Like a Salem witch trial or "swating," anyone can accuse someone of being dangerous. The burden of proof falls on the gun owner to prove they are innocent. What is to stop a vengeful ex-spouse or an antigun neighbor from calling in a "tip." Imagine the lawyer fees with no way to recoup the cost, guilty until proven innocent will cost you $100k.

Who is to define the category of someone who is "high risk? As we covered previously, what's to stop them using "right-wing extremist" or militia member as a potentially high-risk individual. Reminder, some of those traits from the DHS report, were fears of financial collapse, pro-life, veterans, love of the founding fathers, etc... But hey I'm sure no government agency has ever targeted people of a politician ideology *cough *cough IRS *cough Lois Lerner. [280]

States like Maryland, who have passed red flag laws, have found that two-thirds of reports are frivolous and aimed at "getting even." From Oct 2018 to May 2019, officers in Prince George's county have collected more than 132 firearms and 35,000 rounds of ammunition.

Red flag laws are rather new, so it's hard to see any real data on the long-term effectiveness besides the stat I just posted; however, we can look at predictive policing or better put "thought police." Predictive policing is like the umbrella term for things like Red Flag laws and Civil asset forfeiture. It's treating someone as a criminal before a crime has been committed.

Predictive policing has been deemed ineffective by groups like RAND Corp, but that doesn't seem to stop anyone from trying out new, more invasive ideas. One that has been proposed that further merges red flag and background checks are the ideas proposed by New York State Senator Kevin Parker. His plan was in order to purchase a firearm; the buyer would need to submit up to three years of internet search history and submit their social media profiles. Under that proposed legislation, law enforcement officials could investigate:

> "commonly known profane slurs used or biased language used to describe race, national origin, ancestry, gender, religion, disability or sexual orientation; threatening health or safety of another person, or an act of terrorism." [281]

Guess what, though, using racial slurs or mocking a sexual orientation in no way bars someone from owning a firearm. If this were the case, every kid on Xbox live would be barred from possessing a firearm for life. This type of legislation is less about guns and more about social engineering; it is Cultural Marxism at its finest. We may not like the words people use, but if we dictate their Natural Rights on those words, we are the ones in the wrong.

## *Social Credit*

Social Credit is like the Background check taken to dystopian levels. A Social Credit system would be like a credit check, like your FICO credit score. You would get certain hits to your "credit" if you had misdemeanors or perhaps took certain medications, mental health evaluations, buying too many guns or too much ammo would even harm your score. One article I read also suggested including speeding tickets affecting your ability to purchase a firearm. [282]

This social credit system is even beyond red flag laws and precrime. It is social engineering at its finest; this isn't a gun issue as much as it is a general liberty issue. The ability for the government to determine your rights based on social credit should alarm everyone as systems like this are already being implemented in places like China, where social credit will eventually even determine your internet speed. It's a great example of Antonio Gramsci's idea of Cultural Hegemony, where the ruling class manipulates culture.

It's not like we aren't already being manipulated in this way to some extent after all numerous gun owners are already playing into this game where they play by stupid rules in order to keep their gun rights. The obvious example is medicinal marijuana; they cannot use for fear they will lose their ability to carry or own a firearm legally, so they must listen to the nanny state tell them how to medicate. Some gun owners will not attend public rallies for fear of being labeled an extremist. Others withhold their opinions online for fear of being added to a list, which sounds crazy until you see the list of words homeland security monitors. [283] Or they worry that CPS will take their children, this again seems extreme until you do a simple google search of the cases where CPS has investigated gun owners that have been reported for posting pictures of guns or taking their kids to gun ranges. (lawyer up and shut up.)

Again, this whole social credit system should worry everyone; it would take your data from places like Amazon, Google, and everything else on your phone or computer to determine what rewards and punishments you get. In this case, we are talking about firearm purchases, but this means all that data is being collected on everyone, not just gun owners. How long until they decide they can use this on other things besides firearms? Oh, and it would not work; this whole idea once again relies on the notion that criminals go through legal routes to purchase firearms.

### *Stop and frisk*

An option proposed by Donald Trump was to implement "Stop and Frisk." It is no different from proposals like red flag laws, but because Trump said it, ASDM hate it when then-candidate Trump mentioned the idea in Chicago while campaigning democrats blasted him for his unconstitutional scheme.

There isn't much to say about this that we already haven't covered under red flag laws and social credit. It is unconstitutional; it is a way to harass people. [284]

## Guns and Ammo limit

Let's start with a quote from a Slate article:

> "The 27 words of the 2nd amendment don't say anything about how many guns someone can own in America." [285]

Well it does, "infringe" is a rather specific word meaning; to weaken, break, undermine, violate, encroach. I'm sure the author of that Slate piece did not know was that they were stumbling on the age-old argument between the Federalists, Anti-federalists. Anti-federalists believed there needed to be some extra protection against the federal government, namely the Bill of Rights, to further protect the rights of individual Americans and State governments. Federalists believed a list would have people assume these items were the only rights that were covered. Or as Lawrence Hunter better explains:

> "During the Constitutional Convention, Madison resisted a Bill of Rights because he believed that it would be impossible to avoid an unintended and undesirable negative pregnant unless every conceivable right were enumerated. When Madison finally came around to supporting a Bill of Rights, he offered the Ninth and Tenth Amendments as bulwarks against the negative pregnant. These amendments stated explicitly that rights not enumerated in the Constitution were not denied to the people and that powers not enumerated in the Constitution nor prohibited to the states therein were reserved to the states or the people." [286]

Unfortunately, this idea of limiting the number of guns someone can own or amount of ammo is not limited to some incel with a blog, this is an idea promoted by California lawmakers and is praised by ASDM groups like Gifford Law Center. While not a new concept by the ASDM, this has been passed in California and in Virginia. They argue that according to the ATF, a percentage of weapons that have been found at crime scenes have been part of multiple gun purchases — implying that people are buying up guns in bulk and then reselling them to criminals. Newsflash that's already illegal.

These laws focus on small anomalies to push their ideas. They're not stopping gun violence at most they are just shuffling vendors. What gun owners may not know is that when multiple handguns, or more than one handgun in a 10-day period, are purchased, a separate form is filled out by the dealer. The form is completed after the sale and submitted to the ATF. There really is no telling what is done with the form once it is sent to the ATF. This means the ATF already knows who is buying multiple firearms.

Another ASDM argument for limiting the number of firearms a person can purchase is the possibility people are buying them to resell in states where they are illegal. Gifford Law Center says:

> *"States with weak gun laws attract traffickers who make multiple purchases, and then resell those firearms in states with stronger gun laws."* [287]

As almost to prove our point, these gun laws increase the black market. So, wouldn't economics then dictate that supply going down would lead to an increase in price, thereby increasing the incentive to run more firearms to these states? If prices increase and supply is not met, wouldn't it also incentivize other ways to obtain firearms such as theft? What these states have done is penalized law-abiding citizens and just created a market for criminals to make profit.

### Gun Control Would Work but Guns Are Being Trafficked by States with Less Gun Control

Well, then why aren't those states that have more lax gun laws as dangerous? If I'm taking guns from Indiana to go to Chicago to commit a crime, then why don't I stay in Indiana? One answer could be that I can sell guns to criminals in Chicago and make a profit. Although if that's the case, why would gun control stop this practice? You've just increased my profit by reducing supply, and you certainly didn't reduce demand for the product. What you did was decrease the number of law-abiding gun owners while doing nothing about armed criminals.

## *Magazine capacity limits*

For most of us in the gun community, the magazine ban debate is nothing new. States and other countries have pushed bills like this since at least the early '90s and do not seem to be slowing. I would say the first capacity limit that was attempted came from the NFA in 1934 with the original definition they had for a "Machine Gun." The original text said:

> *"Machine gun, means any weapon designed to shoot automatically or semiautomatically twelve or more shots without reloading."*

The theory of limiting magazine capacity is based on the idea that while a person is reloading, a potential victim may have time to rush the assailant or run for cover. While this could be possible, it is assuming that victims are timing the reloads of the attacker, this isn't very feasible considering how fast a firearm can be reloaded. [288] You have just as much time when the shooter is pointing their firearm in the opposite direction. Also, an attacker could carry more firearms that could be readily drawn to cut down on reloads.

What makes a gun useful to criminals is the same thing that makes them sought after and valuable for homeowners, sportsmen, military, and law enforcement. A firearm's controllability, accuracy, capacity, etc. are all key traits that many people look for in a gun. While there are awful events that involve these firearms, there are also homeowners who protect themselves from attacks with multiple assailants. One story that San Diego Judge Roger Benitez cited in his judgment to overturn California's ten-round magazine ban was that of pajama-clad women taking on three attackers, as Benitez wrote:

*"She had no place to carry an extra magazine and no way to reload because her left hand held the phone with which she was still trying to call 911,"* [289]

He ruled that magazines holding more than 10 rounds are *"arms"* under the U.S. Constitution, and that the California law:

*"burdens the core of the 2nd amendment by criminalizing the acquisition and possession of these magazines that are commonly held by law-abiding citizens for defense of self, home, and state."* [290]

He further argued that cases such as the San Bernardino shooting used as fodder by ASDM to enact the ban were rare compared to the number of firearms used in self-defense. Which lines up with a study mentioned in Matthew Larosiere's article below, according to:

*"a 2015 study by the International Journal of Police Science & Management, novice shooters have a 39 percent hit probability over typical engagement distances, compared to 48 percent for intermediate and 49 percent for expert shooters. That, combined with the fact that an assailant is rarely stopped by a single bullet, makes magazine capacity all the more important for effective defensive use of firearms."* [291]

Let's look at the numbers further, a great article I suggest reading in its entirety is Matthew Larosiere's article published by the Cato Institute and can be found on their website. The article is entitled "Losing Count: The Empty Case for High-Capacity Magazine Restrictions." [291]

*"In the Virginia Tech shooting, for several years the deadliest mass shooting in American history, the shooter changed magazines a total of 17 times during the course of his rampage, rapidly and frequently*

*exchanging 10-round magazines that would be compliant with most magazine bans.*

*The Parkland shooter fired 150 rounds over the course of about seven minutes, reportedly using 10-round magazines that would be compliant with almost every current and proposed magazine restriction. Assuming the shooter used fifteen 10-round magazines, he would have reloaded fourteen times over the course of seven minutes. If he had spent three seconds per magazine change (an estimate on the slow side), he would have spent a total of 42 seconds reloading and 378 seconds firing, averaging one shot every 2.5 seconds.*

*Would using 30-round magazines have made him significantly more lethal? Probably not. Reloading four times instead of fourteen while firing the same amount of ammunition would have allowed him to fire one shot every 2.3 seconds. Such a minuscule difference in practical fire rate would be unlikely to have any appreciable effect on lethality. The tiny reduction could be made up for by simply carrying more magazines, as the Parkland shooter did, and continuing the rampage a few seconds longer."*

High capacity is also a misnomer; it's a word that somehow eludes to there being a "standard capacity" magazine. However, using that logic that there are "standard" magazines, then maybe we should look at the first AR15. The first Armalite Rifles used by the military in 1964 came (standard) with 20 rounds. Five years later, they were issued (came standard) with 30 round magazines. So, if we are going to define what is "standard," then it seems to be that 30 round magazines have been issued (as standard equipment) for fifty years, which is quite a precedent.

Also, of note is that not all things are created equal a ten-round mag of 458 SOCOM can just as easily fit thirty rounds of 5.56. Therefore, I could sell ten round 458 mags all day long and be in compliance; this makes zero sense and shows the futility of such laws.

## *Age restrictions*

> *"This difference is ascribed to our superiority in taking aim when we fire; every soldier in our army having been intimate with his gun from his infancy." -Thomas Jefferson* [292]

> *"A militia when properly formed are in fact the people themselves...and include, according to the past and general usage of the states, all men capable of bearing arms... To preserve liberty, it is essential that the whole body of the people always possess arms, and be taught alike, especially when young, how to use them."*
> *- Richard Henry Lee* [293]

Some states have enacted legislation recently and been pushed at the federal level. Laws like this are promoted more heavily after a school shooting. Current federal age limits are 18 for a long gun and 21 for a handgun. The laws that are being proposed, as well as passed in some areas, is to raise the age to 21 for handguns and long guns.

Here is the first problem with age restrictions; firearms are routinely used for home and self-defense. Plenty of people under 21 are living on their own and have a Natural Right to protect themselves. I am speaking from personal experience, I was in the military, living off base, 1,000 miles from family, married, and under 21. I worked 24-hour shifts, leaving my wife home alone for entire evenings every other night. I bought a 12-gauge shotgun, then added two things that would make it an assault rifle under many AWB laws, a pistol grip stock, and a heat shield. Why? Because it would be easier for my petite wife to control and shoot as a novice.

Many people between 18 and 20, have additional responsibilities. Some have their own place; they should be able to defend themselves and their families. The government nor a majority of voters have the right to take that away from them.

It's also ineffective, look no further to the drinking age. According to the CDC, 30% of high schoolers drink. [294] People aged 12 to 20 years drink 11% of all alcohol consumed in the United States. [294] Studies on age restrictions on firearms also show they are ineffective or inconclusive.

Rand Corporation has reported on firearm age requirements: [295]

> -We found no qualifying studies showing that minimum age requirements increased any of the eight outcomes we investigated.
> -Evidence that minimum age requirements for purchasing a firearm may reduce firearm suicides among some people aged 20 or younger is limited. Evidence that such laws affect total suicides is inconclusive, and evidence that minimum age requirements for possessing a firearm affect total suicides and firearm suicides is inconclusive.
> -Evidence for how minimum age requirements for purchasing a firearm affect mass shootings is inconclusive.
> -Evidence for how minimum age requirements for possessing a firearm affect unintentional firearm deaths is inconclusive.
> -Evidence for how minimum age requirements for purchasing or possessing a firearm affect total and firearm homicides is inconclusive.

In an article from the National Shooting Sports Foundation, Criminologist Gary Kleck performed a longitudinal analysis of the impact of the 1968 ban on 18-20-year-olds purchasing handguns. After testing for an effect on the share of violent crime arrests for the adults in this age group, he concluded that the results,

> *"there was no impact of these age restrictions on handgun purchases, on the 18-to-20 share of arrests for homicide, robbery or aggravated assault."* [296]

I said, in the beginning, the legislation to increase the age has gained traction and implemented recently, the latest reason is because of the mass shooting at Parkland High school in Florida. The Shooter, in this case, was only 19 years old. However, of the 23 deadliest shootings in the United States, only three of the shooters were under 21, Sandy Hook, Columbine, and Parkland.

- Sandy hook shooter was 20 years old; it was his mother's legally obtained firearm that he stole, which he also murdered her with that firearm. The age restriction in the Sandy Hook case would not have changed the outcome.
- In the case of the Columbine shooters, they purchased their guns illegally through a straw purchase, during the years of the Assault Weapon Ban. Therefore, the age restriction would not have changed the outcome nor did the AWB.
- Parkland shooting is much less about age and much more about the ineptness of Broward (Coward) County Law enforcement leadership and some of the healthcare providers involved. Approximately forty-five times, police responded to the Shooter's home over seven years, ranging from violent attacks and suicide attempts. Even though he was seen multiple times by clinicians, they chose not to commit him. Since the shooting, the Parkland shooter has attacked a guard and tried to steal the guard's stun gun. Even in prison, under constant supervision, people can commit crimes.

> *Of the 64 mass public shootings from 1998 through March 13, 2018, ten of the sixty-four attacks were done by people under age 21. Four of these ten attacks were done by people under age 18, and thus they were banned from being able to buy either handguns or*

*rifles. In all four of those attacks, the killers had a handgun. The proposed increase in the age limit to 21 wouldn't have changed their ability to buy a gun. The other six were between 18 and 20 and thus banned from buying a handgun, and a handgun was among the weapons used in one of those. Thus, in only 5 of the 64 attacks (8% of the attacks) could the proposed increase in the age limit have in theory prevented them from buying a gun used in their attacks, and those attacks accounted for 5.7 percent of all the casualties (84 out of 1,461). Given that half of these attacks occurred with weapons that the killers were already banned from buying, the question is whether these five sets of attackers who were 18 to 20 could have still obtained weapons even with the higher age limit on purchases, particularly given that these mass public shootings were planned at least six months in advance. -John R. Lott, Jr.* [297]

With the ASDM, it seems to be the norm not to ask enough questions. How many people have used those firearms in a mass shooting, conversely how many have used them in defense? How many guns were legally obtained? How many were gang-related? When they mention suicide, they work to make firearms unavailable for everyone, but again they fail to ask the hard question; why do these kids want to commit suicide? Why do the vast majority, basically all, mass shooters come from homes without a father? Why have almost all, if not all, of mass shooters been on behavior modification drugs? Mental health is, of course, a more complicated issue, so they argue over symptoms. This is not unlike prohibition, where the government tried to solve social problems and crime by going after a symptom and not a root cause. Crime will continue because actual issues are not being addressed; firearm bans, and restrictions will continue when new laws do not fix the problem.

How can all these politicians who believe you shouldn't have a firearm before you turn 21 also continue to approve of sending those under 21 to war? Why do ASDM politicians such as Nancy Pelosi push to lower the voting age to 16, but think you are not responsible enough to own a gun? How can you be responsible enough to take on $200k worth of student loans at 18, but you are not mature enough to protect yourself or your family?

What I've also encountered when arguing against age restrictions is the ridiculous statement, "so you think a nine-year-old should be able to buy semi-automatic rifles." This appeal to the extremes deserves to be answered in the same manner: "Yes, I believe the nine-year-old who saved up $500, then drove to a gun store without their parents, should be able to purchase the firearm." After all, they've demonstrated the maturity to have saved money and operated an automobile. If their parents gave them money or drove them, then they approved of the purchase and therefore facilitated the purchase, which they could do just as easily underage restrictions. The point being is that it is not an actual scenario. Also, I had my first BB gun and compound bow by the time I was ten years old. By twelve, I walked around my grandparents' farm by myself with a .22, then later with a shotgun. Age restrictions didn't save anyone, my dad teaching me respect for those items (as well as the value of human life) did that, as millions of parents still do and have done for centuries.

One of my favorite stories about guns and applies to age restrictions comes from an unlikely place; I originally heard it while he was on the Norm Macdonald Show, it is the story of how comedian and actor David Spade grew up.

> "When we were 8, 10 and 12, my mom was really an on-the-go '70s woman. My dad scrammed. So, you know when you're a single mom in Arizona, we all had guns 'cause we're from Arizona. So, she would take us on the way to work to the end of the desert, and I had a rifle. Andy had a pistol. Bryan had a shotgun.... I was probably 10, so it was safer? joked Spade. "We had a lunch, a canteen and Bactine in case everything went

*wrong. And then, she would pick us up seven miles away at the Chevron station when she got off work.... We had a quarter to call her if there was any problems. But the pay phone was at the Chevron, so we had to get there at least. So we'd just walk, shoot cactus, shoot birds, shoot roadrunners, kill rattlesnakes,"*
*I have no idea Spade's stance on firearms except that he has used a shotgun in self-defense, and he gave Phoenix police $100,000 for them to buy approximately 300 rifles. [298]

## *You're More Likely to Kill a Family Member*

This kind of notion is passed around all the time by the ASDM crowd, and it revolves around one study from Arthur L. Kellerman. The study is well debunked, and while people can argue over the methods, it is simple to read and easy to see the failures. Even though this study is bunk, you can still find it spewed as a fact in many ASDM places like the Democratic Debate and Gifford's Law Center to Prevent Gun Violence. They claim that you are 90% more likely to kill a family member if you have a gun in your home. Just the claim of 90% more likely is highly suspect, so here is what Gifford says:

> *"Another study published in the American Journal of Epidemiology similarly found that "persons with guns in the home were at greater risk of dying from a homicide in the home than those without guns in the home." This study determined that the presence of guns in the home increased an individual's risk of death by homicide by 90%."*

What did that report say? This study's purpose was to study risk factors for homicides in the home. They did conclude that homes with firearms were more likely to have a homicide in them than ones without a gun. Of course, ASDM doesn't want to mention what else the reported. [299]

- Alcohol was more commonly consumed
- Illicit drug use was more common
- More likely to live alone
- More likely to rent rather than own a home
- More likely to have previous violence in the home
- 21% were felony related such as part of a burglary
- 7% were drug deals
- 7% were love triangles.

Translation: it wasn't just the guns! The quip by Gifford's makes you think a completely different conclusion than what the report says. Of the cases reviewed, 174 had a firearm in the home, and 139 did not. Out of all those cases, only 8 of these 444 homicides can the investigators prove that the gun used was the homeowners', so they were not murdered with their firearm. [300]

As mentioned, there were numerous other factors at play, such as domestic violence and drug abuse. The study is reviewing homicides inside the home it is not a study on breaking and entering, it is not a study on violent crime, it is not a study on rape prevention, nor domestic violence. When you read "90% more likely," I bet most of you thought accidental discharge or perhaps a child getting a gun. Frankly, the study does not account for enough factors nor does it study enough areas to make this a reliable case study. Here is justfacts.com reasoning for why they disregard the findings of this study Gifford's organization quotes.

- *The study blurs cause and effect. As explained in a comprehensive analysis of firearm research conducted by the National Research Council, gun control studies such as this (known as "case-control" studies) "fail to address the primary inferential problems that arise because ownership is not a random decision. ... Homicide victims may possess firearms precisely because they are likely to be victimized."*

- *The results are arrived at by subjecting the raw data to statistical processes instead of letting the data speak for itself. For reference, the raw data of this study shows that households in which a homicide occurred were:*
  - *25% more likely to have a firearm (45% vs. 36% for non-homicide households).*
  - *130% more likely have a household member who was previously arrested (53% vs. 23%).*
  - *400% more likely to have a household member who used illicit drugs (31% vs. 6%)*
  - *400% more likely to have a household member who was previously hit or hurt during a fight in the home (32% vs. 6%).*

Saying something like:

> *"living in a home where guns are kept increased an individual's risk of death by homicide by between 40% and 170%"* [299]

Is again misleading, as the report included suicides, (which is not a homicide as the stat suggests) and many of these are domestic abuse cases. Saying that it increases the risk of death makes people think of accidents and not actual crimes. This constant play on words is done on purpose.

The next report often cited says:

> *"individuals who were in possession of a gun were about 4.5 times more likely to be shot in an assault than those not in possession"* [301]

Makes one assume that you are speaking of only legal defensive use of a firearm, once again the story makes a nice sound bite for the ASDM but is completely misleading. The study they are quoting was done in Philadelphia; there is no differentiation on gang affiliation in the report. No telling if it was during a drug deal or other crime, we don't even know if the gun was pulled to use in these cases or if the person died with it holstered or in their vehicle. It is merely a study that focused on people who were shot and had a gun on them. As the study itself states:

> *"shooting case participants were significantly more often Hispanic, more frequently working in high-risk occupations, less educated, and had a greater frequency of prior arrest. At the time of shooting, case participants were also significantly more often involved with alcohol and drugs, outdoors, and closer to areas where more Blacks, Hispanics, and unemployed individuals resided. Case participants were also more likely to be located in areas with less income and more illicit drug trafficking"*
> [301]

This clearly is not a study of the standard licensed concealed carrier.

So far, what the ASDM has proved with these studies is that domestic violence and suicides need to be addressed, and that criminal activity is dangerous. What they did not prove was their initial statement:

> *"a gun is more likely to be used to kill or injure an innocent person in the home than a threatening intruder"*

Last along this line of thinking ASDM say defensive gun use happens far less than what gun advocates say. That claim is incorrect and again justfacts.com provides the crucial data:

- *Based on survey data from a 2000 study published in the Journal of Quantitative Criminology U.S. civilians use guns to defend themselves and others from crime at least 989,883 times per year.*

- *A 1993 nationwide survey of 4,977 households found that over the previous five years, at least 3.5% of households had members who had used a gun "for self-protection or for the protection of property at home, work, or elsewhere." This amounted to 1,029,615 such incidents per year. This excludes all "military service, police work, or work as a security guard."*

- *A 1994 survey conducted by the U.S. Centers for Disease Control and Prevention found that Americans use guns to frighten away intruders who are breaking into their homes about 498,000 times per year*

- *In 2013, President Obama ordered the Department of Health and Human Services and Centers for Disease Control and Prevention to "conduct or sponsor research into the causes of gun violence and the ways to prevent it." In response, the Centers for Disease Control and Prevention asked the Institute of Medicine and National Research Council to "convene a committee of experts to develop a potential research agenda focusing on the public health aspects of firearm-related violence...." This committee studied the issue of defensive gun use and reported:*

  - *"Defensive use of guns by crime victims is a common occurrence, although the exact number remains disputed...."*

  - *"Almost all national survey estimates indicate that defensive gun uses by victims are at least as common as offensive uses by criminals, with estimates of annual uses ranging from about 500,000 to more than 3 million...."*

  - *"Some scholars point to a radically lower estimate of only 108,000 annual defensive uses based on the National Crime Victimization Survey," but this "estimate of 108,000 is difficult to interpret because respondents were not asked specifically about defensive gun use."*

- *"Studies that directly assessed the effect of actual defensive uses of guns (i.e., incidents in which a gun was 'used' by the crime victim in the sense of attacking or threatening an offender) have found consistently lower injury rates among gun-using crime victims compared with victims who used other self-protective strategies...."*

### Assault Weapons are a Huge Problem in the United States.

From the ASDM group Everytown:

> *"A study of mass shooting incidents between 1981 and 2017 found that assault rifles accounted for 86 percent of the 501 fatalities reported in 44 mass shooting incidents."* [302]

AR15 and AK47 are incredibly efficient and reliable platforms. They are designed to be mass-produced, and they were made to be controlled by any skill level. Since they are plentiful and great weapons, people have used them instead of different options. Now to that info Everytown mentioned above: 86% of 501 is 430 deaths; this works out to 12 a year over the 36 years they cite. Now compare that to the fact that more people are killed per year by furniture. [303] twice as many are killed by falling TVs [304], 150 by falling coconuts [305], 15 by icicles [306] , and an insane amount from constipation 900 (and I thought it was just the ASDM that was full of shit) [307].

I do not intend to make lite of those deaths; I'm merely saying in relation to the number of "assault rifles," which there are million: from 2007 to 2016, production of AR15s more than doubled going from 1.6 million to 4.2 million according to the ATF. [308] While horrific it is incredibly uncommon to die at the hands of an "assault rifle." After all the sort of bar for "unlikeliness" is when someone says, "you're more likely to be struck by lightning," well in this case using those figures, you are more likely to be struck by lightning, 55 a year vs. the 12 by an "assault rifle" in a mass shooting. [309]

Moving away from mass shootings, when we look at overall violent deaths, you would think, given the rhetoric, the AR15 would top the charts. The problem is FBI doesn't even have a category specifically for AR15s or "Assault Rifles," it is just listed as rifles. But even including all rifles, you are still more likely to be murdered with a hammer, bat, bare hands, knife, etc... [310]

Every culture and generation have had a version of an "Assault Weapon" a Mongolian short bow was an assault weapon, the Kentucky long rifle was an assault rifle, the lever action was an assault weapon, the M1 carbine was an assault weapon. The AR15, AK47, FAL, etc. are now just the most efficient firearm of the day.

## *Gun Buy Back*

Common sense would dictate that since I did not BUY my guns from you, then you cannot BUY them back from me. I cover a full buyback later when we investigate Australia, in this section, we will cover the more common local buybacks that are done by the police, sometimes with community centers and other times churches.

These buybacks are ridiculous; for one, the person turning them in is usually a person who had no intention of using that gun for harm, it was merely an old gun they had that they lying around. [311] Many of those people think they are getting a dangerous weapon off the street; however, what the turn in place will not tell you is that in some states, these guns cannot be destroyed. By law, they have to resell these firearms to gun dealers and through auction houses. [312]

Second is the other type of people who use these places. It is advertised that no questions are asked, so criminals will take stolen firearms to these locations and use them to launder their goods. These buyback locations are just a fence for stolen goods at that point, encouraging more crime. If you're a criminal do you steal a car stereo or a TV and sell it to a pawn shop that must look out for stolen goods, or do you take firearms so you can sell them risk-free to the police?

## *Nobody Needs a....*

> *"Necessity is the plea for every infringement of human freedom. It is the argument of tyrants; it is the creed of slaves." -William Pitt the Younger* [313]

What someone determines they need is none of your business as long as they aren't hurting anyone. The AR, AK, and similar platforms were designed for a reason. As I've said, they provide great power and controllability; therefore, they are popular; it is why the military uses them and why your local law enforcement has them.

Now, if your local law enforcement has them, then why wouldn't you need them? What threat are they coming across that you couldn't possibly have to deal with on your own? I understand it's not common; however, I also have a new generator in my garage I haven't used for five years, technically I've never "needed" it. I also lock my doors even though no one has ever tried to break in, so you could say I don't "need" to lock my doors. But look, I'm not going to be selling my generator, I'm still locking my doors, and I am certainly keeping my guns.

It boils down to a fundamental difference in mentalities. Two schools of thought one is self-reliance, the other relies on government to intercede. It's no wonder that gun owners typically prefer less governmental interference in our lives while the ASDM crowd is usually in line with government involvement in our lives.

Bottomline, when panic hits one bolt action rifle starts to feel like not enough. 50 rounds of ammo starts to feel like no ammo at all, and 1,000 rounds starts to seem like the bare minimum. In March of 2020 during the Covid-19 panic Americans bought 3.7 million firearms, the most on record. [314] A lot of these were first time gun buyers who quickly changed their stance on what they <u>needed</u> in an emergency.

## *Real Men Don't Need Guns or Compensating for Penis Size.*

To piggyback on the previous topic, this one comes up a lot. Oddly enough you would think the argument that you aren't a real man would be made by male chauvinist, but this is made by the group with preferred pronouns in their bios. For one self-defense is not reserved for males. Second the possible correct lingo would be to say that responsible people (male or females) choose to defend themselves and their loved ones by whatever means they feel necessary.

As far as penis size, I don't know what to tell you. We all saw the scene in Braveheart where the Scots show off their manhood before they go into battle, but a key point to that was after they showed off the length of their poles, they picked up arms to fight.

I don't know how you train but if a group of attackers break into my home, I hope I am armed with more than my penis. Afterall Urban Dictionary defines the term "dick in your hand" as someone stuck in a predicament without the right tools.

Really these are just childish ignorant comments that do not deserve a reply. A person who makes this type of comment has not moved on since middle school and are probably expressing their own insecurities.

## *Guns Don't Stop Mass Shootings*

Some say guns do not stop mass shootings. Do you know why some statistics say they don't? Because they shoot the person before they become mass shootings, so they are left out of the stats of mass shootings. Also, most mass shootings are in gun-free zones. 94% of mass shootings since 1950 have occurred in gun-free zones. [315]

As a side note. It is also interesting how stats that are funded by ASDM affluent businessmen like Bloomberg are considered unbiased. Yet, if a study says anything positive about firearms, the data is associated with the NRA, even if there are no links to the NRA. So why when an ASDM group like Everytown, Bloomberg, or Soros "sponsor" research it is supposedly gospel and not to be questioned. The "research" is parroted by every news agency as if it had settled the question. If you want to know more about this, I suggest John Lott's books "The Bias Against Guns," and "The War on Guns." Both books do a great job and breaking down the propaganda.

### The Founders Meant Muskets! (or they didn't know about repeating arms.)

> "There are other things so clearly out of the power of Congress, that the bare recital of them is sufficient. I mean "rights of conscience, or religious liberty — the rights of bearing arms for defense, or for killing game — the liberty of fowling, hunting and fishing."
> February 22, 1788 Alexander White: Winchester Gazette (VA) (*Notice how he says both for defense and for hunting)

This is a popular argument from the ASDM crowd; it shouldn't be. As we went over prior, the founders meant military-style firearms. Local Massachusetts ordinance specifically mentions not keeping your cannon, howitzer, mortars, grenades, etc. loaded within the city limits due to fire hazard. The penalty for having those loaded, according to the ordinance, was that they would be sold at <u>public</u> auction. They did not say a private government auction, not melted down or smashed, but resold to the public... and without a background check.

The earliest repeating firearms known as a repeater date back to between 1490 and 1530. There were machine guns with 16 round capacities as far back as 1580. A Danish firearm inventor designed a repeating firearm with a capacity of 30 rounds in 1640. Kalthoff repeaters as they were called were copied across the world [316]. We know of the Puckle gun, which held 6 to 11 rounds was patented in 1718 [317]. Another repeating rifle was made to which we know the founders knew about because we have the letter sent to them by Joseph Belton in 1777. Belton claimed the firearm could fire 16 shots in 20 seconds [318]. Yet another example was the Girandonu Rifle patented around 1780 [319], which was carried by Lewis and Clark. The Girandonu could fire twenty-two .46 caliber projectiles with an effective range of over 100 yards. This all means the founders new about repeating arms well before the writing of the 2nd amendment.

## *Cops Will Protect You*

> *"Make no mistake, every single person in America owns a gun. Some of you just pay a guy across town to hold yours and hope he's available to bring it over when you need to protect your family. I prefer to have mine on my hip"* twitter @helengilson_

I can only assume people make this argument live in nice neighborhoods. Because it isn't the reality in Detroit, and it isn't the reality in rural America. Cops cannot be there instantly; some are not able to be there within an hour or two, so no, the police cannot protect you. But more important is that they aren't required to protect you. What is even more infuriating about this is that this is what ALL gun control boils down to, this is what the ASDM is ALL about, the cops protecting you, yet the police do not always have the ability, and they do not ultimately have the responsibility.

> *"Neither the Constitution, nor state law, impose a general duty upon police officers or other governmental officials to protect individual persons from harm — even when they know the harm will occur. Police can watch someone attack you, refuse to intervene and not violate the Constitution."* -Darren L. Hutchinson, a

*professor and associate dean at the University of Florida School of Law.* [320]

- **Hartzler v. San Jose 1975:** The court held that the San Jose police were not liable for ignoring Mrs. Brunell's pleas for help. Ruth Brunell called the police on 20 different occasions to plead for protection from her husband.
  - He was arrested only one time. One evening, Mr. Brunell telephoned his wife and told her he was coming over to kill her. When she called the police, they refused her request that they come to protect her. They told her to call back when he got there. Mr. Brunell stabbed his wife to death before she could had a chance to make that call to the police to tell them that he was there.

- **Warren v. D.C 1981:** The Court ruled the "fundamental principle of American law that a government and its agents are under no general duty to provide public services, such as police protection, to any individual citizen."
  *Warning, this one will make your blood boil*
  - Two women were upstairs in a townhouse when they heard their roommate, a third woman, being attacked downstairs by intruders. They phoned the police several times and were assured that the officers were on the way. After about 30 minutes, when their roommate's screams had stopped, they assumed that the police had finally arrived. When the two women went downstairs, they saw that, in fact, the police never came, but the intruders were still there. As the Warren court graphically states in the opinion:
    *"For the next fourteen hours the women were held captive, raped, robbed, beaten, forced to commit sexual acts upon each other, and made to submit to the sexual demands of their attackers."*

- **Bowers v. DeVito 1982:** The appeal court ruled, "There is no constitutional right to be protected by the state against being murdered by criminals or madmen. It is monstrous if the state fails to protect its residents from predators, but it does not violate the 14th Amendment or, we suppose, any other provision of the Constitution."

- Case summary from Casetext: *"In 1970 Vanda was convicted of aggravated battery with a knife. He was diagnosed at Madden as a "schizophrenic in remission" but must soon have been released because in 1971 he killed a young woman with a knife. This time he was found not guilty by reason of insanity and was committed to Madden. But he was released in April 1976 and a year later murdered Miss Bowers with a knife. The complaint alleges that the defendants knew that Vanda was dangerous when they released him and acted recklessly in doing so."*

- **Castle Rock v. Gonzales 2005:** The Supreme Court ruled that the police did not have a constitutional duty to protect a person from harm, even in the case of a personal protection order/ restraining order.
  - Jessica Gonzales estranged husband kidnapped her daughters and eventually murdered them.

- **Broward County 2018:** Judge ruled officers had no duty to protect students.
  - After 17 students were gunned down it was found that while eight sheriff deputies who raced to the school when they heard gun shots, they all stayed outside the building.

I have pointed these cases out before to other progun individuals on social media and I had some claim that I was taking the cases out of context, however when I asked for correct context they didn't reply in kind. Instead they made a new rebuttal and defense for the police. They claimed that if the court said that law enforcement was responsible then anytime someone was harmed then they could sue the police, law enforcement would be inundated with lawsuits. But that's not what these cases were at all, these cases were not when cops COULD NOT act, these are cases when they DID NOT act. Read Warren v. DC again if you think the cops should not have been held liable.

Now look at the Covid19/ Coronavirus pandemic in 2020. Law Enforcement across the country put out word they will not be responding to property crimes, burglary, vandalism, auto-theft, etc. [321]. Some even made it a point to say they would not be responding to domestic disturbance cases if the other person was not still at the scene. Given the giant spike in gun and ammo purchases during that time, approximately 3.7 million firearms, you can see that a lot of people realized their self-defense was now in their own hands.

> *"Gun laws are an attempt to nationalize the right of self-defense. Politicians perennially react to the police's abject failure to prevent crime by trying to disarm law-abiding citizens. The worse government fails to control crime, the more politicians want to restrict individual rights to defend themselves.*

> *But police protection in most places is typical government work... slow, inefficient, and unreliable. According to laws on the books in many states and cities, government has a specific, concrete obligation to disarm each citizen, but only an abstract obligation to defend each citizen. The government has stripped millions of people of their right to own weapons yet generally left them free to be robbed, raped, and murdered. "Gun control" is on the of the best examples of laws that corner private citizens, forcing them either to put themselves into danger or to be a lawbreaker."*

> *Even the most advanced cellular phone is no substitute for a good .38 Special."*

> *-James Brovard, author of Lost Rights, quoted in "The Boston Gun Bible"* [322]

Look at these stats from gunfacts.info

- *14,196 murder victims, 345,031 robbery victims, and 79,770 rape victims who the police could not help.*
- *There are not enough police to protect everyone. In 1999, there were about 150,000 police officers on duty at any one time.*
  - *This is on-duty police. This includes desk clerks, command sergeants, etc. – far fewer than 150,000 cops are cruising your neighborhood.*
- *There were approximately 271,933,702 people living in the United States in 1999.*
  - *Thus, there is only one on-duty cop for every 1,813 citizens.*
- *Former Florida Attorney General Jim Smith told Florida legislators that police responded to only 200,000 of 700,000 calls for help to Dade County authorities.*
- *The United States Department of Justice found that, in 1989, there were 168,881 crimes of violence for which police had not responded within 1 hour.*
- *95% of the time police arrive too late to prevent a crime or arrest the suspect.*
- *75% of protective/restraining orders are violated and police often won't enforce them unless they witness the violation.*

### *We Need Firearm Registration:*

First, this is a direct infringement of the 2$^{nd}$ amendment. Imagine if the federal government decided to make you register printing presses, or showed up to churches for massive bible registration? There would be outrage as this would be a violation of the 1$^{st}$ amendment. The bottom line is that it is not a "right" if it can be taken away by not submitting a piece of paper or registering an item. If the government regulates it as such, then it is viewing it as a "privilege," not a "right," and self-defense is one of the most basic human rights.

It also doesn't work. One reason it doesn't work is that felons are not required to register their firearms. Haynes v. U.S. ruled registration is a violation of their 5th amendment rights. Since they cannot legally own a firearm registering a firearm would be bearing witness against oneself. Therefore, registration only affects law-abiding citizens.

The ASDM believe that registration will solve crimes, but think about it do you think criminals are dropping their firearms at the scene? If they had to register the weapon, do you think they would leave the item that would link them to the crime?

> *During a 2013 deposition, the Washington, D.C., police chief said that she could not "recall any specific instance where registration records were used to determine who committed a crime." [323]*

Canada attempted a nationwide registration and abandoned it after they realized the cost without a discernable impact on crime. The initial estimated cost was $2 million dollars but grew to $1 billion before it was stopped. [324]

Registration is a violation of the 2nd amendment as the government has no right to dictate what paperwork needs to be completed before owning a firearm. The government has no business knowing what you possess in your house. And they have no business knowing how you choose to protect yourself or your family inside or outside your home.

### *We Regulate Cars and License Drivers!*

Well, maybe if they mean we treat firearms the same as automobiles, then I'll bite. Nick Leghorn from The Truth About Guns has created a helpful list of let's say pluses for treating them the same. [325]

- *Car dealers don't need to be licensed by the federal government. Gun dealers do*

- *Car dealers don't need to keep meticulous records of all transactions under penalty of law. Gun dealers do.*
- *Cars don't require registration to own or licensing to operate. Neither do guns.*
- *Cars can legally be sold across state lines. Selling a gun across state lines is a felony.*
- *Driver's licenses are valid in all states. Concealed carry licenses aren't.*
- *I don't need to tell the ATF when I take my short wheel-base car to another state. I do need to tell them when I take my SBR hunting rifle.*
- *Cars aren't banned just because they look scary. "Assault weapons" are.*
- *I get a tax credit when I buy certain cars. I don't get a tax credit for my new hunting rifle*

Once you regulate a right, you turn it into a privilege. I am always shocked to see some from the gun community supporting ideas like this, or at least a version of federal "drivers" license for firearm owners. It's like they can't grasp that they are falling for all the other gun control measures with all their failures just packaged differently. No, a federal license on firearms is not common sense or a great option for gun owners. These IDs would be akin to registration by identifying yourself as a gun owner to the federal government; this method would still incorporate background checks; it still includes all the criminals obtaining firearms illegally.

The burden of proof for any proposed gun law should be on the supporters of these plans to show what shooting this would've stopped.

Finally, the elephant in the room is that the federal government has no business regulating firearms or implementing these IDs. The 2nd amendment is meant specifically to keep the federal government away from your guns, stop bringing them back into the debate thinking they will save you from your states.

## Saturday Night Specials, *(an argument for cheap guns)*

> *"To ban guns because criminals use them is to tell the law abiding that their rights and liberties depend not on their own conduct, but on the conduct of the guilty and the lawless" -Jeff Snyder* [326]

Jimenez, Raven, Cobra, and the granddaddy of them all Hi-point; no, I am not trying to convince you that these are great firearms, merely saying they serve a legitimate purpose. Not everyone can afford to pay $500 for a handgun. Some in the gun community may scoff at this, believing that the $500 is worth it. While I agree, let's not forget what these sub $200 firearms are. These guns are for personal protection; no one is going to put a thousand rounds (or even a quarter of that) through these firearms.

While these firearms would not be my first choice, cheap guns are all the protection some people have and add that to the fact that many shootings and assaults take place in low-income environments. Those law-abiding citizens have the most to gain from protecting themselves, and if they only can spend $100, then so be it. My question to the ASDM would be, what price range is too cheap? Who will determine how much you must spend on a firearm? What "class" do you need to be in before you're allowed to protect yourself.

What we need to realize is that our guns or self-defense procedures may seem like a "Saturday night special" to other people. It boils down to is the ruling classes dictating what the other classes can use to defend themselves. We are quick in the gun community to point out celebrities & politicians who pitch gun control are surrounded by security, and just because we cannot afford bodyguards, it does not mean we don't deserve the right to defend ourselves. We should also remember that while some people protect themselves with bodyguards, others might protect themselves with a Noveske AR15, and others may only be able to protect their families with an Anderson AR15 or even a Hi-point.

> *"Gun prohibition is the brainchild of white middle-class liberals who are oblivious to the situation of poor and minority people living in areas where the police have given up on crime control. Such liberals weren't upset about marijuana laws, either, in the fifties when the busts were confined to the ghettos. Secure in well-policed suburbs or high-security apartments guarded by Pinkertons (whom no one proposes to disarm), the oblivious liberal derides gun ownership as "an anachronism from the Old West."* Don B. Kates, Jr [327]

Some stats taken from gunfacts.info
> *-Saturday Night Specials" were used in fewer than 3% of crimes involving guns.*
> *-Fewer than 2% of all "Saturday Night Specials" made are used in crimes.*

## *Accessories Are Not Covered by the 2<sup>nd</sup> Amendment*

> *"There is no such thing as the right of some men to vote away the rights of others"*
> *-Ayn Rand*

While the Supreme Court has not heard an argument on magazine capacity, many of the proponents of bills such as these assert that they are constitutional as they believe the 2nd amendment does not pertain to accessories. It is the equivalent of saying the 1st amendment doesn't pertain to the internet, as if the internet is a subset of speech, not actual speech. If your argument is the 2nd amendment does not cover accessories like magazines or ammunition, then you're either a liar or willfully ignorant. It really comes from a perverted understanding of the Constitution, the Bill of Rights, and the 2nd amendment.

*"Gun control advocates attempt to avoid the real issue of gun rights—why the Founders felt so strongly about gun rights that they singled them out for special protection in the Bill of Rights—by demanding that individual rights be balanced against a counterfeit collective right to "security" from things that go bump in the night. But, the Bill of Rights was not a Bill of Entitlements that people had a right to demand from government; it was a Bill of Protections against the government itself. The Founders understood that the right to own and bear laws is as fundamental and as essential to maintaining liberty as are the rights of free speech, a free press, freedom of religion and the other protections against government encroachments on liberty delineated in the Bill of Rights." -Lawrence Hunter* [328]

Context matters, and while the education system in this country is severely lacking, I believe it is still taught that we fought the British to gain independence from a tyrannical king. It shouldn't take a leap of understanding to realize that our constitution was ratified under this shadow. Freemen and free states were not about to trade:

*"one tyrant three thousand miles away for three thousand tyrants one mile away" -Mather Byles 1788 (quoted by Mel Gibson in the Patriot).*

The idea that they would argue for the 2nd amendment as protection against a tyrannical government but then believe that the same government has the right to dictate how they can use that right is absurd. All gun laws including those on accessories are infringements, and enforcers of those gun laws are violating their oaths.

*Nunn v. State held the statute unconstitutional under the 2nd amendment to the federal Constitution. The court held that the Bill of Rights protected natural rights which were fully as capable of infringement by states as* *by the federal government and that the 2nd amendment provided "the right of the whole people, old and young, men, women and boys, and not militia only, to keep and bear <u>arms of every description</u>, and not merely such as are used by the militia, <u>shall not be infringed, curtailed, or broken in on, in the slightest degree;</u> and all this for the important end to be attained: the rearing up and qualifying of a well-regulated militia, so vitally necessary to the security of a free state." Senate committee hearing on the 2nd amendment 1982* [329]

## Bump-stocks

Along the lines of accessories are bump stocks. For those of you who don't know bump stocks (slide fire/ bump-fire) is a product that allows for a faster rate of semi-automatic fire while still only producing one shot per trigger pull. This led to a ruling by the ATF that bump stocks were not subject to NFA regulations. Some claim that bump stocks can attain rates up to 800 rounds per minute, which anyone in the gun world will tell you is a sensationalized claim. The Vegas gunman took about 10 minutes to fire 1,100 rounds, a lot of rounds (110 per minute), but nowhere close to 800 rounds and no more than could be fired without the addition of a bump stock.

More on Vegas since this is where the issue began, the tragic events of that day left 58 dead and 489 wounded. It is a devastating amount from a mass shooting, and if you add those numbers to the other times bump stocks were used since 2010, you will come up with a total of 58 dead and 489 wounded. Yep, as horrible as that event was, the bump stock has never been used in a shooting before [330]. To compare; high school football results in 12 deaths annually, cows, bees, hot water, and auto-erotic asphyxiation all result in more deaths than the bump stock. So why go after bump stocks?

No doubt the argument that is pushed by gun control organizations such as the NRA [331] is something like: "the bump-stock is a useless accessory that can easily be the sacrificial lamb, the goal of gun owners should be National Reciprocity." National Reciprocity is the right of gun owners to carry concealed no matter what state they are in.

However, history shows this will not work, and incidents like this are why the NRA is losing members, upper management, and money. You see, gun control over the last century has not been pleasant to the gun owner in America, not only in its restrictions but in its constant reinterpretations. Example: the 1934 National Firearms Act (NFA) was pushed to go after gangsters and not meant to target citizens; therefore, the committee at the time concluded it did not infringe on the 2nd amendment. This act made gun owners pay the hefty tax of $200 for a shotgun less than 18 inches. As a frame of reference, a shotgun's cost was a mere $6 at that time. A few years later, a case made it to the supreme court, Miller V. United States. The case was regarding a 16-inch barrel shotgun, and at that time, Justice McReynolds ruled a 16-inch barrel shotgun had no MILITARY purpose, therefore, was not protected by the 2nd amendment. Fast forward to the Gun Control Act (GCA) of 1968, where it was ruled a firearm must have a SPORTING purpose; this, of course, isn't the end of the violations but it proves the point that the government words things how they want to, when they want to, in order to get the results, they desire.

This same line of government meddling will be used with the bump-stock ban, and this is where the NRA hurt itself tremendously after the Vegas shooting. One they blamed Obama, which was ridiculous, imagine an organization that said Obama was going to take your guns now saying Obama was too lenient. Then the guy the NRA endorsed as the most pro-gun president, has passed more gun control legislation to date [332] [333]. Look at the NRA's wording in their statement after the Vegas shooting.

> *"The NRA believes that devices designed to allow semi-automatic rifles to function like full-automatic*

*rifles should be subject to additional regulations."*
[234]

Countless people in the gun community saw a pro-gun NRA endorsed president as a way to finally repeal the 1934 NFA and the 1986 Hughes amendment, or at the very least pass the Hearing Protection Act, which would remove suppressors/silencers from the NFA. Over 250,000 of us signed a petition for this administration to repeal the NFA (we never even got a response). However, the NRA's statement clearly shows they believe that these items need additional regulations.

The other issue here is that the NRA is blaming a device. For years the NRA and their talking heads have said accessories such as pistol grips, magazine capacity, collapsible stocks, etc. do not play a role in the deadliness of a firearm. And the dangerous part isn't the firearm at all, as it is only an object or tool. Blaming bump-stocks turns this age-old argument on its head.

What's more, is some states have pushed legislation with proposed language referring to an "increase in cyclic rate." Who gets to distinguish what an increase in cyclic rate is? It's like asking what a "livable wage" is. Items such as triggers can increase the cyclic rate by having a shorter reset; the reset is the minimum length a trigger must return before another pull can take place. Gas tubes can affect cyclic rate, muzzle devices, buffer systems, ammo, and on and on; even gun oil could have some effect on the rate of fire. And now we are seeing states pass bans on what they are calling "Trigger Activators" normally called binary triggers.

Politicians have this nasty habit of continuing down futile paths and promising results only to head further down and continue to attempt to legislate a result. Just look at the spending on the war on drugs that has been lost [334], spending on education even though schools have done worse since the creation of department of education [335], and of course the failed war on terrorism [336]. Just throw more money at it, and if that doesn't work, it throws more and adds more bureaucrats. If one law doesn't work, then we need more laws, and of course they will not repeal any prior failed laws. Let us not forget to look back and realize bump-stocks were explicitly invented because of bad legislation (the NFA).

Ultimately banning bump-stocks will not save any lives. This ban will not be exchanged for National Reciprocity or any positive for gun owners; it will merely be the next legislative placebo used to chip away at our rights and be one more steppingstone for further bans.

By the way according to a FOIA request to ATF, as of April 2019 only 582 bump-stocks have been turned in [337] out of around a million sold (.0582%) [338].

### *Manufacturer Liability*

> *"The rifle itself has no moral stature, since it has no will of its own. Naturally, it may be used by evil men for evil purposes, but there are more good men than evil, and while the latter cannot be persuaded to the path of righteousness by propaganda, they can certainly be corrected by good men with rifles."*
> -Jeff Cooper

It seems almost cliché to say or perhaps small-minded to list all the scenarios where this idea of holding a company accountable for an end-user inappropriately using their product, but more homicides are linked to blunt force than that of firearms, will we be holding Louisville Slugger accountable, perhaps Estwing for their hammers? Is Budweiser or Ford responsible for drunk drivers? Gerber or Kershaw for stabbings? I know this seems absurd; however, the bias is all too evident when it comes to firearms, no other right, no other product, no other amendment is under so much scrutiny.

Hillary Clinton, during her failed 2016 campaign and since her loss (lol) has been one of the most prominent politicians pushing for manufacturer liability, maybe because Bill Clinton also pushed for this as well. Funny that of all people, these two are the ones pushing for accountability [339]. A few of the items pushed by Bill Clinton administration was for firearm manufacturers to include locking devices, limit magazine sizes, and end advertising. Smith and Wesson (S&W) was the first to jump on board in 2000; the result was S&W almost went bankrupt.

Gun owners saw them as sellouts and boycotted their products [340]. If you read papers like the Washington Post [341] or Business Insider [342]you read that this was an awful display by gun owners, "S&W was trying to do the right thing." That, however, is not the whole story. S&W did not "jump on board" they did so in exchange for an end to the legal battles they were embroiled in. In short, they were blackmailed into it. In 2001 however, S&W ownership changed, and George W. Bush supported lawsuit protection for gun manufacturers; this new trajectory for S&W quickly fell apart, and they are now one of the top firearm manufacturers.

We do have legislation passed during this same Clinton administration that we can look to that shows firearm manufacturers may not be as unique as we first thought when it comes to liability protection. In 1996 the Communications Decency Act (CDA) was passed. The CDA is an attempt to deal with obscenity on the internet and may not seem connected to this subject, but there is relevant text to our argument. Section 230 of the CDA states:

> "No provider or user of an interactive computer service shall be treated as the publisher or speaker of any information provided by another information content provider." [343]

What is this saying? It essentially makes online services immune from civil liability for the actions of their users. It is important to note that this doesn't mean they cannot be sued when they are liable, and the gun community is not arguing that firearm manufacturers shouldn't be held responsible when they are actually at fault. On the contrary, the gun community is one of the harshest and most quick to criticize manufacturers when they produce an unsatisfactory or unsafe product.

When numerous state attorney generals called for this section 230 to be removed from the CDA, the ACLU said:

> *"If Section 230 is stripped of its protections, it wouldn't take long for the vibrant culture of free speech to disappear from the web."* [344]

I wonder if they would be as quick to jump in to defend firearm manufacturers from liability.

One thing the ASDM is not considering when they push to sue firearm manufacturers is what these firearm companies mean to the United States. Sure, there is an economic impact on the United States as the firearm industry ranks second amongst sporting good sales (number one fitness equipment, number three is golf). But the other issue is the defense of this country, one of the primary purposes of the 2nd amendment.

For instance, we currently have, to the dismay of the founding fathers, a vast standing army at around 1.3 million, but we are third in size in the world after India and China. It is essential to our homeland defense that we keep our populace well-armed. It is not enough that we are armed, almost equally important is that our country be able to manufacture our arms for our defense. By the term "arms," I do not mean just firearms but ammunition, magazines, optics, etc. Take a look at our arms industry, and you see that innovation that wasn't so much done by the military as the private sector did it and then implemented later by the military. The military may have asked for solutions or changes to said problems, but it relied on manufacturers to compete in the free market. The AR15, for example, was developed by Eugene Stoner, Jim Sullivan, and Armalite, a private company not a military armory.

Frivolous lawsuits harm and stifle manufacturers, they are forced to spend money defending themselves in court instead of spending the money on innovation. We know this is the case, and the great firearm inventor John Browning understood this. Browning sold his designs to companies instead of creating his own factories partially because he saw the nightmare manufacturers like Colt went through as they were in constant legal battles defending their firearm patents.

Again no one in the gun community believes that manufacturers have immunity when it comes to creating faulty products. However, they are in no way liable when an end-user decides to use their product for a different intent. No more responsible than Ryder is responsible for McVeigh, the United States Postal Service for Ted Kaczynski, or Boeing for 9/11.

## *I Support the 2nd Amendment But…*

But… you don't.

Definition of the conjunction "But"
> 1. on the contrary; yet:
> 2. except;
> 3. unless; if not; except that (followed by a clause, often with that expressed) (from dictionary.com)

Or take the definition from urbandictionary.com, where the top definition is "to delay the inevitable" second is "a word used to nullify all the words preceding the sentence."

You know that what is coming after "but" is about to contradict or diminish what was said before. Even if I was to say something like "I support the 2nd amendment, but…my rights are not confined to the constitution." This isn't an antigun, however by adding "but" it is implying that what I am about to say is more important.

When talking about gun rights with others in the gun community, whether online or in person, you will get at least one person inserting a scenario where they believe in gun rights and at the same time believe firearms should be regulated. That of course is no different than the ASDM who have also chosen a level in which they believe the 2nd amendment and a standard to which they think firearms should be regulated.

We've already covered the wording and purpose of the 2nd amendment, so I am not going to do that again here except to take a look at the stringency placed in this text with the words "shall not be infringed."

Infringed:

- To wrongly limit or restrict *Websters*
- Act so as to limit or undermine *Oxford*
- Synonyms: break, encroach, weaken, disobey, meddle

The right of the people to keep and bear Arms, shall not be limited, restricted, undermined, encroached, weakened. If you make the statement that you support the 2nd amendment and then list an infringement then you do not support the 2nd amendment, the logic doesn't follow.

*To clarify, I am not saying you must be gung-ho about the 2nd amendment or the constitution to own firearms, nor am I saying that believing in some gun control means you don't have the right to own firearms. Self-defense is a Natural Right that belongs to all people; it doesn't matter your political beliefs, race, religion, gender, budget, etc.

## We Put Limits on Free Speech, *(you can't yell fire in a crowded theater...)*

> *"It should further be clear from our discussion of defense that every man has the absolute right to bear arms — whether for self-defense or any other licit*

*purpose. The crime comes not from bearing arms, but from using them for purposes of threatened or actual invasion. It is curious, by the way that the laws have especially banned concealed weapons, when it is precisely the open and unconcealed weapons which might be used for intimidation." -Murray Rothbard*

In the words of Stefan Molyneux, "not an argument." This statement is just a strawman fallacy; it does not apply to the debate. To understand, we should look at this idea's origin.

The case where this stems from is Schenck v. United States, and I doubt most people would agree with the decision if they knew the context. The original case was regarding Schenck protesting World War 1 by handing out flyers against the war. I assume most people reading this would at least agree that Schenck had the right to protest freely even if they disagree with the content. Later, this case was somewhat overturned in 1969 with Brandenburg v. Ohio, which defined the limit as "likely to incite imminent lawless action." Even Supreme Court Justice Holmes, who is responsible for the phrase "falsely shouting fire in a theatre and causing a panic," later walked back his statement. [345]

So, to summarize, yelling fire in a crowded theater is used as an example of malicious speech in which the intent is to cause harm, in this example where someone intends to harm is not free speech. This would be like saying the 2nd amendment protects murder if it was done with a firearm, and no gun owner is making that argument.

If you want to read more about the absurdity of laws such as "yelling fire in a crowded theater," then I suggest reading Walter Block's book "Defending the Undefendable." Quite frankly, the real answer to this is that they shouldn't have laws limiting speech either. [346] Audio version of his breakdown of this topic is here: [347]

# Less and Less People are Owning Guns in the US

> *"Since 2007, the number of concealed handgun permits has soared from 4.6 million to over 12.8 million, and murder rates have fallen from 5.6 killings per 100,000 people to just 4.2, about a 25 percent drop."* [348]

Imagine every time you turn on the news; you're made out to be the villain. Open Twitter and see another celebrity or politician calling for a ban on guns and telling people that gun owners are evil. You watch a presidential debate and see candidates saying they are coming for your guns. After all this your phone rings, the person asks, "do you own a gun?" How are you going to answer? Don't you think that statistic they quote might be a little skewed?

First off, who answers their phone nowadays, not just an unknown number but for anyone, certainly not anyone under thirty-five years old. If you do answer, are you going to tell someone what is in your house? That statistic should read, "firearm ownership is down amongst people weird enough to answer an unknown number and provide them with data on how they defend themselves."

Of course, some may say these are online polls, but didn't the media just spend 3 years telling us Russia has interfered with elections by manipulating online polls?

The reason they are saying fewer and fewer Americans are owning firearms is to make it taboo; if people think it is more obscure and perhaps irrational, they will possibly not buy a firearm. It's like a self-fulfilling prophecy. They can use this leverage when lobbyist go to congress and try to sell the ASDM agenda by saying fewer voters are gun owners.

There are a few other things we can look at to see that guns are not going anywhere. One is the ATF report on manufacturing, which has increased dramatically, peaking at the end of the Obama presidency. Second, we can look at the increase in the number of concealed carriers which is up 273% since 2007, that number is even with more states now allowing permit-less carry. [349]

## *"Libertarian" Gun Control: Opting out*

What has been called "Libertarian Gun Control" is a way that anyone, but specifically designed for the suicidal, can opt-out of their gun rights. It works just like opting out of telemarketing calls by registering on a national "do not call list," but instead, it would be a "do not sell list." People could voluntarily add themselves to the list, and if they wanted to get off, they would have to go through a specific process, possibly with different levels. For instance, something as simple as a one-week waiting list all the way to requiring a mental evaluation to get removed off the list. Given the amount of ASDMs arguing that the reason we need things such as waiting periods is due to self-harm and suicides, then this may be an option within our current framework.

Let me preface this a little more; I don't care for inward libertarian arguments. Decoding someone's level of "libertarianess" isn't anything I care about. However, I don't understand why it is called "Libertarian gun control" maybe big "L" libertarian gun control, perhaps minarchist gun control, or possibly republican gun control but I certainly would not say libertarian gun control.

As I said, I do not know how well this will work, but as the system is intended to be 100% voluntary for the person who puts themselves on the list, then if it saves one life, it may be worth it. In this plan, you don't have the other issues where someone may be withheld from getting a firearm when they need it and getting delayed or denied in error based on or other obstructions such as waiting lists, and you are not putting people on a secret list. This system has a clear set of instructions on how they can get their right back that they voluntarily surrendered. But this is of course all in theory.

There are big problems though; this is relying on the framework of a failed unjust background check system. That is why I say it isn't a "libertarian" gun control idea but perhaps better labeled a "republican" gun control idea. If we imagine that NICS does not exist and people were able to opt-in for this no-buy-list, then it becomes more palatable, although we run into a new issue, and that is the other parties involved in the sale, one being the firearm dealer. If it were voluntary, then the dealers would be able to opt-in as well. Ask yourself, though, would you opt-in to a program that could land you in a civil suit?

The "libertarianess" of this idea seems to break down once a dealer is required to check the list. Imagine a scenario where say a person is purchasing a firearm, and the website is down, or possibly a poor internet connection is interfering with looking up the buyer. What if the buyer in this scenario is not on the list and is delayed due to the website? In this scenario, you have dragged in another party that did not opt-in for the no-buy-list. Sites and internet connections do go down, I have seen gun shows grind to a halt when NICS e-check is down and phone hold times are multiple hours long.

If this system is not mandatory and there is no liability, then this system may never get used. After all, how often is that cashier looking for the signature on your credit card? In a scenario where it is not required, and someone tells you their name is not on the list, then you could offend or lose a customer by checking the no-buy-list. So, will the fear of lawsuits and fear of lost sales make it so a dealer would never participate in the program?

I realize no system is perfect, and I'm sure the creators of this idea are not saying it is foolproof but this system fully embraces the failures of the NICS system, and while this program seems acceptable, it's just an expansion of an unconstitutional rights-violating leviathan. A possible unattended consequence of this program being a success would mean the rest of the failed programs from the Brady bill would stay in place.

# How Many Kids Have to Die and Legalize Nuclear Weapons?

> *"Wont somebody please think of the children"* -Helen Lovejoy

This is a logical fallacy, "begging the question." You're assuming one has something to do with the other: "An increase in gun laws will reduce child deaths." However, there are tons of people saved every year by guns, and one of those factors is that criminals fear a person may be armed. Also, in places that enact gun laws such as Great Britain, the criminals move on to other means to inflict violence.

How many kids must die? Well, how many healthy people need to walk around when so many people are in hospitals waiting on organs? If we kill one healthy person that's a liver, two kidneys, a heart, lungs, a pancreas, and that's not even mentioning all that blood they have. That's at least six people we can save by sacrificing one. How many of these sick people need to die before we have common sense human sacrifices?

This outlandish argument is not unlike the "so you believe people can have nuclear weapons?" Well, in the words of the 18th century judge, Sir Michael Foster:

> *"If your enemy or oppressor has a bomb, then get yourself a bomb."*

The point of "How many children have to die" and "legalize nuclear weapons" is trying to come up with some point at which we agree with the ASDM. For instance, if I say, "well obviously no one should own nukes," then I have entered the compromise debate. "So, if people can't have nukes, then you agree there are some limits to the 2nd amendment?" In the words of Admiral Ackbar:

> *"It's a trap!"*

Nuclear Weapons is an absurd argument if you think about it, the US government has spent around $5 trillion since 1940, just maintaining its nuclear arsenal. The average cost of a nuclear warhead is $20 million, and you really need to deliver those with an inexpensive classic B52, that will run you an additional $104 million, not including the fuel. Cruise missiles are cheaper, but then you must get an aircraft carrier, always a catch. You're about $124 million for this "recreational nuke." If you have $124 million, then I bet you can buy one right now, or at least a primo dirty bomb. It turns out a lot of people with $124 million are rather sane individuals that do not want to see total annihilation. Turns out if you have that much money you just come up with more interesting ways to wreck the world like manipulating currencies or oil prices.

### *School Shootings*

It is common in pro-gun circles to cite the idea that for the majority of the 20th century, School Shootings did not happen even though fully automatic machine guns were available mail order with no background checks. This is true; we did not have mass shootings in schools even though you could buy full auto Sten for $17 and kids drove to school with shotguns in their trucks for deer season. But I think it misses at least one point of the debate. It's hard to extrapolate useful data on violence specifically to schools from before the 1970s. The data just wasn't as precise and dependable. Note I am saying "school violence" encompassing: shootings, stabbings, beatings, etc.

As we talked about earlier, the disgraced Senator Thomas Dodd chaired numerous committees related to juvenile delinquency. One of those committees was the first to investigate school violence; from the sample of schools, they found an increase in deaths from 1964 fifteen to twenty-six in 1968. Keep in mind the sample size represented just .05% of the total school districts. I believe the Dodd study to look at school violence was a way to investigate the effects of school desegregation and the increase of violence in schools regarding race, especially after all the riots in the 1960s. To put the Dodd report in perspective, they sampled only 110 schools and came up with twenty-six deaths in 1968. In 1999 the year of the Columbine shooting, the national total from over all 3,000 schools, was thirty-six deaths, and fifteen of those were from Columbine. [350] [351]

Many of these schools that now blame guns for school violence blamed drugs in the '80s and '90s. Before that, they blamed it on race, and in New York, they blamed it on the influx of Puerto Ricans. Always looking for a scape goat, and media is always looking for a story. Data, however, contradicts the current narrative, according to the National Center for Education

Statistics in 2000 reported that students were less than half as likely to be victims of a violent crime at school. The report for 2003-2004 showed young people were fifty times more likely to be murdered and 150 times more likely to commit suicide outside of school. From 1996 to 2018, there were 16 mass shootings in schools that resulted in four or more victims. [351] According to researchers, mass murders (four or more) happen between twenty to thirty times per year, and on average, only one of those occur in a school per year. Also, the research shows that these events have been declining since the 1990s. Professor of Criminology James Alan Fox said:

> "There is not an epidemic of school shootings…more kids are killed each year from pool drownings or bicycle accidents. There are around 55 million school children in the United States, and on average over the past 25 years, about 10 students per year were killed by gunfire at school… The thing to remember is that these are extremely rare events, and no matter what you can come up with to prevent it, the shooter will have a workaround, over the past 35 years, there have been only five cases in which someone ages 18 to 20 used an assault rifle in a mass shooting." [352]

You may wonder why this isn't jiving with what you hear on the news, and from politicians. The answer is they add whatever they can to inflate the numbers, gang shootings, and robberies after school hours, drug deals that went wrong, shootouts after basketball games, room invasions in dorms, shootings involving bb guns, etc. One report showed just how bad the data is inflated; a man killed five people was chased by cops where he ran into a school fence. He took refuge in the school where one child was injured, and the shooter committed suicide, they counted all six as a school shooting. That is just one out of many that you would not consider a quote "school shooting."

### *The Founders Were Just a Bunch of Slave Owners*

Samuel Adams wasn't, neither was John Adams nor was Thomas Paine, John Jay, Benjamin Rush, Gouverneur Morris, John Hancock, or Alexander Hamilton. Benjamin Franklin had two slaves which he freed and became president of an abolitionist group. John Dickinson also freed his slaves.

Thomas Jefferson tried to ban slavery in the Louisiana territory and considered slavery a curse. Madison, Mason, Monroe, and Henry, all Virginians like Jefferson, held similar views yet they still kept slaves. They considered it immoral and evil, believed it would bring judgement from heaven, but didn't know what to do about it. Washington was like his Virginia brethren but freed his slaves in his will. Describing this as a sin or evil was common even into the Civil war:

> *"If it comes to a conflict of arms, the war will last at least four years. Northern politicians do not appreciate the determination and pluck of the south and southern politicians do not appreciate the numbers, resources, and patient perseverance of the north. Both sides forget that we are all Americans. I foresee that the country will have to pass through a terrible ordeal, a necessary expiation perhaps for our national sins." -Robert E. Lee*
> [353]

Other Virginians like Richard Henry Lee, one-time president of the continental congress, attempted to tax slavery out of existence and said Africans were:

> *"equally entitled to liberty and freedom by the great law of nature."* [354]

You can go down the line or founding fathers and see that most were against it and did not own or at least freed their slaves. Of the remaining founders the majority spoke out against slavery and tried to end it. In the end however this really doesn't matter and is just an attempt to go after character when they have nothing else to argue. One should be more concerned about the people who want to take guns out of the hands and return us to dependency on a ruling class.

> *"He is a fool who knows not that swords were given to men that none might be slaves."* -Algernon Sidney

## Felons Should Not be Able to Buy Guns

> *All animals are equal, but some animals are more equal than others.* -George Orwell

Sometimes just the mere exercise of walking through controversial positions can strengthen your own beliefs; it can also help you determine if your view is based on emotions or based on logic. I have no doubt people will not agree with all these positions, and that's fine, echo chambers are not usually great places for growth.

Gun owners are quick to point out the importance of the Natural Right of self-defense as well as the constitutionally protected right of firearms by the 2nd amendment. Yet, once you start wading in the weeds, you find that it isn't as cut and dry for most. They mean that it is a Natural Right and Constitutionally protected right for them, which is why this topic needs review.

"Felons should be able to purchase and possess firearms" admittedly, this isn't the majority or popular opinion, and you can be damn sure it isn't on any bumper stickers; nevertheless, the question remains the same…why? One reason is that not all felons are violent, for example, drug distribution, drug possession in some cases, cybercrimes, fraud, counterfeiting, bribery, tax evasion, and drunk driving are just a few non-violent felonies. Some may argue that these people have committed crimes, they knew what they were doing, and it isn't so much that these felons are not safe owning firearms; it is that they need to still be punished. Or phrased differently (and ignorantly) "play stupid games, win stupid prizes." If this is the case, the question becomes, how long does a person need to be punished for a crime? Generally, people who go to prison and are released are said to have "paid their debt to society" how is that true if their rights are not restored? And at what point is permanent punishment just an acceptable version of the social credit system?

Some politicians have looked to restore voting rights, jury duty, and even allowing ex-felons to run for public office. Of course, not a thought is given by these same lawmakers to allow these people to regain their right to own firearms. We can look in article after article that says the same thing, people who are against restoring the rights of felons continue to insist that the state is in the wrong as they continue to exact punishment and retribution, upon people who have paid their debt to society. But again, these articles mention nothing of restoring gun rights.

It is telling to hear the same people on the left who say voting laws that do not allow felons to vote disproportionately affect the African American vote. But they do not apply this to African Americans who are disproportionately unable to protect themselves and their families with firearms.

Violent offenders bring up more issues, why are we letting them out if we still think they are violent? If these are violent criminals, then haven't they proven they don't obey laws? If felons are not allowed to buy guns, then how would we stop them? Background checks? Is it right to infringe on the rights of everyone so we can stop the sale of a few guns to violent felons who would be able to get the guns through other means anyway through illegal channels? Afterall, according to the Department of Justice study, only 1.9% obtained their firearms legally [355]. Gun control doesn't work; it is legislation that keeps firearms out of the hands of people without due process.

It was about two years ago when I had to flush this out and figure out how I felt about this specific issue, and I came across a list of items that someone posted regarding this question that sums it up well:

*"What scares me way more is what a government would have to do to make that ban viable. They'd need a few logical assumptions and mechanisms in place.*

- *A "felon" is a class of person, not someone who did a thing.*
- *Serving your sentence is not rehabilitation.*
- *We need to interrogate everyone who wants to buy a gun, to make sure none of them are felons.*
- *We need to crack down on person-to-person gun sales, gun show sales, and every sort of legal environment where someone can purchase a gun, to make sure that a felon is not able to buy a gun*
- *We will ignore the black-market gun sales, because those don't fit the narrative.*
- *If someone has committed a crime of a certain magnitude, we can force life-long restrictions on them, beyond jail."*

Lastly and as more of a note, the criminal justice system in this country is so jacked up with nonviolent criminals spending life sentences while rapists are getting house arrest or parole. It further complicates the issue because, in many instances, violent criminals should never see the outside of prison.

One of the great pro-gun organizations is Firearm Policy Coalition, as of this writing, they are taking a case to the supreme court to challenge this very thing. Their client Mr. Medina is labeled a felon for lying on a mortgage application three decades ago, since then the mortgage company has even taken him back. He was never violent, just simply lied on an application. It will be interesting to see how this case unfolds and if the government will declare "lying" is a life sentence. For more on the case check out link [356]

## Gun Owners Should Not be Able to Smoke Weed *(Gun owners and Drugs)*

How about two controversial questions back to back, before we cover this, I want to add the disclaimer that drugs and guns do not mix, and I am not advocating being intoxicated or under the influence while using a firearm.

If you're still stuck on how scary drugs are, I ask that you listen to the first few episodes of the podcast series "Historical Controversies" from the Mises Institute [357] as this discussion is way past legalization of Marijuana.

The more states that legalize Marijuana, the more the question is posed; should gun owners be allowed to use medicinal Marijuana. Part of the reason that this is such a difficult question for most is the number of lies and propaganda that have been told for so long about the dangers of Marijuana and other illicit drugs, which is why I put the link to the podcast series above. It is extremely well done, thorough, and best of all, it includes tons of references.

I've tried to point this out numerous times through this writing that many times, people are all about freedom and liberty when it comes to themselves but are quick to want to reign in the freedom of others, whether it be "what part of infringe don't you understand: *unless you're a felon*" or "marijuana should be legal: *and tax the hell out of it*" type of arguments.

Think of the many ridiculous laws, prohibitions, Jim Crow style, and sin taxes that have been pushed in America just during the 20th century. Many areas still have pointless Blue laws regulating industries and behaviors. Alcohol was probably the most famous prohibition where its users were vilified by numerous groups and politicians, marijuana users are just the most current in a long line of second-class citizens in the eyes of the law.

I realize much of this section is focused on Marijuana, and that was intentional as this is the hot button issue right now; this all still applies to the cocaine, heroin, DMT, LSD, etc. user. Its use doesn't make the user's rights null and void. The response to this is commonly: "druggies end up committing crimes while trying to get money for these drugs" but you do know it's illegal to steal? Will you also be banning drug users from crowbars and bolt cutters? It also is an excellent example of the misconception of drug users. Contrary to cop drama television shows and movies, not everyone who has looked at a drug becomes a rabid uncontrollable druggy hell-bent on larceny.

Congressman Thomas Massie has also discussed this issue when it comes to states that are currently legalizing Marijuana.

> *"I think we've created millions of felons with this question. You can't imagine that everybody in Colorado, who under Colorado state law is legally using marijuana, has never purchased a firearm. That would be completely illogical. Or vice versa. And by the way, whether you purchased it or whether it was a birthday gift, it doesn't matter. Whether you fill out a form 4473 or not, it doesn't matter. You're still committing a crime by possessing a firearm or ammunition in your house if you use marijuana. [The legislation] makes it legal for marijuana users to also be gun owners, is what my bill does. So the question is, when people hear about the bill, "well, if you just take it off the form aren't they still going to be criminals because you haven't changed the underlying statute, which prevents a marijuana users from owning a gun?" But what my bill would do is fix the underlying statute. And I want to remind people that this is a problem for not just recreational users of marijuana, but medical marijuana recipients, according to the federal government, are felons if they possess a firearm. This is something that needs to be fixed."* [358]

### *(insert name) Wants Gun Control*

It doesn't matter who you enter in that line, the argument or more accurately put "the fallacy" remains the same (argumentum ad populum). Who or how many people say something doesn't make it true or not true. Certainly, a statement seems more valid based on who says it or the number of people that agree, but it doesn't make it a fact.

As good as the intentions of celebrities may be, their statements, whether for or against a subject, have little, no, bearing on what is true. Usually, the "arguments" they present are little more than emotional opinions not rooted in fact, again this could be true whether they are for or against firearms.

Now what you could say is you just used a bunch of quotes throughout this eBook, yep. Some quotes are just because the opinions are worded better than my own; others, like quotes from the founders, are used to show what the founders thought about firearms and rights. I'm using their words to prove something about them and their thoughts. All this isn't to say that some people are more authoritative, Stephen Hawkings talking about black holes has a lot more weight than my neighbor who works at home improvement store. So, while it is possible that Hawkings could say something wrong when explaining black holes, I am still going to take his word for it.

Think about it, in Hollywood people are worried when an actor works in a genre that they are not commonly in. A singer that tries to cross from country to pop is also seen as a risk... but no one in Hollywood or Nashville seems to worry when they cross from their job as an entertainer into the roll of political advisor.

### *Compromise*

> *Guy: Would you sleep with me for ten million dollars?*
> *Woman: of course I would.*
> *Guy; How about doing it for fifteen dollars?*
> *Woman (indignant): Why, what do you think I am?*

> *Guy: That's already been established. Now we're just haggling about the price.*

"Shall not be infringed" doesn't allow a lot of room to compromise; more importantly, my rights are not up for compromise. Sure, we could get into a long list of "would you rather" as so many Fudds in the NRA did after Las Vegas when it came to bump-stocks. Saying "we'd rather trade bump-stocks for National Reciprocity," yeah and now you don't have either… see how that works?

Once you compromise, you're setting yourself up for more: short barrels, suppressors, pistol grips, import bans, etc... the list of compromises is never ending. Political theater from the ASDM is always the same; it's easier to explain in terms of numbers. They ask for five things and shout in agony when they don't get it but settle for 2 of ours. Next time they ask for five more crying "think of the children" and attempt to make us look bad for not "being reasonable," we give in another 2, and on and on it goes as we give in over and over with nothing to gain. They ask for the ridiculous knowing our side will settle for some restrictions. They act like they were bulldozed yet we are the ones who keep giving up ground as they continue to gain:

> *"I receive a lot of easily disproven comments on gun control on Facebook. Take, for instance, this whopper: "Nobody wants to take your guns away."*
> *Ironically, it's usually found in the same thread as "those should be banned" and "nobody needs that gun" and "your right to have guns doesn't override my right to feel safe" and "it worked in Australia."*
> *Can't we just acknowledge that there are lots of people in this country, including members of state legislatures and the U.S. Congress, who do in fact "want to take your guns away?"*
> *The honest thing to say is, "they want to take your guns away, but politically it's not feasible, so they'll take what they can get for now."*
> **Why would we give them an inch?"**

## *The NRA Does…*

Full disclosure, I've only been an NRA member for two separate years of my life once a few years ago when I had some confidence in them, and another time when I wanted to go to the NRA show to look at guns (you have to be a member to look around.) I don't believe they do enough for gun rights; my opinion is that the mission has been lost in the maintenance of the monument. You do not just raise $450 million in a year (2016) [359] and then hope politicians stop pushing for gun control legislation. If the NRA is successful in its mission, they will put themselves out of business. [360] And they don't seem like they are trying to do that.

I believe the NRA is a lobbying group for gun manufacturers. My further impression of them is that they create a false sense of security to many gun owners, you pay them to do the fighting for you supposedly. This, unfortunately, allows for lazy men that do not have to think about their rights and instead tout pre-canned slogans like "from my cold dead hands!"

Frankly, the antigun crowd does not understand how good they have it with the NRA. If the NRA were somehow shut down or vanished, you'd have millions of gun owners flock to Gun Owners of American, 2nd amendment Foundation, and Firearm Policy Coalition, these groups have proven they will not compromise. The NRA has become gun-control-lite, when someone hollers for more gun control the NRA plants their feet and proclaims No! Then follows it up with, but what if we gave you (insert bump stocks, background checks, Red flag laws, etc.).

They deserve all the attention they have received regarding how they spend money so poorly [361]. More gun owners should be aware of how so many of those board members have ruined that organization for the sake of money [362].

All that being said they do not deserve the blame for shootings nor the lies that are told about them by the ASDM and reported as facts by the media.

## *The NRA is Responsible for XYZ Shooting.*

I don't believe an NRA member has ever done even one mass shooting. In fact, the NRA has always promoted firearm safety, including training military members dating back to 1871

Claiming they are to blame for these shootings because of their lobbying efforts would also be incorrect when you weigh the deaths compared to the lives saved by firearms. Which becomes much clearer when you look at violent crime rates or countries that have banned firearms entirely that we covered earlier, also in John Lott's book More Guns, Less Crime.

## *The NRA's Money is Paying for all These Politicians and XYZ*

This one is frustrating because there is a large group that drastically outspends the NRA, and that is the ASDM. While gun control advocates chastise the NRA and their evil money, the ASMD is out there spending away. During the 2018 midterm elections, the New York Times reported

> *"Two groups that are focused on gun control, Giffords and Everytown for Gun Safety, spent at least $37 million at the state and federal level in the midterms, compared with at least $20 million by the NRA"* [363]

In 2013 Everytown outspent every gun-rights group, including the NRA 6.3 to 1 on television ads [364]. Everytown can run ads during things like the Super Bowl, which they have, but the NRA is prohibited from running commercials during such events.

What the NRA will also never be able to compete with is the billions in free advertising gun control groups get with the constant publicity and mentions they get in the media. The NRA has no monetarily feasible way to combat the hundreds of millions of dollars' worth of studies that were bought by George Soros and Michael Bloomberg that are regularly reported by the mainstream media.

## *General Gun Control Argument*

> *"The whole aim of practical politics is to keep the populace alarmed by menacing it with an endless series of hobgoblins, all of them imaginary."*
> -H.L. Mencken

I threw this in here because I can't cover every argument, whenever I think I got them all, a new one comes up. For this reason, I'm grouping the general premise of gun control arguments. I believe it comes down to correlation does not imply causation. "Easy access to firearms increases gun violence." Or the lousy analogy from Obama that "guns are easier to get than books" Both are examples of this argument. After all, Firearms used to be able to be purchased by mail, fully automatic machine guns and antitank rifles could be ordered with no paperwork whatsoever. The result was the exact opposite of what was expected. The correlation of access and violence isn't necessarily a cause of an increase in mass shootings (or any shootings).

The real issue is not firearms, the problem is why do people feel the need to kill other people, whether that be an AR15 or a hammer? That may be drug war-related, video games, one-parent homes, behavior drugs, etc. whatever it is, that is where we should be working.

# Gun Control Around the World

With quotes like:

> *"The advantage of being armed, which the Americans possess over the people of all other countries" and that "notwithstanding the military establishments in the several kingdoms of Europe, which are carried as far as the public resources will bear, the governments are afraid to trust the people with arms"* [365]

made by James Madison or like this one from Noah Webster:

> *"Before a standing army can rule, the people must be disarmed, as they are in almost every country in Europe. The supreme power in America cannot enforce unjust laws by the sword; because the whole body of the people are armed and constitute a force superior to any band of regular troops. A military force, at the command of Congress, can execute no laws, but such as the people perceive to be just and constitutional; for they will possess the power, and jealousy will instantly inspire the inclination, to resist the execution of a law which appears to them unjust and oppressive."* [366]

Along with numerous quotes from other founders, you may be able to catch on to a bit of a theme that perhaps America is different, as the joke goes, we stopped caring about Great Britain's opinion in 1776.

Gun control around the world is a tough subject. The hard part being the work it takes, tearing down all the false information that is spread by everyone in the ASDM community from the corporate press to presidents and down to social media NPCs who regurgitate talking points as gospel.

Two of the most annoying things in the gun community regarding this debate; one, the information states the opposite in most cases, yet people will not listen to our side. Second, we don't care how things are done in other countries. Firearms are a part of America and have been since its creation as our goal has been to embrace freedom.

America is great at a lot of things, and one of those things it is great at is collecting data on its citizens, not just bulk meta-data, but data regarding crime stats. The FBI uniform crime report is accessible to everyone and goes back over a decade. It's nicely organized, and as the title suggests "uniform," it doesn't switch titles on us, it is clear on its reporting, and it's clear on its definition of items such as mass shootings. With other countries, this data is not as precise, nor is it uniform. Different reporting requirements and definitions used need to be taken into consideration when trying to argue all these figures.

Take the Small Arms Survey [367] that has been used by numerous people in the ASDM as a key data set, such as the debunked hit piece by Vox (Louder with Crowder has a video with source links destroying their arguments [368]). The Small Arms Survey lists Americans at the highest rate of gun ownership, granted when you tell us that we are proud of it, but that isn't exactly true. It comes down to the definition of "own." We "own" our firearms, but in countries such as Israel and Switzerland, the government "owns" most weapons that are then issued to its citizens, mind you these are all actual military-style as in some are full auto. So, they have a higher rate of people possessing firearms, which is really what the survey is trying to relay with their data, but they twist it and show they have a lower rate than America. Or take homicide rates in the UK; they only report homicides where someone has been charged, where in the US, all homicides are tracked. Wouldn't you think that was a crucial piece of information?

Before we dive in, this isn't a book about other countries' methods. I am not going to explain each thing and will not be covering the details of each law, for instance, Australia's gun laws and firearm categories are ridiculous and no reason to explain precisely how they work. As with the last section on common arguments, some of these topics are too vast to cover here without making this a multivolume encyclopedia. Therefore, I implore you to click on the sources mentioned if you have further questions on this topic. Finally, I chose countries that are most often cited to counter American gun laws as we cannot cover them all.

## *Australia*

The Port Arthur massacre in 1996, which resulted in 35 deaths, forever changed the gun debate not just in Australia but across the western world. Gun control legislation was passed in a mere 12 days, which included the often talked about mandatory buyback of certain semiautomatic rifles and shotguns. That resulted in the round-up of around 650,000 firearms with an average buyback amount of $360, costing Australians $230 million dollars. Take this same program and apply it in America to just the number of AR15s that were manufactured in 2016, and you get a cost of $1.6 Billion. That's just one-year worth of one style of firearm…$1.6 Billion. [369]

Taking it further to explain my point about buybacks, $360 adjusted for inflation is $588, in the recent 2019 democrat debates Rep Eric "Nukem" Swalwell has said we need to buy back the 15 million AR15s presently in civilian hands, that would be $8.8 Billion (Swalwell estimates $15 billion [370]). Never mind the fact he isn't counting the millions of "assault rifles" that are not AR pattern. Nor would the cost only be $15 billion, because most gun owners would not accept $588 for their AR. There would be lawsuits for years.

More importantly, is the low number of people who will comply. New Zealand has had low rates of compliance [371] and complaints about the dollar amount offered during their buyback after the Christchurch mass shooting. US states such as Connecticut, New Jersey, and California also experienced meager rates of turn-ins. New Jersey, for instance, after they banned "high capacity magazines," not one magazine was turned in [372]. During Australia's gun buyback, they had less than half comply. The result is that it is not the billions you will spend buying them; it is the billions you will spend prosecuting and turning peaceful, everyday citizens into criminals.

Here is the something that isn't mentioned and is misunderstood about Australia's gun laws, Australians can have firearms. As of 2016, Australians have more firearms than they did before the Port Arthur massacre [373]. In 1996 Australia had 3.2 million guns, the buyback brought them down to 2.5 million by 1997, but by 2016 the number of firearms was over 3.6 million.

According to an article often cited from the Journal of the American Medical Association (JAMA) [374], Australia has had 13 mass shootings from 1979 to 1996, and from 1997 to 2016, there has been no mass shooting in Australia. The definition they are using for a mass shooting is five or more persons killed. This is one of those areas where different meanings can confuse data, the generally accepted definition in the United States from the FBI is four or more at a single event. Because of this, I added the other shootings that fell into this category.

| YEAR | LOCATION | DEAD | WEAPONS | DESCRIPTION |
|------|----------|------|---------|-------------|
| 1981 | Campsie Murders | 5 | 22 cal rifle | murdered his family |
| 1983 | Inland Motel | 5 | Vehicle | Drove truck though motel bar |
| 1984 | Wahroonga | 5 | 22 cal rifle | murdered his family in their sleep |
| 1984 | Milperra | 7 | firearms and other | Motorcycle gang fight |
| 1987 | Pymble | 4 | firearm | Murdered girlfriend's family |
| 1987 | Top End | 5 | Mini14 | Murdered 5 people over 5 days |
| 1987 | Hoddle Street | 7 | 22, Shotgun, M14 | Fired on passing trafic while hiding behind bilboard |
| 1987 | Canley Vale Huynh | 5 | firearm | Murdered girlfriend's family |
| 1987 | Queen Street | 8 | M1 | Shooting Spree |
| 1988 | Oenpelli | 5 | firearm | murdered his family |
| 1990 | Surry hills | 5 | Shotgun | Shooting Spree |
| 1991 | Strathfield | 7 | SKS | Shooting Spree |
| 1992 | Central Coast | 6 | Shotgun | Shooting Spree |
| 1993 | Greenough | 4 | Axe | murdered his family |
| 1993 | Cangai Siege | 5 | firearm | 5 murders over 9 days |
| 1996 | Hillcrest | 6 | firearm | murdered his family |
| 1996 | Port Arthur | 35 | AR15 and FAL | Shooting Spree |

A few things can be gathered from this simple table; for one, a lot of them involve murdering their families; second, a lot of these are done with rather simple firearms not the kinds that were banned. What is challenging to gather is if these laws would have stopped these killings, it is difficult to go back this far, especially when searching another country to find out how they obtained these weapons and what the exact firearms were. However, in the first case, Campsie Murders, the man bought the rifle legally and received his license from the police station. Others on this list, such as a businessman and a veteran, would more than likely have been able to obtain these firearms legally. The next point the article from JAMA is accurate when it comes to "mass shootings" but not the whole story when you look up all massacres.

| YEAR | LOCATION | DEAD | WEAPONS | DESCRIPTION |
|------|----------|------|---------|-------------|
| 1997 | Richmond | 5 | knife and rifle | Slit the throats of his family then shot himself |
| 2000 | Childers Palace | 15 | Arson | |
| 2003 | Poulson Family | 4 | knife | murdered his family |
| 2005 | Oakhampton Heights | 4 | rifle | murdered her family |
| 2009 | Churchill Fire | 10 | Arson | |
| 2009 | Lin Family | 5 | hammer | murdered his family |
| 2011 | Quakers Hill | 11 | Arson | |
| 2014 | Hunt Family | 5 | firearm | murdered his family |
| 2014 | Cairns | 8 | knife | murdered her family |
| 2016 | Northern Sydney | 4 | Gas | murdered his family using carbon monoxide |
| 2017 | Melbourne | 6 | Vehicle | |
| 2018 | Osmington | 7 | rifle | murdered his family |
| 2018 | Bedford Massacre | 5 | knife | murdered his family |
| 2019 | Darwin | 4 | Shotgun | Was on parole and wearing his GPS anklet |

Again, a lot of disgusting people killing their own families. We see a few firearm deaths in this chart, but we can see that when sick people want to act out, they craft ways around the limitations imposed on them.

As I mentioned above, this article is spread all over as proof of the success of Australia's gun laws; however, this is the actual conclusion from this study:

> **"Conclusions and Relevance** Following enactment of gun law reforms in Australia in 1996, there were no mass firearm killings through May 2016. There was a more rapid decline in firearm deaths between 1997 and 2013 compared with before 1997 but also a decline in total non-firearm suicide and homicide deaths of a

*greater magnitude. Because of this, <u>it is not possible to</u>*
*<u>determine whether the change in firearm deaths can be</u>*
*<u>attributed to the gun law reforms.</u>"*

This is also consistent with what was going on across the rest of the English-Speaking world according to Criminologist Michael Tonry:

> *"There is now general agreement, at least for developed English-speaking countries and western Europe, that homicide patterns have moved in parallel since the 1950s. The precise timing of the declines has varied, but the common pattern is apparent. Homicide rates increased substantially from various dates in the 1960s, peaked in the early 1990s or slightly later, and have since fallen substantially."* [375]

Fact of the matter is that mass shootings aren't the only issue, they just get the most media coverage. So besides mass shootings how have gun control effected Australia:

> *"According to gun control advocates' logic, Australia's buyback should have been followed by a sudden drop in firearm homicides and suicides. After all, access to legal guns ought to have been greatly diminished. Gun control advocates would then have predicted a slow increase in firearm deaths as the ownership rate increased again. No such thing occurred. Firearm homicides and suicides were falling for 15 years prior to the buyback and fell more slowly after the buyback. So, there is no evidence that the buyback actually caused the fall, but it may look that way in the absence of historical context. Armed robbery rates rose after the buyback, and then slowly fell back down to pre-buyback levels as gun ownership increased. This is the exact opposite of what gun control advocates predicted."* - *John Lott Jr* [376]

I would also like to note the double standard I have mentioned before when it comes to accepting research as fact. Regularly I see the claim that NRA funded research or that scholars were on the payroll of the gun industry even when no clear link exists between the data. Yet this JAMA study was completed by three researchers, two of which have direct ties to gun control institutions according to their disclosure statements. Dr. Chapman was a member of the Coalition for Gun Control in Australia from 1993-1996, and Mr. Alpers is the director/editor of GunPolicy.org which according to their website

> "is the world's most comprehensive and accessible Web source for published evidence on armed violence, firearm law and gun control."

This is not to not to insinuate this study is done poorly or that they were biased in their data. The point is that they are connected to the ASDM, yet they do not face the same criticism for their connections as someone that is on the other side of the argument.

Lastly, it would be interesting to see how population density plays into mass killings; Australia, for instance, has a population similar to Florida, yet when it comes to land size, it is almost the same as the continental United States. When we look at murders in the US, we see them concentrated in areas with higher population density. Research from Crime Prevention Research Center (CRC) states that:

> "murders in the United States are very concentrated 54% of counties in 2014 had zero murders, 2% of counties had 51% of the murders... The worst 1% of counties have 19% of the population and 37% of the murders. The worst 2% of counties contain 28% of the population and 51% of the murders. The worst 5% of counties contain 47% of the population and account for 68% of murders. But even within those counties the murders are very heavily concentrated in small areas."
> [377]

Several reasons could be to blame for murders in such a confined area with large populations such as gang-related activity, poverty in inner cities, illegal drug trade, etc. What we can derive from this is that the United States does not have a nationwide problem with firearms nor with homicides. While some want to look at other countries to try to push a particular narrative of the effectiveness of gun control, we could point to our own states and our counties. The Guardian has praised Australia for having a homicide rate of 1 person per 100,000 [378], which is a great achievement, however New Hampshire has had that rate even with their lenient gun laws. North Dakota, Iowa, Idaho, Vermont, Wyoming, Maine, and numerous others are also very similar to Australia's homicide rate. [379]

### *Great Britain*

In 1689 parliament passed the English Bill of Rights which included a right to bear arms.

> *"That the **subjects** which are Protestants may have arms for their defense suitable to their conditions and as **allowed by law**"* [380]

Quite a contrast to

> *"the right of the **people** to keep and bear Arms, **shall not be infringed**."* [381]

Still, they did understand, to an extent, the importance of arms for defense, and this did restore some gun rights that were previously lost before the Glorious Revolution.

While some restrictions were enacted in the 18th and 19th centuries, gun control didn't make many strides until the 20th century, starting with the pistol's act of 1903 requiring a hunting license or pistol license. It still wasn't significant law, but then came the 1920s like our country numerous reasons were given, but many underlying issues probably had a lot to do with its passing. This act required a license to purchase a firearm or ammunition. To obtain this license or certificate, you had to justify your reason for needing one to the chief constable who had the final say.

As always, gun laws don't work, so the government does what they do best and legislates more laws this time in 1933 with the Criminal Use bill. This mostly just increased punishments. It didn't work, so more regulations were "needed;" this ushered in the firearms act of 1937, which regulated smoothbore weapons with barrels shorter than 20 inches and raised the age to 17 to purchase. It seems like comparing gun laws based on other countries is nothing new; both England and the United States passed gun laws in the 1930s, and then again, these criminals were not obeying laws, so they add more gun laws. Come 1968 same year as our gun control act (GCA), they centralized their gun laws.

Significant changes start coming in the late '80s following the 1987 Hungerford Massacre, where a gunman killed 16 people. The Hungerford Massacre lasted around 45 minutes; only four cops total were on duty, and since this is the U.K., none of them had guns. The firearm squad was 40 minutes away; this is why gun owners have a somewhat Newtonian view of mass shootings: "bad guys stay in motion until acted upon by an equal or greater force." The Firearms Act of 1988 that followed banned ownership of semiautomatic centerfire rifles and restricted shotguns to no more than three shells.

As the theme of gun laws continue, these weren't good enough, this time in Scotland. The Dunblane Primary School 1996 shooting resulted in the deadliest shooting in Britain's history, with 18 people killed. Rifles were mostly banned, and shotguns had limits, so this psycho used two handguns. As we've said, you take away one weapon; they go to a different one. You take away all the guns, and they start setting fires or running people over. Dunblane resulted in the firearms act of 1997, which banned the private possession of handguns. One hundred sixty-two thousand pistols and roughly 700 tons of ammunition and accessories were turned in. They weren't done yet though in 2006 they banned mail order BB guns and restricted a few more items such as primers.

So, does this mean there is no gun crime in Great Britain? Nope, let's look at 2010. In 2010, after all those gun laws, states such as Maine, Iowa, Hawaii, Idaho, Montana, New Hampshire, North Dakota, Rhode Island, South Dakota, Vermont, and Wyoming all had less gun-related homicides than England [382]. More significant is the overall crime. Scott McPherson points out it isn't looking good:

> *"It was an illusion. Today the UK is experiencing yet another crime wave, and now holds the dubious honor of having the highest crime rate of any Western industrialized country – higher than the United States. Rapes and murders in the country's largest cities are breaking records. A documentary film-maker complained recently that he had to wear body armor while filming in Birmingham. London is worse; murders have surpassed New York City, averaging about three per week, and it has three times as many rapes. Machete attacks happen an average of every ninety minutes in Britain."* [383]

Great Britain has been a great example of what gun owners have feared. "One more gun law" is never enough, it's always more. Then when the guns are gone, it's onto the next object used in self-defense, which is already happening in London as they have moved on to imposing knife bans [384].

## *Canada*

Canada's gun laws are unique in the fact that it's hard to pinpoint why they passed any legislation. With other countries, the moves were reactionary but not so with Canada. It seems that they passed laws because the U.S. and U.K. were passing laws. We see minor gun laws before but come 1934, Canada begins requiring handguns to be registered, and in 1935, they impose an age requirement of 16. Throughout the 20th century, they passed numerous different laws in 1969 (red flag) in 1977; they began requiring background checks. In 1991 they implemented requirement things such as required safety courses and a 28-day waiting period.

The bill in 1991 (C-17) was significant compared to previous legislation. This was the "military-style" weapons, magazine capacity limits on rifles and handguns. They also banned certain types of ammo.

There has however been some good news for Canadian gun owners, in 2012 the long gun registry was scrapped after years of it being a complete waste of money.

> *"After 1951 when gun control was centralized under the federal government, and automatic weapons were registered, the murder rate began a 30-year march upward, even as gun control measures increased.*
>
> *If gun-control advocates want to claim credit for recent declines in homicide rates, they'll need to explain why they remain blameless for increases in the murder rates that came on the heels of increasing gun controls through much of the 20th century. Of course, in these countries, one could also claim that the lack of sufficiently restrictive gun control was what really caused the increases in homicides mid-century, and that it was the build-up in restrictive laws that finally took effect ten or twenty years ago, thus pushing down homicide rates.*
>
> *However, this could not be applied to the US where gun ownership has expanded in recent years while homicide rates have fallen." Ryan McMaken* [385]

Canada does indeed have a low homicide rate as of 2017; they had a rate of 1.8 per 100,000. But as I've pointed out covering Australia and Great Britain, numerous states have a homicide rate less than that, New Hampshire, Hawaii, Idaho, Maine, Oregon, Utah, Vermont. Idaho, Maine, New Hampshire. Vermont even has constitutional carry, so it is clearly not access to firearms that is the sole issue. Dave Kopel also makes a similar comparison when viewing Canada's gun laws:

> "If one excludes Americans born in Southern states (of all races) from American crime statistics, America's crime rate is comparable to Canada's. American Northerners have far easier access to guns than Canadians do, and commit no more crimes. American Southerners have the same access to guns that American Northerners do and commit far more crime. The important variable in crime rates is not the number of guns available, but the characteristics of the citizenry. (The high Southern crime rate cannot be due mainly to guns, since most of the guns are in rural areas, and most of the crime is in urban areas. Southerners also have an abnormally high non-gun assault rate.)
> Further, despite editorial claims that America is a land of "carnage," most Americans have no more to fear from guns than Canadians do. The overall death rate for non-Hispanic white Americans from all types of shootings (murder, suicide, accident, etc.) is the same as the rate for Canadians.
>
> American Blacks and Hispanics have a much higher death rate from shootings, in part because they are likely to live in poorer, more dangerous neighborhoods, and to receive less protection from the authorities.
>
> Unlike Canada, the U.S. has a large social and racial underclass. Most members of that underclass are disproportionately the victims of crime (and therefore most in need of inexpensive guns for self-defense). A fraction of the underclass population, on the other hand, is the segment of society that most frequently

*perpetrates armed robberies and domestic murders (with and without guns).* [386]

While he originally wrote this in 1989, the article is still accurate. It is ringing true today as we are seeing the same issues now in Canada where crime and homicides have increased due to an increase in gang activity.

Comparing our two countries we find that guns do indeed prevent crime due to the number of Americans being armed. Criminologist Gary Kleck explains:

> *"Only thirteen percent of U.S. residential burglaries are attempted against occupied homes. But this happy fact of life, so taken for granted in the United States, is not universal.*
>
> *The overall Canadian burglary rate is higher than the American one, and a Canadian burglary is four times more likely to take place when the victims are home. In Toronto, forty-four percent of burglaries were against occupied homes, and twenty-one percent involved a confrontation with the victim. Most Canadian residential burglaries occur at night, while American burglars are known to prefer daytime entry to reduce the risk of an armed confrontation.* [386]

The rate of "hot burglaries" (burglaries when the home is occupied) is 13% in the United States, 44% in Canada and 59% in Great Britain [387].

## *Japan*

In an earlier chapter, I mention what true "universal" background checks would mean and the invasion of privacy that would have to take place along with other things. It turns out the Japanese did that. No handguns are allowed, to obtain a long gun, which would only be for hunting or sport, the applicant must attend an all-day class, take a written test, and an accuracy test where they must get at least a 95%. They then need to go to a hospital for a psychiatric evaluation, and a background check is completed not just on them but on their friends and family. All of this must be done every three years. Then this is reviewed by law enforcement who have complete discretion and can search your property at any time. It also means they can search anyone at any time if they "suspect" them to have a gun.

> *"If ye love wealth better than liberty, the tranquility of servitude better than the animating contest of freedom, go home from us in peace. We ask not your counsels or arms. Crouch down and lick the hands which feed you. May your chains set lightly upon you, and may posterity forget that ye were our countrymen." - Samuel Adams* [388]

The two biggest things besides lack of access to firearms are culture and the police state under which they leave. This police state conducts routine house calls done up to twice a year, which includes filling out a residential card with all of your information [389]. Quite frankly, this love for the nanny state that the Japanese have is a million miles removed from the reality that is the United States.

Since one of the main arguments made by the ASDM is suicides, it is fair to mention that Japan's suicide rate has, for years, been much higher than the United States. In 2016 the US had a rate of 12.6 while Japan, although at a 22-year low, still had a rate of 15.1. [390]

I believe Japan and many Asian countries are not as often used to compare to the United States because even the ASDM knows that it is far beyond just gun control that they possess. It is an entirely different culture that Americans would never accept. The rioters in Hong Kong have decided they do not accept this type of authority and have protested with signs wishing they had gun rights.

*"In Japan, the total murder rate is almost 1 per 100,000. In the U.S., there are about 3.2 murders per 100,000 people each year by weapons other than firearms. This means that even if firearms in the U.S. could be eliminated, the U.S. would still have three times the murder rate of the Japanese. -gunfacts.info*

## *Summary: Gun Control Around the World*

A summary is better said by Dr. Gary Mauser paper titled "The Failed Experiment
Gun Control and Public Safety in Canada, Australia, England and Wales"

*"This brief review of gun laws shows that disarming the public has not reduced criminal violence in any country examined here: not in Great Britain, not in Canada, and not in Australia. In all cases, disarming the public has been ineffective, expensive, and often counterproductive. In all cases, the means have involved setting up expensive bureaucracies that produce no noticeable improvement to public safety or have made the situation worse. The results of this study are consistent with other academic research, that most gun laws do not have any measurable effect on crime (Kleck 1997: 377; Jacobs 2002). As I have argued elsewhere (Mauser 2001a), the history of gun control in both Canada and the Commonwealth demonstrates the slippery slope of accepting even the most benign appearing gun control measures. At each stage, the government either restricted access to firearms or prohibited and confiscated arbitrary types of ordinary firearms. In Canada, registration has been shown to mean eventual confiscation. As well, police search powers have been increased. The expansion of the state's search and seizure powers should be taken very seriously by all civil libertarians concerned about the erosion of Canadians' individual rights. Canada's democratic institutions may also have been damaged by*

*the transfer of what many would consider legislative*
*powers to both the police and cabinet under firearm*
*legislation."* [391]

As has been said throughout this book, the issue shouldn't be
solely an argument about gun violence; it should be about
violence in general. It should be about crime, whether that be a
shooting, rape, assault, or a hot burglary. Is it worse to have a
person murdered with a handgun rather than a knife, or rather
than a bat, or even fists? Is it worse to survive a mass shooting
or be violated by rape or burglary where your family is
threatened and assaulted? It doesn't seem to make sense to want
to trade one type of crime for another, especially when one such
as gun control means I lose a method of self-defense that is used
by Americans countless times a year. Does anyone want to live
in an unobtainable idea that is absolute security in exchange for
their freedom?

In Patrick Henry's biography, he laments the plight of the slave,
seeing it as evil and inconsistent with morality, even pointing
out that slavery is keeping Virginia behind northerners who
have been able to produce more without the use of slave labor.
Yet, he also wrestled with the thought that without them (slave
owners), the slaves would be worse off; killed by Native
Americans, he believed they would not be able to provide for
themselves, which may be why he taught his slaves many skills
rather than just manual labor. Point being Patrick Henry's
incorrect view that African Americans would be better off as
slaves than freemen was much like the false idea presumed by
the ASDM in believing that the only way to make people safe is
to take away their freedoms. Their view being freemen cannot
handle the responsibility of protecting themselves and need a
master to rule over them.

You cannot get around the fact that besides some states having
more guns than entire countries, they have fewer crimes than
those same countries that have implemented extreme gun
control measures. When all things are equal more guns, equal
less crime; when they are not equal, you have to deduce that

there are differences that go beyond firearms, one of those things is culture. Not only do all these countries have different cultures than our own, but our states also have different cultures from other states, even counties and cities inside states can have vastly different cultures. Take Pennsylvania, which is known not only for its cities like Philadelphia and Pittsburgh but also for its large Amish community. Illinois isn't just Chicago the rest of the state is rows and rows of Dekalb corn. Do you think Portland has the same culture as Oregon City? Even if gun control did work, why would you believe the same gun laws needed in Miami would also apply in Bismarck? Why do we pretend that one city, which is one of the most violent (Washington DC), can dictate the lives of 350 million Americans? And why should a congresswoman in the Bronx be able to dictate one detail of a person's life way out in Montana?

Federal gun control does not work, is unconstitutional, and turns everyday citizens into criminals and the natural prey of bureaucrats and agencies that must prove their worth and budgets. These laws have been passed with bipartisan support and approved by politically motivated judges that are looking to advance their own agendas. Just because a judicial activist in a black robe says something is constitutional, it doesn't make it so. As Thomas Jefferson said:

> *"The judiciary of the United States is the subtle corps of sappers and miners constantly working underground to undermine the foundations of our confederated fabric."*
> [392]

# Section 4: Discourse

*"After having thus successively taken each member of the community in its powerful grasp and fashioned him at will, the supreme power then extends its arm over the whole community. It covers the surface of society with a network of small complicated rules, minute and uniform, through which the most original minds and the most energetic characters cannot penetrate, to rise above the crowd. The will of man is not shattered, but softened, bent, and guided; men are seldom forced by it to act, but they are constantly restrained from acting. Such a power does not destroy, but it prevents existence; it does not tyrannize, but it compresses, enervates, extinguishes, and stupefies a people, till each nation is reduced to nothing better than a flock of timid and industrious animals, of which the government is the shepherd."*
*- Alexis de Tocqueville* [393]

In this section we will cover
- Solutions
- Civil Disobedience
- 80% (unfinished firearms)
- Defense Distributed/ Cody Wilson (Ghost Guns)
- Firearm Manufacturers
- State Nullification
- Law Enforcement Nullification

## Solutions

*"1. So, disturbed kids are taking guns to school and killing teachers and classmates. We better make sure kids can't get guns.*

*2. So, disturbed kids are taking guns to school and killing teachers and classmates. We better*

*find out what's making these kids want to kill, fix
that, and then they won't want to use guns to kill
teachers and classmates.*

*See what I did there? Which statement makes more
sense? Don't bring up politics. Don't refer to statistical
data. Don't nervously look at your cell phone. Just read
the two statements and be honest with yourself. We can
do better. We're smarter than this. WAKE UP."*
*-Aaron B. Powell* [394]

What are we to do? This is really two questions and those are:

1.    What do we as gun owners do to restore our rights?
2.    How do we decrease violence?

I'm not arrogant enough to believe I have all the answers, and
I'm certainly not optimistic enough to think enough people will
read this and act. I do, however, feel that if I am expressing in
this book all the things that didn't and won't work, I should
perhaps present some ideas that I believe will work.

### *First up what do gun owners do?*

> *"If the Tenth Amendment were still taken seriously, most
> of the federal government's present activities would not
> exist. That's why no one in Washington ever mentions
> it." -Tom Woods*

Two words Nullification and Decentralization. The exact
opposite of what is being done now in the gun debate. Stop
believing the federal government is the answer. The federal
government is like the story of Leprechauns. If you catch one,
they are supposed to grant you a wish. The hitch is that it always
comes at an unforeseen cost like the Leprechaun grants your
request for a new BMW, but the cops arrive shortly after and
arrest you for auto theft. It is also the case when you get a "win"
from the federal government. So great, we get national

Reciprocity, but the hitch is handgun licenses are issued by the federal government, which includes a national registry. (Please stop asking for this.) Even the Firearm Owners Protection Act was accompanied by the Hughes amendment.

Embrace free state projects like Wyoming and New Hampshire, push Nullification of gun laws like Kansas and Missouri. Push Sheriffs to declare publicly that they will not enforce gun laws. Take a cue from marijuana legalization. Marijuana legalization failed at the federal level, but so many people were on the side of medicinal marijuana; the states caved and disregarded what the federal government had to say. Yes, people got in trouble at first, but soon the tide shifted, now it's not just legalized for medicinal purposes but recreation — all against the federal government.

Read Nullification by Thomas E Woods Jr and his podcast the Tom Woods show
Check out the Tenth Amendment center and their podcast Paths to Liberty; it is full of examples of how Nullification works.

### *How do we get to officials to nullify and what else can we do?*

- o Attend town halls and encourage others to so.
- o Join gun clubs and state gun groups.
- o Invite your congressman and representatives to shoot, encourage them to get their CPL.
  - Pool your money together with others in your club and pay for the class; it's not about the class. It's about the eight hours you will get to spend with them. If they like it, invite them to other training classes. Be a rational human being with common sense; if you are talking to your democratic congressman, don't wear an "Make America Great Again" hat. Don't have them shoot a S&W 500 the first time they shoot. Invite their interns. Show

them that a suppressor is not Hollywood quiet.
- Get involved in shooting sports, invite others, take friends and family shooting.
- Don't treat gun ownership as a taboo; it's normal to own guns, so talk about guns.
- If you are an instructor offer to give the class to schoolteachers for free (don't forget college professors), ask gun clubs, gun rights organizations, and local gun shops for donations. Advertise to first-timers, ladies only, college students over 21, Muslims, Blacks, Asians, Hispanics, Jews, etc. look at your area and pick a demographic, it can help your business and push the cause. Get with other instructors to develop a PowerPoint or some course material that you can all share and devote an hour to just statistics and why firearm ownership is essential from a purely self-defense position.
  - Rick Ector of Legally Armed in Detroit does this, he started off with 50 women trained in a weekend and has grown it to almost a 1,000.
- Don't have a gun group or pro-gun organization near you? See if you can create a new chapter of an existing group or start from scratch. Don't know where to start? Start a non-profit that focuses on cleaning up parks or abandoned property, do it while open carrying a sidearm. Call it "helping arms" or something. Create a positive image that will attract others, and it will grow. Look at what is needed in your community and do it, all while being a firearm advocate.
- You don't even need to be a non-profit just get with other gun owners and pick up trash, clean up a park, build some picnic tables… all while open carrying. Just say you are gun owners doing your civic duty.

- Join a local civic club or local networking groups like Business Network International (BNI) or Toastmasters.
- Are you an introvert? I certainly am, so write blogs, start a podcast, make a YouTube channel, make memes, draw cartoons. Whatever your skillset is, you can be helpful; maybe it is knowing Microsoft suite well, I mentioned earlier about designing a PowerPoint for CPL class. Perhaps set up a website or Facebook page that lets gun owners know of local events and town halls. Good with video or animation then do that.
- Wear pro-gun shirts (I didn't say you had to buy mine) it may seem stupid, and some people like to remain low key, but it is a simple way to show people there are a lot of us.
- Stalk a tyrant, hang them from a prominent location as a warning to others, repeat as often as necessary.

Okay, so that last one is a joke, the bottom line is the best thing you can do is at the lowest level and grow from there. The lowest level is the most important because it's the easiest thing for you to do right now. We don't all have the ability to march on DC or the ability to spend a couple hundred grand taking on the Supreme Court.

We won't win over the majority of this country overnight, but we can take on people, cities, counties, and states. The Tenth Amendment Center has done most of the work for us on this issue. Go to the reference at the end of this paragraph and start emailing and writing your state representatives. Sample legislation is included for your reps along with other model ordinances that have passed. This is a simple step that will take you a few minutes, a quick link is even included on the page for you to locate your state rep and senator. Don't forget your sheriff, local law enforcement, and county reps. [395]

## Second, The Harder Question, How Do We Decrease Violence?

- End the drug war
- End gun free zone

I focus on "violence" because eliminating gun deaths at the cost of increased assaults, robberies, and rapes does not seem like much of a positive. Nor do I think anyone could come up with a compelling argument that a certain number of rapes is better than a certain amount of murders. So how do we eliminate overall violence, the assaults, mass shootings, gang violence, and murders? Well, I don't, but I do know where we can start.

Alcohol prohibition is widely regarded as a failure and an absurd idea. Yet somehow so many people still jump on board supporting drug prohibition. I am not advocating drug use any more than I am promoting alcohol use. What I am saying is that these two are the same situations just the drug war has lasted so long people actually believe in it, they bought into all the scary stories and hype. Billions are spent every year with nothing to show except for dead bodies and a prison system larger than the rest of the world. It not only is destroying inner cities, but its effects on Mexico is undeniable, which is likely why Mexico is looking into complete legalization. [396]

The drug war in inner cities has resulted in widespread gang violence as they fight over distribution areas. The ASDM loves to point to overall handgun violence numbers to push their cause while leaving out that the vast majority of those deaths are gang-related (hint: gangbangers don't seem to be good at following laws.)

Not only does the drug war spur gang-violence, but it also spreads further than that. We know that most murderers come from single-parent homes. The drug war has taken generations of fathers out of their homes and into prisons also eliminating a second income for a lot of these families. When they get out, they are generally unable to get decent-paying jobs, and the cycle continues all because someone chose to smoke weed. Some may say that's all well and good for marijuana, but what about heroin, coke, meth, etc. In the words of Ron Paul:

> *"I don't know how to run your life, I don't want to run your life, and the constitution doesn't give me the authority to run your life"*

Treat the addiction as a mental health issue and not a criminal one. Legalizing also brings in stricter controls on drugs at the manufacture and distribution level; for instance, alcohol is under more scrutiny now than when it was made in bathtubs and the woods. The free market incentivizes businesses to create clean, safe products. (I said free market, not crony capitalism)

Speaking of mental health issues and drugs, when are we going to investigate legal prescription drugs and the effect on mental health in adolescents. Why do so many want to sue Remington and Smith & Wesson but not looking into Pfizer or Barr? Almost all mass shooters were seen by psychiatrists and on prescription drugs.

Next, we should look at where these mass shootings take place, around 94% in gun-free zones. I am not against businesses deciding they want to be gun-free, I don't agree, but that's their decision. You can choose not to shop there and encourage other to not shop their as well. I am, however, against the government dictating gun-free zones such as schools. There is a reason gun-free zones are the subject of so many memes; it is a laughable concept that criminals who intend on killing people are going to be worried about a sign.

The arming teachers' argument gets a lot of flak for being an ignorant policy. Partly because of the different cases that have been posed, one being requiring all teachers to be armed, the other allowing teachers to carry. I agree with the second, and I disagree that it should be mandatory. School shootings have been stopped by teachers who used personal firearms. Also, numerous schools allow teachers to carry; you haven't heard about it because it's not an issue.

## Civil Disobedience

> *"Passive resistance and boycotting are now prominent features of every great national movement." -Benjamin Tucker* [397]

> *What country before ever existed a century and half without a rebellion? And what country can preserve its liberties if their rulers are not warned from time to time that their people preserve the spirit of resistance? Let them take arms. The remedy is to set them right as to facts, pardon and pacify them. What signify a few lives lost in a century or two? The tree of liberty must be refreshed from time to time with the blood of patriots and tyrants. It is its natural manure.*
> *-Thomas Jefferson* [398]

While there have been "reformations" in the past, none of them stand out quite like "Protestant Reformation." It may seem odd to explain the reformation to you in this topic on Civil Disobedience, but it will make sense the deeper we dive. To do that, we must do a little history. Don't Worry; this whole section is not about the reformation

History lesson: in 1517, the then Catholic Monk Martin Luther famously nailed his 95 theses to the door at Wittenberg, 95 theses was a list of grievances or issues he had with the Catholic church at the time. Interesting note and not as well-known was that Luther's last straw was Johan Tetzel. Tetzel's famous line was "for every coin in the coffer rings a soul in purgatory springs" (coffer being the box that collected the offering to bring to Pope Leo). The reason this infuriated Luther was, he believed this to be a downright lie and contrary to the scripture. His thesis was to point out the errors and "reform" or correct the current path or position of the Roman Church. He wasn't the first to do this either, John Wycliffe and Jan Hus made these stands as well. To give some context to the stakes he was up against Hus was executed for it, Wycliffe's bones were exhumed and burned. Thus, Luther's stance "here I stand, I can do no other" is a clear example of Civil Disobedience, his aim was not violence, it was disobeying what he believed to be unjust and incorrect. The result was the largest group of protesters in the world, the Protestants (Lutherans, Presbyterians, Baptist, Methodist, etc.). He spawned resistance not only during his time but centuries later in a name that would become synonymous with civil disobedience, Martin Luther King Jr (MLK).

Michael King Sr. MLK's father visited Germany in 1934 and learned about the reformer Martin Luther, his father was so inspired he changed his name, as well as his son's. MLK is now perhaps the first thing people think of when they hear Civil Disobedience (sorry Henry David Thoreau) his statements on civil disobedience are numerous and "Letters from a Birmingham Jail" [399] in my opinion was him at his best. Letters from a Birmingham Jail is where he penned:

*"Injustice anywhere is a threat to justice everywhere."*

It might sound weird to say, but I think the letter gives the best example of his intelligence, my reason in believing that is that he wrote so well and referenced cases so clearly without the use of source material or a library of resources, after all, he was in jail. He was writing about civil disobedience while acting out civil disobedience.

*"We know through painful experience that freedom is never voluntarily given by the oppressor; it must be demanded by the oppressed. Frankly, I have never yet engaged in a direct-action movement that was "well timed" according to the timetable of those who have not suffered unduly from the disease of segregation. For*

*years now I have heard the word "wait." It rings in the ear of every Negro with a piercing familiarity. This "wait" has almost always meant "never."*

I have heard people from inside the gun community say that by not turning in an item, such as a bump stock or high capacity magazine, then you are breaking the law, and you are a criminal, and further saying this is not civil disobedience. However, this action is precisely that; it is civil disobedience. It is asinine to believe that just because a thing is labeled a "law" that it somehow becomes "just." Countless cases can be offered as an example. People such as Harriet Tubman, Corrie ten Boom, MLK, and I would say to an extent more controversial people like Daniel Ellsberg, Edward Snowden, Julian Assange, or even Irwin Schiff and Ross Ulbricht. However, it is easier to argue over older scenarios and their morality because the stigma is gone; the fruits of disobedience are now evident in the historical examples.

At this moment, many do not consider an infringement of the 2nd amendment to be immoral; in fact, I would say they believe they have the moral high ground as they do not understand Natural Rights. Even people who you would think would be on our side are pushing not to disturb the status quo, and again in MLK's Letters from jail he seems to answer

> *"You express a great deal of anxiety over our willingness to break laws. This is certainly a legitimate concern. Since we so diligently urge people to obey the Supreme Court's decision of 1954 outlawing segregation in the public schools, it is rather strange and paradoxical to find us consciously breaking laws. One may well ask, "How can you advocate breaking some laws and obeying others?" The answer is found in the fact that there are two types of laws: there are just laws, and there are unjust laws. I would agree with St. Augustine that "An unjust law is no law at all."*

**At what point do you want to reform and at what point can you no longer reform, at that point,** you must revolt? I, for one, would prefer to attack low hanging fruit and reform while we still have the means instead of waiting for things to deteriorate further.

Between Martin Luther and MLK, we had Henry David Thoreau, who literally wrote the book on Civil Disobedience. He argued Civil Disobedience is the "deliberate violation of laws for reason of conscience." (Notice he didn't say they had to be public displays of resistance) Thoreau believed that no law should command blind obedience and that non-cooperation with unjust laws is both morally correct and socially beneficial. An interesting quote that ties Reformation and Civil Disobedience is from Thoreau's famous work, in it he says:

> *"They think that, if they should resist, the remedy would be worse than the evil. But it is the fault of the government itself that the remedy is worse than the evil. It makes it worse. Why is it not more apt to anticipate and provide for reform? Why does it not cherish its wise minority? Why does it cry and resist before it is hurt? Why does it not encourage its citizens to be on the alert to point out its faults, and do better than it would have them? Why does it always crucify Christ, and excommunicate Copernicus and Luther, and pronounce Washington and Franklin rebels?"*

This essay, when I originally wrote it, was meant to explain that the gun community as a whole needed reformation, and to get my point across, I was going to compare it to the protestant reformation. As I was writing this originally in Dec 2018 for my blog, New Jersey was beginning its newest rounds of gun laws. Unfortunately, a lot of figures in the gun world argued for New Jersey gun owners to comply, some explicitly saying that it was not an act of Civil Disobedience to not comply. While rushing in to explain that it was, in fact, Civil Disobedience, I found that what I was writing about the reformation and the act of Civil Disobedience went hand in hand. Thoreau, in the previous quote in his book on civil disobedience references Luther and MLK in his letter from a Birmingham Jail, quotes St Augustine, who said: "an unjust law is no law at all." Luther was a monk dedicating himself to the "Augustinian" order, Wycliff who I also mentioned shortly, was known as "John of Augustine" because he loved him so much, and Hus was Wycliff's student... In other words, St Augustine was born in the mid 300's yet the same belief that was true in his day was true in Wycliffe's, it was true for Hus, true for Luther, true for Thoreau, true for MLK and you can be sure it's true for you, and that is DISOBEY UNJUST LAWS! Civil disobedience is nothing new; it has just grown out of favor as a means because men have grown to rely so heavily on politicians for justice that they neglect their own abilities.

What every great generation or leader has had in common was that they had a breaking point, a point where they said, "here I stand, I can do no other," what made movements out of those moments was that other people got on board and simultaneously had the last straw. A more current example or at least an honorable mention would be the comparison of Bundy Ranch Standoff and the Oregon BLM Standoff. Bundy Ranch garnered the support of around 5,000 armed men, while in Oregon, the group never amassed much of a real following. I believe Bundy Ranch succeeded for a couple of reasons; the case was rather simple, so it was easy to explain and hard to spin, Bundy Ranch was in 2014 while Obama was still in office and gun owners were on alert. By the time Oregon standoff came around, the reason for the standoff was unclear; there were so many confusing stories, it became hard to pick out the facts. The issue wasn't clear to the majority of Americans who don't understand that the US government owns and controls a lot of land in the west and the impact on ranchers because of this. It also was at a time where Trump had just taken office, and gun owners once again let their guard down and thought a politician would take care of them. You could guarantee the Oregon Standoff would have grown to thousands if Hillary was in office at the time. People tend to be ok with oppression when it is the person, they think is on their side doing the oppressing.

I made it a point to explain Luther's last straw earlier, Johan Tetzel conning the poor out of money in the name of church for the benefit of Pope Leo X. My reason behind this was that it is like an issue we face in the gun community; you could argue unfounded fines and taxes were also the last straw for the founders as well. The core of this is violating or ignoring convictions for financial gain, now as I write this it has been brought to light that there have been numerous "pro 2a" businesses that have donated to antigun politicians, more than likely in an attempt to get large government contracts. Social media Gun-celebs have fallen in this trap as well. Too many in the industry have let their pocketbook direct their beliefs instead of the truth. Even gun rights organizations like the NRA have lost their mission 400 million dollars in annual donations (under Obama and the fear of Hillary in 2016) results in numerous people clamoring to keep their jobs and putting the principle to the side to make way for profit. Outside of the NRA, we have too many people who claim to be supporters of the constitution and gun rights who make statements like "don't blame me I just enforce the law I didn't write it." People who make such claims that they are just enforcers are in direct opposition to their duty to protect the people, and in violation of their oaths to uphold the constitution.

I urge you to read MLKs letter not only because of the content but because of who the letter addressed. I think the message is more powerful because he was writing to his fellow pastors. People who should have been next to him standing with him, but instead stayed safely away — people who Thoreau said: sit by waiting for others to remedy the evil.

MLK had so much to say in regard to Civil Disobedience that it would be a shame not to have more quotes from Letter from a Birmingham Jail as many can be applied to the gun debate:

> "Now, what is the difference between the two? How does one determine when a law is just or unjust? A just law is a man-made code that squares with the moral law, or the law of God. An unjust law is a code that is

*out of harmony with the moral law. To put it in the terms of St. Thomas Aquinas, an unjust law is a human law that is not rooted in eternal and natural law. Any law that uplifts human personality is just. Any law that degrades human personality is unjust. All segregation statutes are unjust because segregation distorts the soul and damages the personality. It gives the segregator a false sense of superiority and the segregated a false sense of inferiority. To use the words of Martin Buber, the great Jewish philosopher, segregation substitutes an "I - it" relationship for the "I - thou" relationship and ends up relegating persons to the status of things. So segregation is not only politically, economically, and sociologically unsound, but it is morally wrong and sinful. Paul Tillich has said that sin is separation. Isn't segregation an existential expression of man's tragic separation, an expression of his awful estrangement, his terrible sinfulness? So I can urge men to obey the 1954 decision of the Supreme Court because it is morally right, and I can urge them to disobey segregation ordinances because they are morally wrong"*

*"Let us turn to a more concrete example of just and unjust laws. An unjust law is a code that a majority inflicts on a minority that is not binding on itself. This is difference made legal. On the other hand, a just law is a code that a majority compels a minority to follow, and that it is willing to follow itself. This is sameness made legal."*

*"Of course, there is nothing new about this kind of civil disobedience. It was seen sublimely in the refusal of Shadrach, Meshach, and Abednego to obey the laws of Nebuchadnezzar because a higher moral law was involved. It was practiced superbly by the early Christians, who were willing to face hungry lions and the excruciating pain of chopping blocks before submitting to certain unjust laws of the Roman Empire.*

*To a degree, academic freedom is a reality today because Socrates practiced civil disobedience."*

*"We can never forget that everything Hitler did in Germany was "legal" and everything the Hungarian freedom fighters did in Hungary was "illegal." It was "illegal" to aid and comfort a Jew in Hitler's Germany. But I am sure that if I had lived in Germany during that time, I would have aided and comforted my Jewish brothers even though it was illegal. If I lived in a Communist country today where certain principles dear to the Christian faith are suppressed, I believe I would openly advocate disobeying these anti-religious laws."*

## 80% Firearms

Make a law, and someone will figure out a way around it, the market always finds a way. Bump-stocks, arm-braces, solvent traps, binary triggers, and 80% build kits are just a few examples of the ingenuity in the gun community. Every time the government makes a law a work around or a black market opens. While the current "craze" of do-it-yourself 80% build kits probably started somewhere in 2013 the law that makes the kit legal goes back to the Gun Control Act of 1968.

*"18 U.S.C, Chapter 44 states that an unlicensed individual can make a firearm for personal use, but not for the intent of sale or distribution. Said firearm must conform to N.F.A standards and you must be legally able to be in possession of a firearm. "80% receiver," "80% finished," "80% complete," "unfinished receiver" are all terms referring to an item that some may believe has not yet reached a stage of manufacture that meets the definition of firearm frame or receiver found in the Gun Control Act of 1968 (GCA). These are*

*not statutory terms or terms ATF employs or endorses."*
[400]

As I mentioned above, the 80% AR started gaining traction in 2013. Kits were available beforehand, but most of them were for AK pattern firearms or demilled military surplus. What seemed to get the 80% trend into the mainstream of the gun community was the perfect storm of bad publicity. It is joked that Obama was the greatest gun salesman of all time, and if we look back, this isn't a joke, gun sales soared. The gun community was in a constant state of panic buying with the belief that Obama would take our guns, this led many gun owners to look for non-conventional ways to get firearms. Now add to that one the most played video "clips" amongst gun owners. In 2014 Democrat Kevin de Leon attempted to scare people with his statement on what he called Ghost Guns:

> *"This right here has the ability with a .30-caliber clip to disperse 30 bullets within half a second. Thirty magazine clip in half a second."* [401]

Yes, that is what he said. Unwittingly what de Leon did was produce the perfect advertisement for 80% firearms that spread like wildfire.

Less than a year later, more publicity ensued. This time the publicity that was mainly kept inside the gun community, this time from Ares Armor and one of the most outspoken proponents of 80% firearms and the previous owner of Ares, Dimitri Karras. The ATF and DOJ fought Ares over selling 80% lowers specifically EP Armory Polymer lower AR-style receivers. To summarize what happened, the ATF sought to obtain the customer records of everyone who purchased a lower receiver from Ares or EP Armory. Ares was able to get a restraining order against the ATF, however after pressure from the ATF and DOJ that restraining order was overturned. This new ruling resulted in the raid of Ares, EP Armory's storefront, the owner's home had already been raided. The ATF in full kit raided Ares and brought a locksmith to open the safe where customer records were sealed. They also confiscated 6,000 lowers from Ares.

Dimitri, a former Marine, told Reason.tv about the raid

> *"This isn't just a 2nd amendment issue, it's not just a firearms issue. It's an issue of an overreaching government that wants to come into your kitchen, that wants to come into your living room, and just see what you're doing…. It's an object that's in the shape of a receiver, but it hasn't been completed to a point that it would be considered a firearm, This was a nice way for them to get their arm inside of the business and grab the information that they are actually looking for. To think that this is over a piece of plastic is ludicrous."* [402]

This was back in 2014, and what Dimitri has said has proven to be accurate, the ATF returned all the receivers, except for 18 that the ATF said went missing. Funny that the guy they said was dangerous didn't lose any firearms, yet the government lost 18 [403]. What was less expected by the ATF was, in fact, Dimitri himself. His letter explaining 80% firearms is a thing of lore, and that's not it, Dimitri has also pushed it so far that he sold 80% firearms by the road outside of his local ATF branch. More importantly, was that this ended up being bad press for the ATF and more publicity for unserialized receivers.

For an AR receiver to be USABLE, it must the trigger and OOPS!! wrong hammer ← use this one ☺ ←Weapon ← Receiver of weapon If this part → requires machining to accept these parts trigger hammer IT IS NØT A Receiver!

Dimitri still sells 80% firearms, EP armory is still in business, and the gun community at large has fully embraced this option. It has moved from a niche market to a popular choice, even showing up at the most significant industry show put on by National Shooting Sports Foundation, SHOT. You can now find 80% kits for every configuration of AR, AK, Glock, 1911, Sig P320, even the Ruger 10/22 can be purchased as a "build your own kit."

Many new offerings jumped into the 80% market to get around the State Departments ITAR requirement of $2,240 a year. This is a separate fee from the ATF and is required of firearm manufacturers. This fee has been a hindrance to many new companies. It is an example of how the government's attempt at controlling an industry only opens backdoors in ways they never thought possible. This has resulted in a considerable benefit to the gun community, one example is Polymer80 who produces a Glock comparable option that many see as not a way around a law, as many still register their 80%, but instead as a way to get options that Glock was not offering. They removed what is commonly referred to as the "Glock hump," eliminated finger grooves as well as other improvements. And now at least five other companies are currently producing 80% Glock kits, including a metal version.

80% build kits create a sort of black hole for gun control. For one the 80% like its cousin, the 3D printed firearm, defies all form of background checks. It defies the requirement for all firearms to have serial numbers, as it is impossible to guarantee all 80% will be serialized. Some may look at this and see loopholes that need to be shut, others see new options. After all the 80% was born out of a loophole, close this one, and like Hydra, two more replace it. That may be 3D printers, pourable firearm molds for plastics or metals, or at home CNC machines that any layman can use which all exist already.

## Defense Distributed

There is not a more controversial subject in the gun world over the last decade than that of 3D printed firearms. It ignited not only gun rights advocates but also free speech advocates. Who would have thought a guy in his twenties and less than 50sq ft of rented office space would cause so much havoc for the government? From the state department to the ATF and up.

Enter Cody Wilson, along with his company Defense Distributed, in late 2012, early 2013 introduced DEFCAD. DEFCAD was designed to be a free space platform to share files that were banned by the company Makerbot. What was a display of free speech and a physical representation of libertarian philosophy, they made available numerous 3D gun files including their legal and printable "Liberator pistol." Of course, the State Department basically shut down the sharing of these files not long after they became available. Still, as we all know, once these files became available, there was no way to make them unavailable. I personally remember when they became available, I had no experience whatsoever with a 3D printer. I just knew the government wanted them taken down, so I saved all the files. Numerous people who had the files shared them regularly while DEFCAD was down. Not only that, more and more people have added to these files creating a sea of information.

> *"It's speech control to regulate the gun culture" -Cody Wilson*

During his five-year court battle with the Obama administration, these files were not to be shared, not that it stopped thousands of forums from sharing the files, however when Obama left office the case fell rather flat. The new administration wasn't interested in pursuing it further and basically dropped the case. In the meantime, Cody didn't stop innovating ways to piss them off, launching the infamous Ghost Gunner CNC machine. Capable of finishing 80% receivers with the push of a button. Making legal unserialized firearms from the comfort of your own home. This basically became the business, and 3D files became a cause.

> *"The technology will break gun control. I stand for freedom" -Cody Wilson*

Cody Wilson is a character that the press could not handle. They couldn't trap him into saying something stupid, they couldn't pigeonhole him into taking a political side. They were unable to understand this form of anarchy, it was counter all their talking points. Ultimately what he said though happened.

> *"If the state is going to move against you, it's going to move against you...I hope when they finally do get me, it's obvious that they just made it up."*

In 2018 Cody Wilson was charged and arrested with soliciting sex from a minor. The case was rather suspect from the beginning. Cody Wilson hooked up with a girl using a dating app that is for adults over 21 years of age. It is unclear if money was later exchanged directly for sex, but what happened then was the girl ended up going to the police to report the incident. The girl's friend supposedly alerted Cody, and he caught the first flight to Taiwan. What is unclear is how a city in Texas was able to negotiate the return of a suspected criminal in Taiwan, a country with no extradition treaty with the United States. Although the site is for adults over 21, it appears Texas law does not deem that as an excuse. Again, it's interesting how the case went down and how it happened at basically the peak of Cody's fame. The case recently concluded with Cody going free with probation.

He doesn't seem to be slowing down as the next generation ghost gunner will be able to complete AK receivers, and Defense Distributed is back up with all new designs that are well beyond the first 3D printed liberator. A ton of new designers have also popped up putting out reliable 3D printed firearms which are now also available at Defense Distributed. The price of entry into this is a printer less than $200 and a spool of PLA filament for about $20.

What Cody Wilson has been able to accomplish in less than a decade in the firearms industry on a shoestring budget is remarkable. When I mentioned him starting in a 50sqft office, I was somewhat exaggerating; it was probably less space, seriously. He created a roadblock that even the antigun politicians couldn't jump over, and that was regulating free information on the internet. He also aggravated the gun communities' old guard, which is a cage that needed rattling. Wilson represents this eras gun owner, the gun owners that have been labeled as villains by the mainstream and political left. He represents the growing trend of gun owners who are skeptical of government and not set on a mainstream political ideology.

# Firearm Industry

What seems apparent is that changes are made incrementally, they are at the local levels. They involve first with a shift in thinking. Most important is the change in thinking or the challenging of what appears to be the standard mode of doing things. These manufacturers, however, have done just the opposite.

Anyone in the firearms industry, probably any industry, will tell you that the goal is contracts or bulk sales. After all, if I have one customer buying 500 items, that means I can focus on that one customer rather than searching for 500 customers to buy 1 item. In the firearm industry, that means you have only a few places to look, Law Enforcement and Military being the primary two. Imaginably this is why the majority of manufacturers and dealers placate to these groups. So, when you see companies in this industry doing the opposite, it makes you take notice.

In walks Barrett Firearms, and it's President Ronnie Barrett. In 2003 California decided to ban the .50 caliber rifle. Mr. Barrett was in attendance that day at a council meeting, and there were a few items that seemed to irk him a little more than others, one example in his own words written to LAPD police chief:

> "At that council meeting, I was very surprised to see an LAPD officer seated front and center with a Barrett 82A1 .50 cal rifle. It was the centerpiece of the discussion. As you know, there have been no crimes committed with these rifles, and most importantly, current California law does not allow the sale of the M82A1 in the state because of its detachable magazine and features that make it an "assault weapon." This rifle was being deceptively used by your department. The officer portrayed it as a sample of a currently available .50 cal rifle, available for sale to the civilians of Los Angeles. One councilman even questioned how this rifle

*was available under current laws, but as I stated, facts were ineffective that day...."* [404]

He goes on to explain his further dismay:

*"When I returned to my office from Los Angeles, I found an example of our need for mutual cooperation. Your department had sent one of your 82A1 rifles in to us for service. All of my knowledge in the use of my rifle in the field of law enforcement had been turned upside down by witnessing how your department used yours. Not to protect and serve, but for deception, photo opportunities, and to further an ill-conceived effort that may result in the use of LA taxpayer monies to wage losing political battles in Washington against civil liberties regarding gun ownership.*
*Please excuse my slow response on the repair service of the rifle. I am battling to what service I am repairing the rifle for. I will not sell, nor service, my rifles to those seeking to infringe upon the Constitution and the crystal-clear rights it affords individuals to own firearms."*

My favorite part of this letter is this sentence:

*"I will not sell, nor service, my rifles to those seeking to infringe upon the Constitution and the crystal clear rights it affords individuals to own firearms."*

Simply put, Ronnie Barrett gets it. The company still holds this stance that they will not sell or service one of their firearms to a law enforcement agency that resides in an area where their fellow citizens cannot purchase.

Barrett has not stopped with California, here is a quote regarding New York's laws:

*"By current law, Barrett cannot be an accomplice with any lawbreaker, therefore, cannot and will not service or sell to New York government agencies. Barrett also*

*applies this stance to the individual elected official who, as a matter of public record, has voted for or created regulation that violates the constitutional rights of their citizens."* [405]

Barrett set a new precedent and made it ok for others to do likewise. Ronnie Barrett wasn't only risking money from agencies throughout California. He was risking angering numerous lawmakers that could possibly put an end to his multiple military contracts. It is telling of him that he put the existence of his company on the line to take a stand.

A giant of a company like Barrett Firearms doing what is right over doing what is profitable is incredibly admirable. He not only sent a message from his company but since his stand, other manufacturers took up a similar stance. Including Hornady Ammunition, that stopped selling their ammo through Walmart years before Walmart took up their antigun position. [406]

For further reference, please take a look at the letters he sent to these agencies. I encourage you to look into Barrett's vast array of firearms that extend beyond their iconic 50 cal, including the AR15 platform. I also encourage you to support companies that take a firm stance on the 2nd amendment like Barrett, such as: Turner Armament, Radian, Noveske, and others.

## States

*"Nullification is the Jeffersonian idea that the states of the American Union must judge the constitutionality of the acts of their agent, the federal government, since no impartial arbiter between them exists. When the federal government exercises a particularly dangerous power not delegated to it, the states must refuse to allow its enforcement within their borders."*

Imagine if the states acted how they were initially designed, independent from the federal government. Well, a few states have decided to do just that. They have invoked their powers of the 10th amendment and nullification.

In Alaska, this was tried before the current firearm bill and pushed by now political prisoner Schaeffer Cox. Alaska's legislation mentions the 10th amendment explicitly.

> *" the Tenth Amendment to the Constitution of the United States guarantees to the states and their people all powers not granted to the federal government elsewhere in the constitution and reserves to the state and people of Alaska certain powers as they were intended at the time that Alaska was admitted to statehood in 1959; the guaranty of those powers is a matter of contract between the state and people of Alaska and the United States as of the time that the compact with the United States was agreed to and adopted by Alaska and the United States in 1959;"*

These states are smart. They have used the perverted justification the government gave to regulate firearms, which they claim is their power over interstate commerce. Borrowing the wording again from Alaska's state legislation:

> *"A personal firearm, a firearm accessory, or ammunition that is possessed in this state or manufactured commercially or privately in this state and that remains in the state is not subject to federal law or federal regulation, including registration, under the authority of the United States Congress to regulate interstate commerce as those items have not traveled in interstate commerce."* [407]

What these states are saying is that it is up to their state how they will regulate firearms. Since these items have not passed over borders, they are not subject to any federal laws. They are out of the federal government's jurisdiction.

Idaho was one of the first states back in 2009 to tell the federal government they were out of line:

> *"NOW, THEREFORE, BE IT RESOLVED by the members of the First Regular Session of the Sixtieth Idaho Legislature, the House of Representatives and the Senate concurring therein, that members of the United States Congress cease and desist attempting to enact federal legislation impinging on the individual right of every American to keep and bear arms in any manner."*

Kansas has also been at the forefront of this issue since the federal government charged Jeremy Kettler with a felony. Jeremy, a US Army veteran, and resident of Kansas purchased a suppressor under this law in the state of Kansas. This case has been taken on by Gun Owners of America and is challenging the federal government's reach. According to Gun Owners of America (GOA):

> *"Jeremy's petition first challenges the legitimacy of the National Firearms Act, which was passed in 1934, and thereafter upheld by the Supreme Court in 1937 under the constitutional power of Congress to "lay and collect taxes." The petition argues that the NFA as it exists today no longer can be justified as a so-called "tax."*
> [408]

> *"(He) challenges the Tenth Circuit's absurd holding that the 2nd amendment applies only to "bearable arms" — but not firearm accessories, such as suppressors. The petition points out that the Second, Third, Seventh, and Ninth Circuits all have concluded that the 2nd amendment extends beyond actual firearms to ammunition, magazines, the ability to purchase firearms in gun stores, and the right to practice at shooting ranges."*

Sadly, Solicitor General Noel Francisco urged the Supreme Court not to take the case, so the Supreme Court never tried the case or rendered an opinion. This should not discourage states, they should continue to press the issue and gain back their sovereignty. What should be telling as to the ineptness of both parties is that there are numerous states that currently have veto proof republican majorities and yet these politicians who are supposed to care about "states' rights" are not looking to enact legislation blocking the federal government's control on guns. Presently (2020) these are the states that have veto proof majority:

- Alabama
- Arkansas
- Idaho
- Indiana
- Kansas
- Kentucky
- Missouri
- Nebraska
- North Dakota
- Ohio
- South Dakota
- Tennessee
- Utah
- West Virginia
- Wyoming

## Law Enforcement

Along with State nullification, the 10th Amendment, and jury nullification there lies another option. That is Law enforcement upholding their oaths and refusing to enforce unconstitutional and immoral laws.

We've already described state nullification so just to explain Jury nullification quickly, Cornell Law describes it as:

*"A jury's knowing and deliberate rejection of the evidence or refusal to apply the law either because the jury wants to send a message about some social issue that is larger than the case itself, or because the result dictated by law is contrary to the jury's sense of justice, morality, or fairness."* [409]

Wikipedia describes it:

*"Jury nullification is a concept where members of a trial jury find a defendant not guilty if they do not support a government's law, do not believe it is constitutional or humane, or do not support a possible punishment for breaking the law. This may happen in both civil and criminal trials."* [410]

Either way, the example is rather clear. Nullification can be applied to other positions as well, such as in our scenario with Law enforcement. One example of this was Michigan's law on automatic knives. The State Police gave testimony that the law was not being evenly enforced, and the misdemeanor that came with the charge was unnecessary. This resulted in an overturn of the original ban making it once again legal. But honestly, the knives were readily available all over the state, and tons of people carried them, it just wasn't enforced.

This should happen much more often in cases like Magazine bans, featureless grips, barrel lengths, etc. Unconstitutional laws should be worthless with law enforcement refusing to enforce these gun laws.

Truth be told, there are cops out there who are doing just that. One example comes from New Mexico after a law was sent to the governor for signature on background checks on private purchases. Numerous counties and their Sheriffs have refused to enforce the law, and those counties have begun to be called. "2nd amendment Sanctuary Counties."

The Chairman of the New Mexico Sheriff's Association has said:

> *"The key thing to remember is this is all a burden on responsible gun owners... We're here to protect people's individual rights."* [411]

New Mexico Sheriffs are not alone; more than half of Washington state's sheriffs have publicly refused to enforce new gun control measures. Several counties in the state have passed local resolutions opposing the enforcement. Some sheriffs have gone so far as to say that not only will they not enforce these laws, they would prevent other agencies from attempting to implement them as well.

What I find interesting in both of these states, as well as others, is that they are predominantly the rural county sheriffs that are refusing to enforce these laws. Rural counties have typically lengthier response times, which is even more reason to have a firearm in the house for an emergency. Also, in all the articles I read, I saw attacks insinuating these sheriffs were alt-right, linking them to the NRA, and that the counties' "ideas of supremacy over the state" was akin to white supremacy. What I did not read in those articles was who these new gun laws would've saved or what cases or data they consulted. My guess is that while they attacked these Sheriffs for being in the pocket of the NRA, they were getting their information from some Bloomberg paid gun group.

Many articles regarding New Mexico sheriffs brought up the Parkland high school shooting. Yet, the New Mexico gun control law is in regard to background checks on private sales, the Parkland shooter passed a background check and purchased it at a store. That is clearly an appeal to emotion and not weighted in any logic. Also, to claim that what these men are doing is linked to white supremacy or the KKK should be embarrassing for the journalist even to write. One could easily switch this around and show the roots of gun control as racist from keeping arms from freed slaves to attacking Huey Newton's group of Black Panthers.

Gun owners need to start taking a more active role in fighting for their rights. Given the relationship between firearm owners and law enforcement, this should be an easier demographic to speak with. Sheriffs, in particular, are elected officials that are more likely to listen than those appointed.

### *The tricky relationship between gun owners and police.*

> *"How long would authority exist, if not for the willingness of the mass to become soldiers, policemen, jailers, and hangmen"* -Emma Goldman [412]

I can't put a date on it, but sometime in the last fifty years supporting the police, gun ownership, and supporting republicans became a package deal. If you support the police, you're instantly labeled a pro-life republican who is against gay marriage and voted for Trump. If you say one thing derogatory about the police, you're a liberal gender-confused socialist snowflake.

What I don't see is either side thinking thoroughly about the role of law enforcement. On one side, you have the ASDM and liberals who love to point out the faults and scandals of law enforcement yet believe those same officers should be the only ones with guns and believe those officers will protect you. On the other side are gun owners who have a blue line "back the blue" sticker on their Toyota Tacoma next to a don't tread on me or a come and take it sticker. Both groups are obviously inconsistent.

That being said, I Frankly don't know how to handle this topic properly. I cannot fully write about the issue of law enforcement in one section. It is a vast topic and encourage you to read the book "Rise of the Warrior Cop" by Radley Balko it's a good place to start. Since I don't think I will do it justice, I instead believe you should think about this on your own and ask yourself some questions.

- If law enforcement has enforced every other gun law, then why do you think they won't enforce the next one, or enforce a complete gun confiscation? If you believe Law enforcement will not enforce or participate in gun confiscation or unconstitutional laws, then what do you think is their line in the sand?
- If you don't know their line in the sand, then what makes you so sure they won't confiscate your firearms?
- If you do not believe they will enforce unconstitutional gun laws, then why are you worried about who is in congress or the Whitehouse? Why do you check on barrel length, overall length, etc.?
- On the other hand, if you think they will confiscate your firearms or enforce unconstitutional gun laws, then why do you support them?
- If they act unconstitutionally, then are they really public servants, or are they just political enforcers?
- If they truly do not support unconstitutional gun laws, then should more law enforcement organizations be vocal about it? Shouldn't they make it public that they will not support any gun laws?
- Does a large majority of the gun community as far as dealers, manufacturers, and accessory companies support law enforcement just because they see them as a meal ticket, and they just want them to buy their products?
- Why can we continuously talk about how poorly politicians are doing, or we can speak of lawyers and tax collectors but give their enforcement arm a pass? Just doing your job has never been an adequate defense.

No doubt, people will get mad at these questions, but the reason they are upset is because of the answers or the struggle they must go through to figure out logical answers. These questions are important because a "gun confiscation" is not what will be passed, at least not anytime soon.

What will happen is a continuation of what has been happening, and that is the small wins for the ASDM, and those small wins add up. Cops might even believe they won't confiscate firearms. But when it comes down to it, they won't believe they are…instead they will say: they are taking "assault weapons" from "dangerous people" or taking "weapons of war" away from potential "cop killers." Or they will just be small incremental laws like we see above. As Ayn Rand puts it:

> *"Many men are capable of dying on the barricades for a big issue, but few, very few are able to resist the gray suction of small, unheralded, day-by-day surrenders."*
> *-Ayn Rand* [413]

Propaganda campaigns against guns will continue, we see this all over with comments like "only mass murderers need" or "these are only used by hitmen." These tactics were used against Marijuana, used by slave owners against blacks, and a million other situations where propaganda made it ok to do something immoral. They undermine reality until people feel what is going on is acceptable.

This is why law enforcement needs to draw a line in the sand; the constitution doesn't change based on the majority's opinion. Rights don't change because of popular opinion. Instead of saying, "I know my (insert relation) is a cop, and they would never..." ask them what they would do. I see everyone always telling people to write to their congressmen in DC, but what they need to do is write their local congressional leaders, write their sheriffs and city officials. More of these officials need to learn about the power of Nullification and gun owners need to stop applying blanketed support to people who do not support them.

# Further Info

I'm making this resource list a bit different in that I didn't want it to be just a list of books to read or podcasts to listen to. In no specific order:

- Tom Woods (Thomas E Woods Jr): He is a historian, author, and podcaster that I listen to every day. My criteria for this section was that they had to fit in both categories Liberty and Firearms. Tom fits this not just because he has his own eBook on gun rights but because his liberty focused show explains many ideas about rights and the Constitution. Also, his great book "Nullification" should be read by every gun owner and examined by pro-gun groups.

- Michael Boldin: He is the man behind the Tenth Amendment Center and the podcast Path to Liberty. I really enjoy the Tenth Amendment Center website and blog posts from guys like Mike Maharrey and Ryan McMaken. They are super informative and deal with gun rights consistently. When I first subscribed to Boldin's podcast, I had no idea how often he would handle gun rights, and now I don't believe there is another podcast that does it this well. Like Tom Woods, the tenth amendment center shows how nullification can be used to get our rights back. Currently, Boldin is working with the Libertarian Mises Caucus and others to help gun owners in Texas.

- Brion McClanahan: A great place to go for everything constitution. You can find him in several places such as his self-titled podcast, the Liberty classroom, McClanahan academy, and numerous books. Besides his politically incorrect guides, I like his book "Founding Fathers Guide to the Constitution" the most.

- John Lott Jr: I talked a little about him before, but he's worth mentioning again. "More Guns, Less Crime" is a great well documented and in-depth book on firearm statistics. Besides his other books, you can read more at his website crimeresearch.org which is updated continuously. You used to be able to find him more regularly on tv, but I think since you can't stump him, they stopped inviting him. However, you should go check out his previous appearances, which you can find on YouTube.

- Gun Rights Organizations: Firearm Policy Coalition and Gun Owners of America. I would stay away from the NRA at least until they remove Wayne and numerous board members, that place is currently cancer.

- Last but not least: There are a lot of great resources out there, so I'm going to lump a bunch of them all together right here.

  - Dave Smith: Look at his podcast "Part of the Problem." Also, on Twitter and frequent guest on Fox Business's show Kennedy Nation.
  - Pete Quinones: His podcast is "Free Man Beyond the Wall." You can also find him at the Libertarian Institute, where you can read guys like Sheldon Richman, who wrote "The Tyranny of Gun Control."
  - Mises.org: this is not solely an economics website; it has a ton of resources covering everything Liberty.

# Quotes

*"That the said Constitution shall never be construed to authorize Congress to infringe the just liberty of the press or the rights of conscience; or to prevent the people of the United States who are peaceable citizens from keeping their own arms."* -Sam Adams

*"I prefer dangerous freedom over peaceful slavery"* is a translation of a Latin phrase that Thomas Jefferson used: *"Malo periculosam, libertatem quam quietam servitutem."* It has also been translated as, *"I prefer the tumult of liberty to the quiet of servitude.*
http://tjrs.monticello.org/letter/86

*"Guard with jealous attention the public liberty. Suspect everyone who approaches that jewel. Unfortunately, nothing will preserve it but downright force. Whenever you give up that force, you are ruined.... The great object is that every man be armed. Everyone who is able might have a gun."*
- Patrick Henry, Speech to the Virginia Ratifying Convention, June 5, 1778

*"As civil rulers, not having their duty to the people before them, may attempt to tyrannize, and as the military forces which must be occasionally raised to defend our country, might pervert their power to the injury of their fellow citizens, the people are confirmed by the article in their right to keep and bear their private arms."*
- Tench Coxe, Philadelphia Federal Gazette, June 18, 1789

*"Conceived it to be the privilege of every citizen, and one of his most essential rights, to bear arms, and to resist every attack upon his liberty or property, by whomsoever made. The particular States, like private citizens, have a right to be armed, and to defend by force of arms, their rights, when invaded."*
-Roger Sherman, Debates on 1790 Militia Act

*"The people are not to be disarmed of their weapons. They are left in full possession of them."*
*-Zachariah Johnson, Virginia Ratifying Convention, June 25, 1788*

*"Who are the original minds and the energetic characters of our day? Who is out there challenging the status quo in defense of liberty?"*

*"Lex malum, lex nulla: A bad law is no law"*

*"In all free states the constitution is fixed" -Samuel Adams*

*"When we hear about rent control or gun control, we may think about rent or guns but the word that really matters is 'control.' That is what the political left is all about, as you can see by the incessant creation of new restrictions in places where they are strongly entrenched in power, such as San Francisco or New York." -Thomas Sowell*

*"Their conscious dignity, as citizens enjoying equal rights, to invade the rights of others. The danger from armed citizens, is only to the government, not to the society; as long as they have nothing to revenge in the government, there are many advantages in their being accustomed to the use of arms and no possible disadvantage." -Joel Barlow*

*"It is a natural right which the people have reserved to themselves, confirmed by the [English] Bill of Rights, to keep arms for their own defense; and as Mr. Blackstone observes, it is to be made use of when the sanctions of society and law are found insufficient to restrain the violence of oppression." - Boston Journal of the Times 1768*

*"it was in the law of nature for every man to defend himself, and unlawful for any man to deprive him of those weapons of self-defense."*
*Boston independent Chronicle 1787*

*"But it is not necessary, for this purpose, that individuals should relinquish all their natural rights. Some are of such a nature that they cannot be surrendered. Of this kind are the rights of conscience, the right of enjoying and defending life, so in forming a government on its true principles, the foundation should be laid in the manner I before stated, by expressly reserving to the people such of their essential rights, as are not necessary to be parted with."*
New York journal 1787

*"That a well-regulated militia is the proper, natural and safe defense of a free government"*
-Delaware Bill of Rights (Virginia, Maryland, New Hampshire and the New York and Rhode Island Convention also say natural)

*"It is the duty of all men to have arms" -Sir John Fortescue*

*"It is the right and duty of all freemen to have arms of defense and peace" - Henry de Bracton*

*"There are acts which the federal, or state legislature cannot do, without exceeding their authority. There are certain vital principles in our free republican governments, which will determine and overrule an apparent and flagrant abuse of legislative power; as to authorize manifest injustice by positive law; or to take away that security for personal liberty, or private property, for the protection whereof the government was established. An act of the legislature (for I cannot call it a law), contrary to the great first principles of the social compact, cannot be considered a rightful exercise of legislative authority. The obligation of a law, in governments established on express compact, and on republican principles, must be determined by the nature of the power on which it is founded"*
-Calder V Bulll

*"Yet the statutory and constitutional law, that is manufactured in this ridiculous and fraudulent manner, is claimed to be the*

*will of "the supreme power of the state;" and even though it purports to authorize the invasion, or even the destruction, of the natural rights of large bodies of the people,—men, women, and children,—it is, nevertheless, held to have been established by the consent of the whole people, and to be of higher authority than the principles of justice and natural law. And our judges, with a sanctimony as disgusting as it is hypocritical, continually offer these statutes and constitutions as their warrant for such violations of men's rights, as, if perpetrated by them in their private capacities, would bring upon them the doom which they themselves pronounce upon felons." -Lysander Spooner*

*"Liberty is not an Idea belonging to Volition or preferring; but to the Person having the Power of doing, or forbearing to do, according as the Mind shall chuse or direct." -John Locke(E2-5 II.xxi.10: 2a38)*

*"Liberty...is the power a Man has to do or forbear doing any particular Action, according as its doing or forbearance has the actual preference in the Mind, which is the same thing as to say, according as he himself wills it." -John Locke(E1-5 II.xxi.15: 241)*

*"The limits of tyrants are prescribed by the endurance of those whom they oppress."*
*- Frederick Douglas*

*"I didn't know I was a slave until I found out I couldn't do the things I wanted."*
*-Frederick Douglas*

*"The man who asks of freedom anything other than itself is born to be a slave."*
*Alexis de Tocqueville*

*"It's not an endlessly expanding list of rights - the "right" to education, the "right" to health care, the "right" to food and housing. That's not freedom, that's dependency. Those aren't*

*rights, those are the rations of slavery - hay and a barn for human cattle."*
-Alexis de Tocqueville

*"Make yourself sheep and the wolves will eat you."*
-Ben Franklin

*"The revolution occurs when the victims cease to cooperate."*
-Karl Hess

*"The Declaration of Independence is so lucid were afraid of it today. It scares the hell out of every modern bureaucrat, because it tells them there comes a time when we must stop taking orders"*
-Karl Hess

*"All who love liberty are enemies of the state"*
-Karl Hess

*"The most revolutionary thing you can do is get to know your neighbors."*
-Karl Hess

*"They [anarchists] spring from a single seed, no matter the flowering of their ideas. The seed is liberty. And that is all it is. It is not a socialist seed. It is not a capitalist seed. It is not a mystical seed. It is not a determinist seed. It is simply a statement. We can be free. After that it's all choice and chance."*
-Karl Hess

*"Democracy is the most vile form of government... democracies have ever been spectacles of turbulence and contention... incompatible with personal security or the rights of property."*
-James Madison

*"Do not separate text from historical background. If you do, you will have perverted and subverted the Constitution, which*

*can only end in a distorted, bastardized form of illegitimate government."*
*-James Madison*

*"The urge to save humanity is almost always a false front for the urge to rule."*
*-HL Mencken*

*"The kind of man who wants the government to adopt and enforce his ideas is always the kind of man whose ideas are idiotic"*
*-HL Mencken*

*"Whenever 'A' attempts by law to impose his moral standards upon 'B', 'A' is most likely a scoundrel."*
*-HL Mencken*

*"Now all acts of legislature apparently contrary to natural right and justice, are, in our laws, and must be in the nature of things considered as void" -George Mason*

## Patrick Henry, St. John's Church, Richmond, Virginia March 23, 1775.

*I just like this speech he gave and think you should read it:

Mr, President, no man thinks more highly than I do of the patriotism, as well as abilities, of the very worthy gentlemen who have just addressed the House. But different men often see the same subject in different lights; and, therefore, I hope it will not be thought disrespectful to those gentlemen if, entertaining as I do, opinions of a character very opposite to theirs, I shall speak forth my sentiments freely, and without reserve. This is no time for ceremony. The question before the House is one of awful moment to this country. For my own part, I consider it as nothing less than a question of freedom or slavery; and in proportion to the magnitude of the subject ought to be the freedom of the debate. It is only in this way that we can hope to arrive at truth, and fulfill the great responsibility which we hold to God and our country. Should I keep back my opinions at such a time, through fear of giving offense, I should consider myself as guilty of treason towards my country, and of an act of disloyalty toward the majesty of heaven, which I revere above all earthly kings.

Mr. President, it is natural to man to indulge in the illusions of hope. We are apt to shut our eyes against a painful truth, and listen to the song of that siren till she transforms us into beasts. Is this the part of wise men, engaged in a great and arduous struggle for liberty? Are we disposed to be of the number of those who, having eyes, see not, and, having ears, hear not, the things which so nearly concern their temporal salvation? For my part, whatever anguish of spirit it may cost, I am willing to know the whole truth; to know the worst, and to provide for it.

I have but one lamp by which my feet are guided; and that is the lamp of experience. I know of no way of judging of the future but by the past. And judging by the past, I wish to know what there has been in the conduct of the British ministry for the last ten years, to justify those hopes with which gentlemen have been pleased to solace themselves, and the House? Is it that insidious smile with which our petition has been lately received? Trust it not, sir; it will prove a snare to your feet. Suffer not yourselves to be betrayed with a kiss. Ask yourselves how this gracious reception of our petition comports with these war-like preparations which cover our waters and darken our land. Are fleets and armies necessary to a work of love and reconciliation? Have we shown ourselves so unwilling to be reconciled, that force must be called in to win back our love? Let us not deceive ourselves, sir. These are the implements of war and subjugation; the last arguments to which kings' resort. I ask, gentlemen, sir, what means this martial array, if its purpose be not to force us to submission? Can gentlemen assign any other possible motive for it? Has Great Britain any enemy, in this quarter of the world, to call for all this accumulation of navies and armies? No, sir, she has none. They are meant for us; they can be meant for no other. They are sent over to bind and rivet upon us those chains which the British ministry have been so long forging. And what have we to oppose to them? Shall we try argument? Sir, we have been trying that for the last ten years. Have we anything new to offer upon the subject? Nothing. We have held the subject up in every light of which it is capable; but it has been all in vain. Shall we resort to entreaty and humble supplication? What terms shall we find which have not been already exhausted? Let us not, I beseech you, sir, deceive ourselves. Sir, we have done everything that could be done, to avert the storm which is now coming on. We have petitioned; we have remonstrated; we have supplicated; we have prostrated ourselves before the throne, and have implored its interposition to arrest the tyrannical hands of the ministry and Parliament. Our petitions have been slighted; our remonstrances have produced additional violence and insult; our supplications have been disregarded; and we have been spurned, with contempt, from the foot of the throne. In vain, after these things, may we indulge the fond hope of peace and reconciliation. There is no longer any room for hope. If we wish to be free² if we mean to preserve inviolate those inestimable privileges for which we have been so long contending²if we mean not basely to abandon the noble struggle in which we have been so long engaged, and which we have pledged ourselves never to abandon until the glorious object of our contest shall be obtained, we must fight! I repeat it, sir, we must fight! An appeal to arms and to the God of Hosts is all that is left us!

They tell us, sir, that we are weak; unable to cope with so formidable an adversary. But when shall we be stronger? Will it be the next week, or the next year? Will it be when we are totally disarmed, and when a British guard shall be stationed in every house? Shall we gather strength by irresolution and inaction? Shall we acquire the means of effectual resistance, by lying supinely on our backs, and hugging the delusive phantom of hope, until our enemies shall have bound us hand and foot? Sir, we are not weak if we make a proper use of those means which the God of nature hath placed in our power. Three millions of people, armed in the holy cause of liberty, and in such a country as that which we possess, are invincible by any force which our enemy can send against us. Besides, sir, we shall not fight our battles alone. There is a just God who presides over the destinies of nations; and who will raise up friends to fight our battles for us. The battle, sir, is not to the strong alone; it is to the vigilant, the active, the brave. Besides, sir, we have no election. If we were base enough to desire it, it is now too late to retire from the contest. There is no retreat but in submission and slavery! Our chains are forged! Their clanking may be heard on the plains of Boston! The war is inevitable²and let it come! I repeat it, sir, let it come.

It is in vain, sir, to extenuate the matter. Gentlemen may cry, Peace, Peace²but there is no peace. The war is actually begun! The next gale that sweeps from the north will bring to our ears the clash of resounding arms! Our brethren are already in the field! Why stand we here idle? What is it that gentlemen wish? What would they have? Is life so dear, or peace so sweet, as to be purchased at the price of chains and slavery? Forbid it, Almighty God! I know not what course others may take; but as for me, give me liberty or give me death!

Source: Wirt, William. Sketches of the Life and Character of Patrick Henry. (Philadelphia) 1836, as reproduced in The World's Great Speeches, Lewis Copeland and Lawrence W. Lamm, eds., (New York) 1973.

# A Declaration of Position on the People's Right to Bear Arms Unmolested by the State

At a time where it has become evident that the fundamental, inalienable right to self-defense, and self-preservation, accomplished by the bearing of arms regardless of design or function, is increasingly infringed upon, willfully disregarding the existence of this right endowed by the Laws of Nature and of Nature's God, it is the right of the people, their duty to object to these usurpations.

The American People have long suffered under the despotic ignorance, the trampling disrespect of the 2nd Amendment of the United States Bill of Rights by statist acts and unjust violations of the very marrow of a right that exists whether penned by men or not. The right of the people to keep and bear arms, is not endowed nor removable by any governing body.

Fully understanding the technological advancements capable, as witnessed in their time, having defeated the powerful, tyrannical British Empire, the acknowledgement of the perpetually existing right to take up and bear modern arms was penned as the 2nd Amendment within the Bill of Rights, by those who founded this Nation.

The People have patiently endured the long train of abuses and usurpations of this natural right. We now peacefully declare objection to the past, present and future infringements and usurpations of this natural law, this God given right by setting forth here an immovable position held by those signed.

We will not recognize nor concede to any ordinance, statute, act, bill, rule, or law further molesting and harassing those exercising the fundamental and inalienable right of firearms ownership. Furthermore, we shall grant no respect or honor any law discriminating against firearms by make, model, function, operation, mechanism or design nor acknowledge the legislative criminalization of those possessing firearms deemed illegal by government.

Being that the very natural, inalienable right to bear modern firearms exists outside of the dominion of government, and where it is not governments to bestow nor to remove, prohibit, disallow or suppress this natural liberty, we the People hereby state that we shall never allow the confiscation, nor willfully surrender or turn over firearms regardless of such demand put forth by any legislative body or government.

This is our position; any violent incursion or aggressive, force exercised by government bent on molesting the people, persecuting or tormenting citizens in possession of firearms will be regarded as an assault against the Laws of Nature and of Nature's God, as well as insult against the very fundamental Liberties of which this nation was founded.

-Denny Ducet

# Works Cited

[1]     G. Mason, "Liberty Tree," [Online]. Available: http://libertytree.ca/quotes/George.Mason.Quote.C321.

[2]     "Wikipedia," [Online]. Available: https://en.wikipedia.org/wiki/Natural_law.

[3]     T. Jefferson, "Founders Online," [Online]. Available: https://founders.archives.gov/documents/Jefferson/98-01-02-5212.

[4]     Aristotle, "The Daily Progress," [Online]. Available: https://www.jstor.org/stable/44797179?seq=1.

[5]     Cicero. [Online]. Available: https://www.libertarianism.org/columns/ciceros-natural-law-political-philosophy#:~:text=.

[6]     Cicero, "Praxeology," [Online]. Available: http://praxeology.net/cicero.htm#:~:text=.

[7]     J. Adams, "Fee," [Online]. Available: https://fee.org/articles/why-the-founders-favorite-philosopher-was-cicero/#:~:text=.

[8]     T. Aquinas, "Essentail Life Skills," [Online]. Available: https://www.essentiallifeskills.net/thomasaquinasquotes.html#:~:tex

t=.

[9]    T. Aquinas, "Columbia," [Online]. Available: http://www.columbia.edu/acis/ets/CCREAD/etscc/aquin.html#:~:text=.

[10]    T. Aquinas, "New Advent," [Online]. Available: http://www.newadvent.org/summa/2091.htm.

[11]    A. Sidney, "Fee," [Online]. Available: https://fee.org/articles/algernon-sidney-forgotten-founding-father/.

[12]    A. Sidney, "Eighteenth Century Collections online," [Online]. Available: https://quod.lib.umich.edu/e/ecco/004874429.0001.000/1:6.1.2?rgn=div3;view=fulltext.

[13]    A. Sideny, "Online Library of Liberty," [Online]. Available: https://oll.libertyfund.org/quotes/395.

[14]    T. Jefferson, "Founders Early Access," [Online]. Available: https://rotunda.upress.virginia.edu/founders/default.xqy?keys=FOEA-print-04-02-02-5007.

[15]    A. Sidney, "Readers Digest," [Online]. Available: https://www.rd.com/culture/meaning-behind-every-state-motto/page/3/.

[16]    J. Locke, "Republican Government," [Online]. Available: http://press-pubs.uchicago.edu/founders/print_documents/v1ch4s1.html.

[17]    J. Locke, "Online Library of Liberty," [Online]. Available: https://oll.libertyfund.org/quotes/317.

[18]    J. Locke, "Ohio University," [Online]. Available: https://www.ohio.edu/ethics/tag/right-to-lifeliberty/index.html#:~:text=.

[19]    J. Locke, "Property," [Online]. Available: http://press-pubs.uchicago.edu/founders/documents/v1ch16s3.html.

[20]    J. Locke, "Libertarianism," [Online]. Available: https://www.libertarianism.org/publications/essays/property-government.

[21]    R. Paul, "Mises Institute," [Online]. Available: https://mises.org/library/liberty-defined-2.

[22]    T. Paine, "US History," [Online]. Available: https://www.ushistory.org/paine/rights/c1-013.htm.

[23]    A. O. Aldridge, "Thomas Paine's American Idealogy," in *University of Delaware Press*, 1984, p. 127.

[24]    Founders, "Live Science," [Online]. Available: https://www.livescience.com/4995-declaration-independence-changed-world.html.

[25]    T. Jefferson, "Claremont Review," [Online]. Available: https://claremontreviewofbooks.com/digital/jefferson-locke-and-the-

declaration-of-independence/.

[26]     J. Locke, "An Essay Concerning Human Understanding".

[27]     T. Jefferson, "Monticello," [Online]. Available:
         http://tjrs.monticello.org/letter/1380.

[28]     J. Locke, "Right of Revolution," [Online]. Available: http://press-
         pubs.uchicago.edu/founders/documents/v1ch3s2.html.

[29]     L. Spooner, "Mises institute," [Online]. Available:
         https://cdn.mises.org/Left%20and%20Right_3_1_7.pdf?token=sIltQ
         y8R.

[30]     T. Paine, "The Writings of Thomas Paine," p. 125.

[31]     R. Raico, "Mises Institute," [Online]. Available:
         https://mises.org/library/what-classical-liberalism.

[32]     M. Malice, "Twitter," [Online]. Available:
         https://twitter.com/michaelmalice/status/876218352804524036?lang
         =en.

[33]     T. Sowell, "Youtube," [Online]. Available:
         https://www.youtube.com/watch?v=3_EtIWmja-4.

[34]     B. Franklin, "Online Library of Liberty," [Online]. Available:
         https://oll.libertyfund.org/quotes/484.

[35]     T. Jefferson, "Monticello," [Online]. Available:
         https://www.monticello.org/site/research-and-
         collections/tje/famous-quotations.

[36]     J. Tucker, "A Treatise Concerning Civil Government," 1781, p. 101.

[37]     T. Hodgskin, "Libertarianism," [Online]. Available:
         https://www.libertarianism.org/publications/essays/excursions/thom
         as-hodgskin-versus-jeremy-bentham.

[38]     G. Smith, "The System of Liberty," Cambridge University Press,
         2013, p. 162.

[39]     "The Founders Constitution," [Online]. Available: http://press-
         pubs.uchicago.edu/founders/documents/amendIIs7.html.

[40]     T. Hobbes, "Leviathan," Hackett Publishing, 1994, p. 198.

[41]     M. N. Rothbard, "The Ethics of Liberty," NYU Press, 2015, p. 77.

[42]     S. P. Halbrook, "That Every an be Armed," unm press, 2013, pp. 9-
         10.

[43]     S. P. Halbrook, "That Every Man be Armed," unm press, 2013, p.
         24.

[44]     "Sortition," [Online]. Available:
         http://sortition.com/Second%20Amendment/Cicero/cicero.html.

[45]     T. Hobbes, "Leviathan," university press, 1904, p. 156.

[46]     L. Adams, "The Second Amendment Primer," Skyhorse Publishing,
         2013, p. 21.

[47]     D. Kopel, "Cato.org," [Online]. Available:
         https://www.cato.org/publications/commentary/algernon-sidney-
         father-declaration-independence.

[48]    S. Adams, "hanover.edu," [Online]. Available:
        https://history.hanover.edu/texts/adamss.html.

[49]    C. Beccaria, "Liberty Tree," [Online]. Available:
        http://libertytree.ca/quotes/Cesare.Beccaria.Quote.E215.

[50]    W. Grassi, "Austrian Economics," 2010, p. 160.

[51]    G. H. Smith, "The System of Liberty," Cambridge University Pres,
        2013, p. 164.

[52]    V. Pareto, "Cours D'Economie Politique," 1896, p. 397.

[53]    F. Bastiat, "Mises.org," [Online]. Available:
        https://mises.org/profile/claude-fr%C3%A9d%C3%A9ric-bastiat.

[54]    L. Hunter, "Forbes," [Online]. Available:
        https://www.forbes.com/sites/lawrencehunter/2012/07/29/both-
        james-madison-and-the-anti-federalists-were-right-about-standing-
        armies/#4d84979e75a0.

[55]    M. Maharrey, "Tenth Amendment Center," [Online]. Available:
        https://tenthamendmentcenter.com/2018/07/14/dont-blame-the-
        constitution-for-your-loss-of-liberty/.

[56]    T. Arms, "youtube," [Online]. Available:
        https://youtu.be/8enTHRDq9r8.

[57]    A. Hamilton, "Yale Law," [Online]. Available:
        https://avalon.law.yale.edu/18th_century/fed84.asp.

[58]    M. Maharrey, "Constitution Owners Manual," 2020, pp. 169-170.

[59]    "Constitution Center," [Online]. Available:
        https://constitutioncenter.org/interactive-
        constitution/amendment/amendment-ix.

[60]    T. Jefferson, "Founder Online," [Online]. Available:
        https://founders.archives.gov/documents/Jefferson/98-01-02-3562.

[61]    J. Madison, "Yale Law," [Online]. Available:
        https://avalon.law.yale.edu/18th_century/fed39.asp.

[62]    "National Archives," [Online]. Available:
        https://www.archives.gov/founding-docs/declaration-transcript.

[63]    "Library of Congress," [Online]. Available:
        https://www.loc.gov/item/92838253/.

[64]    J. Marshall, "Legal Informtion Institute," [Online]. Available:
        https://www.law.cornell.edu/supremecourt/text/32/243.

[65]    T. Jefferson, "Founders Online," [Online]. Available:
        https://founders.archives.gov/documents/Jefferson/98-01-02-4313.

[66]    T. J. DiLorenzo, "Constitution Society," [Online]. Available:
        https://www.constitution.org/14ll/truth_14th.htm.

[67]    S. F. Miller, "Legal Information Institute," [Online]. Available:
        https://www.law.cornell.edu/supremecourt/text/83/36.

[68]    J. Waite, "Justia," [Online]. Available:
        https://supreme.justia.com/cases/federal/us/92/542/.

[69]    "Justia US Supreme Court," [Online]. Available:

https://supreme.justia.com/cases/federal/us/259/530/.

[70]    Frankfurter, "Constitution Conflicts," [Online]. Available: http://law2.umkc.edu/faculty/projects/ftrials/conlaw/adamson.html.

[71]    Harlan. [Online]. Available: http://law2.umkc.edu/faculty/projects/ftrials/conlaw/duncan.html.

[72]    K. R. Gutzman, "Tenth Amendment Center," [Online]. Available: https://tenthamendmentcenter.com/2009/06/15/the-2nd-amendment-and-the-states/.

[73]    L. H. R. Jr., "Mises.org," [Online]. Available: https://mises.org/library/what-we-mean-decentralization.

[74]    A. d. Tocqueville, "Democracy in America," Regnery Publishing, p. 306.

[75]    "Constitution Annotated," [Online]. Available: https://constitution.congress.gov/browse/article-6/clause-2/.

[76]    M. Maharrey, "Constitution Owners Manual," 2020, p. 33.

[77]    J. Madison, "Yale Law," [Online]. Available: https://avalon.law.yale.edu/18th_century/fed45.asp.

[78]    A. Hamilton, "Yale Law," [Online]. Available: https://avalon.law.yale.edu/18th_century/fed33.asp.

[79]    J. Madison, "Yale Law," [Online]. Available: https://avalon.law.yale.edu/18th_century/virres.asp.

[80]    J. Story, "University of Chicago," [Online]. Available: http://press-pubs.uchicago.edu/founders/documents/amendIIs10.html.

[81]    A. Scalia, "Mises.org," [Online]. Available: https://mises.org/library/matter-interpretation-federal-courts-and-law-antonin-scalia.

[82]    "Constitution Center," [Online]. Available: https://constitutioncenter.org/interactive-constitution/amendment/amendment-ii.

[83]    J. N. Schulman, "Constitution Society," [Online]. Available: https://www.constitution.org/2ll/schol/2amd_grammar.htm.

[84]    "Legal Information Institute," [Online]. Available: https://www.law.cornell.edu/supct/html/07-290.ZO.html.

[85]    S. Sherman, "Tenth Amendment Center," [Online]. Available: https://tenthamendmentcenter.com/2018/08/22/how-heller-botched-the-second-amendment/.

[86]    J. Madison, "Founders Online," [Online]. Available: https://founders.archives.gov/documents/Madison/04-03-02-0333.

[87]    K. Hess, "Guns Magazine," 1959. [Online]. Available: https://gunsmagazine.com/wp-content/uploads/2018/12/G0259.pdf.

[88]    C. Center, "Constitution Center," [Online]. Available: https://constitutioncenter.org/interactive-constitution/amendment/amendment-i.

[89]    C. Center, "Constitution Center," [Online]. Available:

https://constitutioncenter.org/interactive-constitution/amendment/amendment-iv.

[90]    D. Vandercoy, "Michael Maharrey," [Online]. Available: https://www.michaelmaharrey.com/constitution-101-the-2nd-amendment-militia-962/.

[91]    B. Adler, "Hippo Reads," [Online]. Available: https://hipporeads.com/plato-and-aristotle-on-the-american-state/.

[92]    M. T. Cicero, "Constitution Society," [Online]. Available: https://www.constitution.org/rom/de_officiis.htm.

[93]    K. H. II, "Constitution society," [Online]. Available: https://www.constitution.org/eng/assizarm.htm.

[94]    "Britannica," [Online]. Available: https://www.britannica.com/topic/fyrd.

[95]    U. States, "The Statutes at Large and Treaties of the United States of America," 1792, p. 271.

[96]    "The Right to Keep and Bear Arms," in *Report of the Subcommittee on the Constitution of the Committee on the Judiciary, United States Senate, Ninety-seventh Congress*, 1982, p. 1.

[97]    "The Right to Keep and Bear Arms," in *Report of the Subcommittee on the Constitution of the Committee on the Judiciary, United States Senate, Ninety-seventh Congress*, 1982, p. 46.

[98]    H. Cox, "The Archer's Register," 1892, p. 33.

[99]    P. E. Volokh, "UCLA.edu," [Online]. Available: https://www2.law.ucla.edu/volokh/beararms/comment.htm.

[100]    L. Adams, The Second Amendment Primer, Simon and Schuster, 2013.

[101]    "Seventeenth Century Isle of Wight County, Virginia:," Heritage Books, p. 86.

[102]    "The Right to Keep and Bear Arms," in *Report of the Subcommittee on the Constitution of the Committee on the Judiciary, United States Senate, Ninety-seventh Congress*, p. 53.

[103]    J. R. Reynolds J. D. Jack, "A People Armed and Free," AuthorHouse, 2003, p. 67.

[104]    M. Farmer, "University Chicago," [Online]. Available: http://press-pubs.uchicago.edu/founders/documents/a1_8_12s26.html.

[105]    G. Mason, "The debates in the several state conventions on the adoption of the Federal constitution, as recommended by the general convention at Philadelphia in 1787:," p. 355.

[106]    D. B. K. G. A. M. M. P. O. Nicholas J. Johnson, "Firearms Law and the Second Amendment," Wolters Kluwer Law & Business, 2017, p. 319.

[107]    N. H. Cogan, The Complete Bill of Rights, Oxford University Press, 2015.

[108]    J. Madison, "Yale Law School," [Online]. Available:

https://avalon.law.yale.edu/18th_century/debates_629.asp.

[109]   J. Madison, "Yale Law School," [Online]. Available:
https://avalon.law.yale.edu/18th_century/fed46.asp.

[110]   T. Coxe, "The James Madison Research Library and Information
Center," [Online]. Available:
http://www.madisonbrigade.com/t_coxe.htm.

[111]   T. Coxe, "Founders Online," [Online]. Available:
https://founders.archives.gov/documents/Madison/01-15-02-0423.

[112]   S. Adams, "Samuel Adams Heritage Society," [Online]. Available:
http://www.samuel-adams-heritage.com/documents/samuel-adams-
to-james-warren-1776.html.

[113]   N. Webster, "The James Madison Research Library and Information
Center," [Online]. Available:
http://www.madisonbrigade.com/n_webster.htm.

[114]   Brutus, "University of Chicago," [Online]. Available: http://press-
pubs.uchicago.edu/founders/documents/a1_8_12s23.html.

[115]   D. T. Hardy, "Guncite," [Online]. Available:
https://guncite.com/journals/hardhist.html.

[116]   J. Elliot, "he debates in the several state conventions on the adoption
of the Federal constitution, as recommended by the general
convention at Philadelphia in 1787," 1836, p. 363.

[117]   "Compiled Statues of the United States, 1913," West Publishing
Company, 1914, p. 3043.

[118]   R. H. Lee, "Teaching American History," [Online]. Available:
https://teachingamericanhistory.org/library/document/federal-
farmer-xviii/.

[119]   "The Right to Keep and Bear Arms," in *Report of the Subcommittee
on the Constitution of the Committee on the Judiciary, United States
Senate, Ninety-seventh Congress*, US government printing office,
1982, p. 56.

[120]   R. Kilburne, "Choice Presidents upon all Acts of Parliament,
relating to the Office and Duty of a Justice of Peace," Mary Tonson,
1694, p. 532.

[121]   U. S. C. S. C. o. t. J. S. o. t. Constitution, "The Right to Keep and
Bear Arms," U.S. Government Printing Office, 1982, p. VI.

[122]   G. Mason, "The James Madison Research Library and Information
Center," [Online]. Available:
http://www.madisonbrigade.com/g_mason.htm.

[123]   E. Gerry, "The James Madison Research Library and Information
Center," [Online]. Available:
http://www.madisonbrigade.com/e_gerry.htm.

[124]   P. Henry, "University of Chicago," [Online]. Available: http://press-
pubs.uchicago.edu/founders/documents/a1_8_12s27.html.

[125]   A. Hamilton, "Yale Law School," [Online]. Available:

https://avalon.law.yale.edu/18th_century/fed29.asp.

[126]   G. Washington, "Independent Institute," [Online]. Available:
        https://www.independent.org/news/article.asp?id=1495.

[127]   Cato, "Independent Institute," [Online]. Available:
        https://www.independent.org/news/article.asp?id=1495.

[128]   H. Security, "Rightwing Extremism:," [Online]. Available:
        https://fas.org/irp/eprint/rightwing.pdf.

[129]   "National Priorities Project," [Online]. Available:
        https://www.nationalpriorities.org/campaigns/us-military-spending-
        vs-world/.

[130]   "Rand Corporation," [Online]. Available:
        https://www.rand.org/pubs/research_briefs/RB3005.html.

[131]   "The New York Times," [Online]. Available:
        https://www.nytimes.com/interactive/2017/03/22/us/is-americas-
        military-big-
        enough.html?mtrref=www.google.com&assetType=REGIWALL&
        mtrref=undefined&gwh=559815E67F022819AFD39806574BB0BA
        &gwt=pay&assetType=REGIWALL.

[132]   "World Atlas," [Online]. Available:
        https://www.worldatlas.com/articles/29-largest-armies-in-the-
        world.html.

[133]   "Politico," [Online]. Available:
        https://www.politico.com/magazine/story/2015/06/us-military-
        bases-around-the-world-119321.

[134]   "Reuters," [Online]. Available: https://www.reuters.com/article/us-
        usa-pentagon-audit/pentagon-fails-its-first-ever-audit-official-says-
        idUSKCN1NK2MC.

[135]   A. Gregg, "Washington Post," [Online]. Available:
        https://www.washingtonpost.com/business/2018/11/21/first-full-
        pentagon-financial-audit-details-bureaucratic-noncompliance-no-
        fraud/.

[136]   T. Jefferson, "Monticello," [Online]. Available:
        https://www.monticello.org/site/research-and-collections/private-
        banks-spurious-quotation.

[137]   T. B. David M Kennedy, "The American Spirit," Cengage Learning,
        2009, p. 161.

[138]   A. d. Tocqueville, "Online Library of Liberty," [Online]. Available:
        https://oll.libertyfund.org/quotes/586.

[139]   T. Knighton, "Bearing Arms," [Online]. Available:
        https://bearingarms.com/tom-k/2019/08/04/anti-gunners-hate-hong-
        kong-residents-long-second-amendment/.

[140]   A. Hamilton, "Yale Law School," [Online]. Available:
        https://avalon.law.yale.edu/18th_century/fed28.asp.

[141]   M. Bernstein, "Oregon Live," [Online]. Available:
        https://www.oregonlive.com/oregon-

standoff/2018/08/state_police_officer_who_fatal.html.

[142]    "District of Nevada," [Online]. Available:
         https://www.justice.gov/usao-nv/pr/arizona-man-pleads-guilty-
         conspiracy-impede-or-injure-federal-officer-during-2014-armed.

[143]    "Free Schaeffer," [Online]. Available:
         https://freeschaeffer.com/story/.

[144]    J. Elliot, "The Debates in the Several State Conventions on the
         Adoption of the Federal Constitution, as Recommended by the
         General Convention at Philadelphia,," J.B. Lippincott Company,
         1891, p. 94.

[145]    C. Ingraham, "The Washington Post," [Online]. Available:
         https://www.washingtonpost.com/news/wonk/wp/2018/06/19/there-
         are-more-guns-than-people-in-the-united-states-according-to-a-new-
         study-of-global-firearm-ownership/.

[146]    "bjs.gov," [Online]. Available:
         https://www.bjs.gov/content/pub/pdf/fleo08.pdf.

[147]    "Pew Research Center," [Online]. Available:
         https://www.pewresearch.org/fact-tank/2017/01/11/police-report-q-
         and-a/.

[148]    S. Gutowski, "The Washington Free Beacon," [Online]. Available:
         https://freebeacon.com/issues/gun-group-3-percent-californians-
         assault-weapons-registered-latest-gun-law/.

[149]    J. J. Smith, "Hudson Valley One," [Online]. Available:
         https://hudsonvalleyone.com/2016/07/07/massive-noncompliance-
         with-safe-act/.

[150]    J. Atmonavage, "NJ.com," [Online]. Available:
         https://www.nj.com/news/2019/09/nj-gun-owners-are-storing-
         thousands-and-thousands-of-banned-gun-magazines-in-a-steel-
         vault.html.

[151]    L. Correia, "Monster Hunter Nation," [Online]. Available:
         http://monsterhunternation.com/2018/11/19/the-2nd-amendment-is-
         obsolete-says-congressman-who-wants-to-nuke-omaha/.

[152]    J. Risen, "The New York Times," [Online]. Available:
         https://www.nytimes.com/2013/09/29/us/nsa-examines-social-
         networks-of-us-citizens.html.

[153]    N. Michel, "Forbes," [Online]. Available:
         https://www.forbes.com/sites/norbertmichel/2018/11/05/newly-
         unsealed-documents-show-top-fdic-officials-running-operation-
         choke-point/#64f80df61191.

[154]    F. Buckley, "Wall Street Journal," [Online]. Available:
         https://www.wsj.com/articles/social-credit-may-come-to-america-
         11567033176.

[155]    J. Snead, "The Heritage Foundation," [Online]. Available:
         https://www.heritage.org/research/reports/2014/03/civil-asset-
         forfeiture-7-things-you-should-know.

[156]    T. Brewster, "Forbes," [Online]. Available: https://www.forbes.com/sites/thomasbrewster/2019/09/06/exclusive -feds-demand-apple-and-google-hand-over-names-of-10000-users- of-a-gun-scope-app/#600ac1842423.

[157]    R. Manning, "The Hill," [Online]. Available: https://thehill.com/blogs/pundits-blog/uncategorized/212468- extremism-in-the-defense-of-liberty-is-still-no-vice.

[158]    J. Arceneaux, "USA Today," [Online]. Available: https://www.usatoday.com/story/news/nation- now/2016/02/06/deacons-of-defense-robert-hicks/78955042/.

[159]    "History.com," [Online]. Available: https://www.history.com/topics/civil-rights-movement/black- panthers.

[160]    "History.com," [Online]. Available: https://www.history.com/news/black-panthers-gun-control-nra- support-mulford-act.

[161]    K. Schilchter, "Townhall," [Online]. Available: https://townhall.com/columnists/kurtschlichter/2019/05/02/be-a- rooftop-korean-n2545651.

[162]    P. Hsieh, "Forbes," [Online]. Available: https://www.forbes.com/sites/paulhsieh/2018/04/30/that-time-the- cdc-asked-about-defensive-gun-uses/#3cf30f77299a.

[163]    J. Madison, "Yale Law School," [Online]. Available: https://avalon.law.yale.edu/18th_century/fed45.asp.

[164]    "Constitution Annotated," [Online]. Available: https://constitution.congress.gov/browse/article-1/section-8/clause- 3/.

[165]    C. Thomas, "Cornell Law School," [Online]. Available: https://www.law.cornell.edu/supct/html/93-1260.ZC1.html.

[166]    C. Thomas, "Cornell Law School," [Online]. Available: https://www.law.cornell.edu/supct/html/03-1454.ZD1.html.

[167]    D. F. Lucido, "Angel Justice," [Online]. Available: http://angeljustice.org/angel/Who_is_Angel_Raich_files/Declaration %20of%20Frank%20Henry%20Lucido,%20M.D.%20October%203 0,%202002.pdf.

[168]    S. D. O'Conner, "Cornell Law," [Online]. Available: https://www.law.cornell.edu/supct/html/03-1454.ZD.html.

[169]    "Casetext," [Online]. Available: https://casetext.com/case/us-v- stewart-168.

[170]    W. L. C. Cox, "NRA," [Online]. Available: https://home.nra.org/joint-statement.

[171]    T. Dickinson, "Rolling Stones," [Online]. Available: https://www.rollingstone.com/politics/politics- features/mindboggling-spending-at-the-national-rifle-association- 836980/.

[172]    "The Right To Keep and Bear Arms," US Government Printing Office, 1982, p. 20.

[173]    H. Weinstein, "Los Angeles Times," [Online]. Available: https://www.latimes.com/archives/la-xpm-2000-jun-15-mn-41294-story.html.

[174]    "Bureau of Alcohol, Tobacco, Firearms and Explosives (BATFE)," U.S. Government Printing Office, 2006, p. 8.

[175]    D. A. Graham, "The Atlantic," [Online]. Available: https://www.theatlantic.com/politics/archive/2012/06/eric-holder-contempt-of-congress-and-fast-and-furious-what-you-need-to-know/258783/.

[176]    K. Pavlich, "Fast and Furious: Barack Obama's Bloodiest Scandal and Its Shameless Cover-Up," Regnery Publishing, 2012.

[177]    T. Balaker, "Reason," [Online]. Available: https://reason.com/podcast/aft-fights-cigarette-smuggling-by-smuggl/.

[178]    N. Bertrand, "Business Insider," [Online]. Available: https://www.businessinsider.com/this-american-life-story-on-the-atf-2014-12.

[179]    C. Friedersdorf, "The Atlantic," [Online]. Available: https://www.theatlantic.com/politics/archive/2013/12/feds-paid-a-teen-to-get-a-neck-tattoo-of-a-giant-squid-smoking-a-joint/282279/.

[180]    C. Marcos, "The Hill," [Online]. Available: https://thehill.com/blogs/floor-action/house/234811-republican-bill-would-abolish-atf.

[181]    S. Schwinn, "SCOTUS blog," [Online]. Available: https://www.scotusblog.com/2017/08/symposium-time-abandon-anti-commandeering-dont-count-supreme-court/.

[182]    S. Alito, "Constitution Daily," [Online]. Available: https://constitutioncenter.org/blog/on-this-day-the-supreme-court-reinforces-the-10th-amendment.

[183]    M. Maharrey, "Tenth Amendment Center," [Online]. Available: https://blog.tenthamendmentcenter.com/2013/10/state-governors-admit-feds-need-state-help-with-most-federal-programs/.

[184]    M. Maharrey, "Tenth Amendment Center," [Online]. Available: https://tenthamendmentcenter.com/2013/12/28/states-dont-have-to-comply-the-anti-comandeering-doctrine/.

[185]    S. Court, "Cornell Law," [Online]. Available: https://www.law.cornell.edu/supct/html/91-543.ZS.html.

[186]    S. D. O'Conner, "Cornell Law," [Online]. Available: https://www.law.cornell.edu/supremecourt/text/505/144.

[187]    A. Scalia, "Cornell Law," [Online]. Available: https://www.law.cornell.edu/supct/html/95-1478.ZO.html.

[188]    J. Roberts, "Cornell Law," [Online]. Available: https://www.law.cornell.edu/supremecourt/text/11-393.

[189]    J. R. L. jr, "Crime Prevention Research Center," [Online].
          Available: https://crimeresearch.org/.

[190]    S. C. N. DeDino, "Fordham Law Review," 2004. [Online].
          Available:
          https://ir.lawnet.fordham.edu/cgi/viewcontent.cgi?article=4021&con
          text=flr.

[191]    p. 424, "Hathi Trust," [Online]. Available:
          https://babel.hathitrust.org/cgi/pt?id=mdp.35112203944048&view=
          1up&seq=432.

[192]    C. U. Press, "Cambridge Academic Content Dictionary Reference
          Book," Cambridge University Press, p. 790.

[193]    A. Hamilton, "Yale Law School," [Online]. Available:
          https://avalon.law.yale.edu/18th_century/fed29.asp.

[194]    "The Statutes at Large of Pennsylvania from 1682 to 1801," State
          Printer of Pennsylvania, 1906, p. 209.

[195]    "Private and Special Statutes of the Commonwealth of
          Massachusetts," Wright & Potter Print, 1805, p. 43.

[196]    "The Charter of the City of Boston, and Ordinances Made and
          Established by the Mayor, Aldermen, and Common Council, with
          Such Acts of the Legislature of Massachusetts, as Relate to the
          Government of Said City," True and Greene, 1827, p. 137.

[197]    "The Statutes of the State of Mississippi of a Public and General
          Nature, with the Constitutions of the United States and of this
          State:," E. Johns & Company, 1840, p. 676.

[198]    "PBS," [Online]. Available:
          https://www.pbs.org/opb/historydetectives/feature/politics-and-
          pistols-dueling-in-america/.

[199]    "Duke Law," [Online]. Available:
          https://web.law.duke.edu/gunlaws/1776/pennsylvania/468024/.

[200]    "Duke Law," [Online]. Available:
          https://web.law.duke.edu/gunlaws/1779/pennsylvania/468026/.

[201]    "Duke Law," [Online]. Available:
          https://web.law.duke.edu/gunlaws/1821/tennessee/468103/.

[202]    "Reports of Cases in Law and Equity, Argued and Determined in the
          Supreme Court of the State of Georgia," 1847, p. 251.

[203]    "Constitution Society," [Online]. Available:
          https://www.constitution.org/2ll/court/sta/bliss_v_ky.htm.

[204]    T. Jefferson, "Monticello," [Online]. Available:
          https://www.monticello.org/site/research-and-collections/firearms.

[205]    J. Ostrowski, "Mises.org," [Online]. Available:
          https://mises.org/library/dilorenzo-and-his-critics-lincoln-myth.

[206]    "Duke Law," [Online]. Available:
          https://web.law.duke.edu/gunlaws/?search=&subject%5B%5D=398
          92&jurisdiction%5B%5D=39888&jurisdiction%5B%5D=39895&ju

risdiction%5B%5D=39897&jurisdiction%5B%5D=39900&jurisdict
ion%5B%5D=39901&jurisdiction%5B%5D=39904&jurisdiction%5
B%5D=39906&jurisdiction%5B%5D.

[207]   "Duke Law," [Online]. Available:
        https://web.law.duke.edu/gunlaws/?search=&subject%5B%5D=399
        09&jurisdiction%5B%5D=39888&jurisdiction%5B%5D=39895&ju
        risdiction%5B%5D=39897&jurisdiction%5B%5D=39900&jurisdict
        ion%5B%5D=39901&jurisdiction%5B%5D=39904&jurisdiction%5
        B%5D=39906&jurisdiction%5B%5D.

[208]   C. E. Cramer, "Clayton Cramer," 1993. [Online]. Available:
        http://www.claytoncramer.com/scholarly/racistroots.htm.

[209]   N.-s. Congress, The Right to Keep and Bear Arms, U.S.
        Governemnt Printing Office, 1982.

[210]   J. Ross, "Unintended Consequences," Accurate Press, 1996, p. 356.

[211]   "Harrison Narcotics act," [Online]. Available:
        http://www.naabt.org/documents/Harrison_Narcotics_Tax_Act_191
        4.pdf.

[212]   S.-t. Congress, "National Firearms Act:," in *Second Session, on H.
        R. 9066*, U.S. Government Printing Office, p. 1934.

[213]   D. S. D'Amato, "The Future of Freedom Foundation," [Online].
        Available: https://www.fff.org/explore-freedom/article/gold-clause-
        cases/.

[214]   R. Higgs, "Mises Institute," [Online]. Available:
        https://mises.org/library/how-fdr-made-depression-worse.

[215]   T. J. DiLorenzo, "Mises Institute," [Online]. Available:
        https://mises.org/library/new-new-deal.

[216]   J. G. Hornberger, "The Future of Freedom Foundation," [Online].
        Available: https://www.fff.org/2009/01/15/fdrs-infamous-
        courtpacking-scheme/.

[217]   "Cornell Law School," [Online]. Available:
        https://www.law.cornell.edu/supremecourt/text/307/174.

[218]   "Military Factory," [Online]. Available:
        https://www.militaryfactory.com/smallarms/detail.asp?smallarms_id
        =488.

[219]   "A&A Gaines Antiques," [Online]. Available:
        http://aagaines.com/inventory/blunderbuss.html.

[220]   C. W. B. Ann Mc Reynolds Bush, "Executive Disorder," Cornelia
        Wendell Bush, p. 241.

[221]   N.-s. Congress, "The Right to Kccp and Bear Arms," U.S.
        Government Printing Office, 1982, p. 17.

[222]   "The National Firearms Act," [Online]. Available:
        https://www.atf.gov/file/58141/download.

[223]   J. M. Edgar Walters, "The Texas Tribune," 2018. [Online].
        Available: https://www.texastribune.org/2018/12/07/texas-civil-

asset-forfeiture-legislature/.

[224]   P. A. Clark, "Western Criminology Review," 2007. [Online].
        Available:
        https://www.westerncriminology.org/documents/WCR/v08n2/clark.
        pdf.

[225]   "Hearings Before the Subcommittee to Investigate Juvenile
        Delinquency of the Committee on the Judiciary, United States
        Senate," in *Handgun Crime Control*, 1967, p. 137.

[226]   "Congressional Record," 1967, p. 17068.

[227]   "The New York Times," 197. [Online]. Available:
        https://www.nytimes.com/1971/05/25/archives/exsenator-dodd-is-
        dead-at-64-censured-in-1967-by-colleagues.html.

[228]   W. Vizzard, "Jews for the Preservation of Firearms Ownership,"
        [Online]. Available: http://jpfo.org/articles-assd02/gca68-nra4.htm.

[229]   N. Congress, "Federal Firearms Legislation," 1968, p. 479.

[230]   "Hathi Trust," [Online]. Available:
        https://babel.hathitrust.org/cgi/pt?id=mdp.39015005397099&view=
        1up&seq=3.

[231]   M. Boldin, "Tenth Amendment Center," [Online]. Available:
        https://tenthamendmentcenter.com/2016/05/01/the-founders-word-
        void/.

[232]   R. Farago, "The Truth About Guns," [Online]. Available:
        https://www.thetruthaboutguns.com/1986-machine-gun-ban-was-a-
        parliamentary-scam/amp/.

[233]   D. Kopel, "Reason," [Online]. Available:
        https://reason.com/2018/08/07/the-1986-plastic-gun-panic/.

[234]   C. Cox, "NRA-ILA," [Online]. Available:
        https://www.nraila.org/articles/20180731/nra-statement-on-3-d-
        printers-and-plastic-firearms.

[235]   G. Galles, "Mises Institute," [Online]. Available:
        https://mises.org/wire/dickinson-we-cannot-be-happy-without-
        being-free.

[236]   "The New York Times," 1989. [Online]. Available:
        https://www.nytimes.com/1989/03/15/us/us-bans-imports-of-
        assault-rifles-in-shift-by-bush.html.

[237]   M. Cox, "Business Insider," [Online]. Available:
        https://www.businessinsider.com/air-force-receives-gau-5a-self-for-
        pilots-who-eject-2020-2.

[238]   J. Chasmar, "The Washington Times," [Online]. Available:
        https://www.washingtontimes.com/news/2013/jan/27/homeland-
        security-seeking-7000-assault-weapons-per/.

[239]   J. Haughey, "Outdoor Life," 2017. [Online]. Available:
        https://www.outdoorlife.com/gun-news-week-atf-says-assault-rifle-
        is-bogus-term/.

[240] "Congress.gov," [Online]. Available: https://www.congress.gov/103/bills/hr4296/BILLS-103hr4296pcs.pdf.

[241] C. S. Koper, "NCJRS," 2004. [Online]. Available: https://www.ncjrs.gov/pdffiles1/nij/grants/204431.pdf.

[242] "Investors Business Daily," [Online]. Available: https://www.investors.com/politics/editorials/we-banned-assault-weapons-before-and-it-didnt-work/.

[243] "Rand Corporation," 2018. [Online]. Available: https://www.rand.org/research/gun-policy/analysis/ban-assault-weapons.html.

[244] R. Saaverda, "Daily Wire," 2020. [Online]. Available: https://www.dailywire.com/news/bloomberg-school-of-public-health-no-evidence-assault-weapon-bans-reduce-mass-shootings.

[245] J. R. L. jr, "Wall Street Journal," [Online]. Available: https://www.wsj.com/articles/SB10001424127887323468604578245803845796068.

[246] "RAINN," [Online]. Available: https://www.rainn.org/statistics/criminal-justice-system.

[247] R. Reagan, "The New York Times," [Online]. Available: https://www.nytimes.com/1991/03/29/opinion/why-i-m-for-the-brady-bill.html.

[248] D. B. Kopel, "Cato Institute," [Online]. Available: https://www.cato.org/publications/commentary/why-wait-buy-gun.

[249] M. Marshall, "University of Virginia," [Online]. Available: https://www.law.virginia.edu/news/2003_spr/cook.htm.

[250] "Politifact," [Online]. Available: https://www.politifact.com/factchecks/2015/apr/27/van-wanggaard/no-evidence-waiting-period-handgun-purchases-reduc/.

[251] "National Center for Biotechnology Information," [Online]. Available: https://www.ncbi.nlm.nih.gov/pmc/articles/PMC1730662/pdf/v006p00245.pdf.

[252] "CDC," [Online]. Available: https://www.cdc.gov/mmwr/PDF/rr/rr5214.pdf.

[253] T. C. P. Matthew D Makarios, "Sage," [Online]. Available: http://jonathanstray.com/papers/Gun%20Violence%20Meta-analysis.pdf.

[254] "RAND," [Online]. Available: https://www.rand.org/research/gun-policy/analysis/waiting-periods.html.

[255] "Naitional Constitution Center," [Online]. Available: https://constitutioncenter.org/blog/on-this-day-the-supreme-court-reinforces-the-10th-amendment.

[256] A. P. Napolitano, Lies the Government Told You, Thomas Nelson Inc; 5th edition, 2010.

[257] "Gun Owners of America," 2016. [Online]. Available: https://gunowners.org/fs08112016/.

[258] "National Criminal Justice Reference Service," [Online]. Available: https://www.ncjrs.gov/pdffiles1/bjs/grants/239272.pdf.

[259] C. Neiweem, "The Hill," [Online]. Available: https://thehill.com/blogs/pundits-blog/defense/295484-va-is-restricting-veterans-gun-rights-without-due-process.

[260] D. Sherfinski, "The Washington Times," 2017. [Online]. Available: https://www.washingtontimes.com/news/2017/feb/15/senate-votes-undo-obama-administration-gun-rule/.

[261] K. Johnson, "USA Today," [Online]. Available: https://www.usatoday.com/story/news/nation/2016/01/19/fbi-guns-background-checks/78752774/.

[262] J. Schladebeck, "Daily News," [Online]. Available: https://www.nydailynews.com/news/crime/ny-atf-security-guard-14-years-stealing-agency-guns-20190828-i6kf6s5kojg2pbz4u4bxkbeu2a-story.html.

[263] "Monticello," [Online]. Available: https://www.monticello.org/site/research-and-collections/laws-forbid-carrying-armsspurious-quotation.

[264] "BBC News," [Online]. Available: https://www.bbc.com/news/uk-england-london-43610936.

[265] T. Knighton, "Bearing Arms," [Online]. Available: https://bearingarms.com/tom-k/2018/08/16/shopify-ceo-deletes-pro-free-speech-comments-companies-impacted/.

[266] J. E. David, "CNBC," 2015. [Online]. Available: https://www.cnbc.com/2015/09/27/angela-merkel-caught-on-hot-mic-pressing-facebook-ceo-over-anti-immigrant-posts.html.

[267] "Community Financial Services Association of America," 2018. [Online]. Available: https://www.cfsaa.com/news/operation-chokepoint/unsealed-government-documents-prove-federal-coverup-in-operation-choke-point.

[268] N. J. M. Ph.D., "The Heritage Foundation," 2018. [Online]. Available: https://www.heritage.org/markets-and-finance/commentary/newly-unsealed-documents-show-top-fdic-officials-running-operation.

[269] "National Shooting Sports Foundation," 2015. [Online]. Available: https://www.nssf.org/fdic-reverses-course-on-operation-choke-point/.

[270] S. Jacobs, "The Libertarian Institute," 2019. [Online]. Available: https://libertarianinstitute.org/articles/state-gun-control-in-america-a-historic-guide-to-major-state-gun-control-laws-and-acts/.

[271] [Online]. Available: https://thefederalistpapers.org/posters/thomas-paine/thomas-paine-the-supposed-quietude-of-a-good-man-allures-the-ruffian.

[272]    B. Clinton, "govinfo," [Online]. Available:
         https://www.govinfo.gov/content/pkg/PPP-1998-book2/html/PPP-
         1998-book2-doc-pg2002-2.htm.

[273]    "The New York Times," [Online]. Available:
         https://www.nytimes.com/1998/11/08/us/clinton-calls-for-closing-
         big-loophole-in-gun-law.html.

[274]    A. J. C. &. J. D. Eisen, "Ammoland," [Online]. Available:
         https://www.ammoland.com/2018/05/black-market-guns-anti-gun-
         laws-create-them/#axzz6IQ5fSHVb.

[275]    P. Wegmann, "Washington Examiner," 2018. [Online]. Available:
         https://www.washingtonexaminer.com/think-twice-about-that-
         bipartisan-no-fly-no-buy-gun-control-bill.

[276]    C. A. Hina Shamsi, "ACLU," 2016. [Online]. Available:
         https://www.aclu.org/blog/national-security/discriminatory-
         profiling/use-error-prone-and-unfair-watchlists-not-way.

[277]    J. Napolitano, "FAS," [Online]. Available:
         https://fas.org/irp/eprint/rightwing.pdf.

[278]    L. M. B. P. J. Butcher, "The Heritage Foundation," 2019. [Online].
         Available: https://www.heritage.org/education/commentary/father-
         parkland-victim-what-could-have-stopped-the-tragedy.

[279]    M. C. Eden, "National Review," 2018. [Online]. Available:
         https://www.nationalreview.com/2018/02/parkland-shooting-
         broward-county-schools-policy-report-fewer-infractions-to-police/.

[280]    B. A. Smith, "Wall Street Journal," 2018. [Online]. Available:
         https://www.wsj.com/articles/the-unresolved-irs-scandal-
         1525905500.

[281]    K. Timpf, "National Review," [Online]. Available:
         https://www.nationalreview.com/2018/12/allowing-new-york-state-
         to-search-gun-seekers-social-media-accounts-terrible-idea/.

[282]    "Gun Owners of America," 2017. [Online]. Available:
         https://gunowners.org/a-massachusetts-police-officer-talks-about-
         how-an-unpaid-traffic-ticket-could-result-in-a-gun-ban/.

[283]    R. Cohen, "Forbes," 2012. [Online]. Available:
         https://www.forbes.com/sites/reuvencohen/2012/05/26/department-
         of-homeland-security-forced-to-release-list-of-keywords-used-to-
         monitor-social-networking-sites/#6cf83b47acd0.

[284]    C. Takei, "ACLU," 2018. [Online]. Available:
         https://www.aclu.org/blog/criminal-law-reform/reforming-
         police/president-trump-stop-and-frisk-both-unconstitutional-and.

[285]    D. Pennington, "Slate," 2017. [Online]. Available:
         https://slate.com/news-and-politics/2017/10/a-two-guns-per-person-
         limit-would-protect-americans-lives-and-liberty.html.

[286]    L. Hunter, "Forbes," 2012. [Online]. Available:
         https://www.forbes.com/sites/lawrencehunter/2012/01/16/the-
         paradox-of-rights-granted-us-by-government/#bbcd5a867670.

[287]    "Giffords Law Center," [Online]. Available:
         https://lawcenter.giffords.org/gun-laws/policy-areas/crime-
         guns/bulk-gun-purchases/.
[288]    Firearms101usa, "youtube," 2013. [Online]. Available:
         https://youtu.be/b2Upjn5DR0o.
[289]    O. France, "jurist," 2019. [Online]. Available:
         https://www.jurist.org/news/2019/04/federal-judge-strikes-down-
         california-ban-on-high-capacity-magazines/.
[290]    "Washington Free Beacon," [Online]. Available:
         https://freebeacon.com/national-security/federal-judge-rules-calif-
         magazine-confiscation-law-unconstitutional/.
[291]    M. Larosiere, "Cato Institute," 2018. [Online]. Available:
         https://www.cato.org/publications/legal-policy-bulletin/losing-
         count-empty-case-high-capacity-magazine-restrictions#full.
[292]    T. Jefferson, "Founders Online," [Online]. Available:
         https://founders.archives.gov/documents/Jefferson/01-02-02-0066.
[293]    R. H. Lee, "The James Madison Research Library," [Online].
         Available: http://www.madisonbrigade.com/rh_lee.htm.
[294]    "CDC," [Online]. Available: https://www.cdc.gov/alcohol/fact-
         sheets/underage-drinking.htm.
[295]    "Rand," [Online]. Available: https://www.rand.org/research/gun-
         policy/analysis/minimum-age.html.
[296]    L. Keane, "National Shooting Sports Foundation," [Online].
         Available: https://www.nssf.org/raising-age-requirement-rifles-
         wont-protect-kids-will-violate-constitutional-rights/.
[297]    J. R. L. Jr, "Crime Prevention Research Center," [Online].
         Available: https://crimeresearch.org/2018/03/push-ban-guns-21-
         years-age-share-mass-public-shootings-done-age-21/.
[298]    "UPI," [Online]. Available:
         https://www.upi.com/Entertainment_News/2008/12/24/Dave-Spade-
         helps-police-buy-guns/42491230152921/.
[299]    F. P. R. N. B. R. J. G. B. D. T. R. J. T. F. A. B. L. J. P. B. B. H. a.
         G. S. Arthur L. Kellermann, "The New England Journal of
         Medicine," [Online]. Available:
         https://www.nejm.org/doi/full/10.1056/NEJM199310073291506.
[300]    J. R. L. Jr, "Scientific American," [Online]. Available:
         https://www.scientificamerican.com/article/more-guns-mean-more-
         violent-crime-or-less-a-researcher-aims-at-scientific-american1/.
[301]    P. a. T. S. R. P. C. D. P. C. P. T. R. T. H. P. M. a. D. J. W. P.
         Charles C. Branas, "US National Library of Medicine National
         Institutes," [Online]. Available:
         https://www.ncbi.nlm.nih.gov/pmc/articles/PMC2759797/.
[302]    "Everytown," [Online]. Available:
         https://everytownresearch.org/assault-weapons-high-capacity-
         magazines/.

[303]  "US Consumer Product Safety Commission," [Online]. Available: https://www.cpsc.gov/content/the-tipping-point-highest-number-of-tv-and-furniture-tip-over-deaths-recorded-by-cpsc-in.

[304]  "Anchor It," [Online]. Available: https://www.anchorit.gov/news/anchor-for-safety-tv-and-furniture-tip-over-related-deaths-and-injuries-not-slowing-down/.

[305]  "Docastaway," [Online]. Available: http://paradise.docastaway.com/falling-coconut-deaths/.

[306]  SIMA, "Snow and Ice Management Association," [Online]. Available: https://www.sima.org/news2/2016/10/25/death-by-snow-ice.

[307]  K. T. Sonnenberg A1, "US National Library of Medicine National Institutes of Health," [Online]. Available: https://www.ncbi.nlm.nih.gov/pubmed/2910654.

[308]  C. Eger, "guns.com," [Online]. Available: https://www.guns.com/news/2018/09/17/nssf-ar-15-ak-numbers-top-16-million.

[309]  D. Rice, "USA Today," [Online]. Available: https://www.usatoday.com/story/weather/2018/01/02/lightning-deaths-all-time-record-low-2017/996949001/.

[310]  "FBI Uniform Crime Report," [Online]. Available: https://ucr.fbi.gov/crime-in-the-u.s/2018/crime-in-the-u.s.-2018/tables/expanded-homicide-data-table-8.xls.

[311]  D. Horn, "USA Today," [Online]. Available: https://www.usatoday.com/story/news/nation/2013/01/12/gun-buybacks-popular-but-ineffective/1829165/.

[312]  B. E. a. M. Hicken, "CNN Money," [Online]. Available: https://money.cnn.com/2015/10/21/news/police-selling-seized-guns/.

[313]  W. Pitt, "Forbes," [Online]. Available: https://www.forbes.com/quotes/10136/.

[314]  C. Riotta, "Independent," [Online]. Available: https://www.independent.co.uk/news/world/americas/gun-sales-us-background-checks-coronavirus-firearms-trump-record-march-a9442861.html.

[315]  J. Lott, "Crime Prevention Research Center," 2018. [Online]. Available: https://crimeresearch.org/2018/06/more-misleading-information-from-bloombergs-everytown-for-gun-safety-on-guns-analysis-of-recent-mass-shootings/.

[316]  "Wikipedia," [Online]. Available: https://en.wikipedia.org/wiki/Kalthoff_repeater.

[317]  "Wikipedia," [Online]. Available: https://en.wikipedia.org/wiki/Puckle_gun.

[318]  "Wikisource," [Online]. Available: https://en.wikisource.org/wiki/Correspondence_between_John_Belt

on_and_the_Continental_Congress.

[319] "Wikipedia," [Online]. Available:
https://en.wikipedia.org/wiki/Girandoni_air_rifle.

[320] R. McMaken, "Mises Institute," [Online]. Available:
https://mises.org/power-market/police-have-no-duty-protect-you-
federal-court-affirms-yet-
again?page=11&fbclid=IwAR1gDz0IeU4qRcb8DDDdKM6lRTmX
47BoFqp_q69Yx3jJjSj04DcvL-ZknDM.

[321] "CNN," March 2020. [Online]. Available:
https://www.cnn.com/2020/03/18/us/police-departments-
coronavirus-response-trnd/index.html.

[322] B. T. Party, "Boston's Gun Bible," Javelin, p. 396.

[323] J. R. L. Jr, "Trib live," [Online]. Available:
https://triblive.com/opinion/john-lott-jr-pa-gun-registry-waste-of-
money-resources/.

[324] D. Fisher, "Forbes," 2013. [Online]. Available:
https://www.forbes.com/sites/danielfisher/2013/01/22/canada-tried-
registering-long-guns-and-gave-up/#50d427465a1b.

[325] N. Leghorn, "Truth About Guns," [Online]. Available:
https://www.thetruthaboutguns.com/debunking-guns-treated-like-
cars-analogy/.

[326] J. Snyder, "Firearms and Liberty," [Online]. Available:
https://www.firearmsandliberty.com/snyder.aw.ban.html.

[327] M. N. Rothbard, "Mises Institute," [Online]. Available:
https://mises.org/wire/rothbard-gun-regulation-explained.

[328] L. Hunter, "Forbes," [Online]. Available:
https://www.forbes.com/sites/lawrencehunter/2012/12/28/gun-
control-tramples-on-the-certain-virtues-of-a-heavily-armed-
citizenry/#5c64c47a32fb.

[329] "Hati Trust," [Online]. Available:
https://babel.hathitrust.org/cgi/pt?id=mdp.39015005397099&view=
1up&seq=1.

[330] D. Codrea, "Ammoland," [Online]. Available:
https://www.ammoland.com/2019/05/government-foia-flouting-
responsible-for-one-bump-stock-conspiracy-
theory/#axzz6InT7Ybry.

[331] A. Shamaya, "Keep and Bear Arms," 2002. [Online]. Available:
http://www.keepandbeararms.com/information/XcIBViewItem.asp?
ID=3247.

[332] l. Jacobson, "Politifact," [Online]. Available:
https://www.politifact.com/factchecks/2019/aug/08/donald-
trump/donald-trump-says-hes-done-more-other-presidents-s/.

[333] D. Jackson, "Courthouse News," [Online]. Available:
https://www.courthousenews.com/trump-administration-steps-up-
prosecution-of-gun-crimes/.

[334]   H. Clark, "the Hill," [Online]. Available:
        https://thehill.com/opinion/healthcare/417228-another-decade-lost-
        to-the-global-war-on-drugs.

[335]   J. Borowski, "FreedomWorks," 2011. [Online]. Available:
        http://www.freedomworks.org/content/abolishing-department-
        education-right-thing-do.

[336]   S. Horton, "Amazon," [Online]. Available:
        https://www.amazon.com/Fools-Errand-Time-End-Afghanistan-
        ebook/dp/B07566KR46.

[337]   D. Sherfinski, "Washington Times," [Online]. Available:
        https://www.washingtontimes.com/news/2019/oct/6/bump-stock-
        ban-failure-omen-gun-buyback-plan/.

[338]   M. Kaste, "NPR," [Online]. Available:
        https://www.npr.org/2019/02/04/691287471/bump-stocks-will-
        soon-be-illegal-but-thats-not-slowing-sales.

[339]   P. Schweizer, "amazon," [Online]. Available:
        https://www.amazon.com/Clinton-Cash-Foreign-Governments-
        Businesses/dp/0062369296.

[340]   "The New York Times," [Online]. Available:
        https://www.nytimes.com/2000/03/18/us/gun-makers-see-betrayal-
        in-decision-by-smith-wesson.html.

[341]   [Online]. Available: https://www.washingtonpost.com/.

[342]   "Business Insider," [Online]. Available:
        https://www.businessinsider.com/smith-and-wesson-almost-went-
        out-of-business-trying-to-do-the-right-thing-2013-1.

[343]   W. A. Sodeman, "Britannica," [Online]. Available:
        https://www.britannica.com/topic/Communications-Decency-Act.

[344]   L. R. Gabe Romman, "ACLU," [Online]. Available:
        https://www.aclu.org/blog/national-security/privacy-and-
        surveillance/new-proposal-could-singlehandedly-cripple-free.

[345]   J. Waimberg, "National Constitution Center," [Online]. Available:
        https://constitutioncenter.org/blog/schenck-v-united-states-defining-
        the-limits-of-free-speech/.

[346]   W. Block, "Defending the Undefendable," Ludwig von Mises
        Institute, 2003, p. 71.

[347]   W. Block, "Mises Institute," 2009. [Online]. Available:
        https://mises.org/library/10-person-who-yells-fire-crowded-theatre.

[348]   K. Howell, "The Washington Times," [Online]. Available:
        https://www.washingtontimes.com/news/2015/jul/14/murder-rates-
        drop-as-concealed-carry-permits-soar-/.

[349]   "Crime Prevention Research Center," [Online]. Available:
        https://crimeresearch.org/2018/08/new-study-17-25-million-
        concealed-handgun-permits-biggest-increases-for-women-and-
        minorities/.

[350]   A. Fuentes, "Verso," 2018. [Online]. Available:

https://www.versobooks.com/blogs/3705-a-brief-history-of-school-violence-in-the-united-states-2011.

[351]    A. N. a. L. Petronio, "News@northeastern," 2018. [Online]. Available: https://news.northeastern.edu/2018/02/26/schools-are-still-one-of-the-safest-places-for-children-researcher-says/.

[352]    R. McMaken, "Mises Institute," 2018. [Online]. Available: https://mises.org/wire/there-are-fewer-school-shootings-now-during-1990s.

[353]    S. H. Society, "Southern Historical Society Papers," Virginia Historical Society, 1883, p. 426.

[354]    R. H. Lee, "The James Madison Research Library and Information Center," [Online]. Available: http://www.madisonbrigade.com/rh_lee.htm.

[355]    P. a. L. G. Mariel Alper, "Department of Justice," [Online]. Available: https://www.bjs.gov/content/pub/pdf/suficspi16.pdf.

[356]    "Firearms Policy Coalition," [Online]. Available: https://www.firearmspolicy.org/scotus-brief-nonviolent-felons-have-2a-rights.

[357]    C. Calton, "Mises Institute," [Online]. Available: https://mises.org/library/historical-controversies?page=7.

[358]    K. Jaeger, "Marijuana Moment," [Online]. Available: https://www.marijuanamoment.net/gop-congressman-wants-marijuana-consumers-to-be-able-to-legally-purchase-guns/ .

[359]    H. Timmons, "Quartz," [Online]. Available: https://qz.com/1214787/how-the-nras-money-forces-republicans-to-fight-gun-control/.

[360]    W. H. R. T. B. Philip Elliot, "Time," 2018. [Online]. Available: https://time.com/5181212/nra-republicans-gun-control/.

[361]    D. Zimmerman, "The Truth About Guns," 2019. [Online]. Available: https://www.thetruthaboutguns.com/editorial-its-time-to-de-fund-the-nra/.

[362]    "The Washington Post," [Online]. Available: https://www.washingtonpost.com/.

[363]    "The New York Times," [Online]. Available: https://www.nytimes.com/2018/11/16/us/politics/nra-gun-control-fund-raising.html.

[364]    J. R. L. Jr, "The War on Guns," Simon and Schuster, 2016.

[365]    J. Madison, "Yale Law," [Online]. Available: https://avalon.law.yale.edu/18th_century/fed46.asp.

[366]    N. Webster, "The James Madison Research Library and Information Center," [Online]. Available: http://www.madisonbrigade.com/n_webster.htm.

[367]    G. Soros, "Small Arms Survey," [Online]. Available: http://www.smallarmssurvey.org/.

[368] Brodigan, "Louder with Crowder," 2016. [Online]. Available: https://www.louderwithcrowder.com/vox-gun-rebuttal/.

[369] V. Mehtra, "Federalist," 2015. [Online]. Available: https://thefederalist.com/2015/06/25/the-australia-gun-control-fallacy/.

[370] I. Richardson, "Des Moines Register," 2019. [Online]. Available: https://www.desmoinesregister.com/story/news/elections/presidential/caucus/2019/04/12/election-2020-eric-swalwell-assault-weapon-ban-buyback-iowa-state-mental-health-democrat-candidate/3436741002/.

[371] A. Stockler, "Newsweek," 2019. [Online]. Available: https://www.newsweek.com/new-zealand-buyback-program-guns-1469405.

[372] J. Crump, "Ammoland," [Online]. Available: https://www.ammoland.com/2019/04/foia-request-confirms-zero-standard-capacity-magazines-turned-in-to-nj-state-police/#axzz6JFDFPMsV.

[373] B. Hall, "The Sydney Morning Herald," 2019. [Online]. Available: https://www.smh.com.au/national/more-guns-in-australia-now-than-before-the-port-arthur-massacre-report-20190327-p5188m.html.

[374] P. A. M. J. Simon Chapman, 2016. [Online]. Available: https://jamanetwork.com/journals/jama/fullarticle/2530362.

[375] R. McMaken, "Mises Institute," 2019. [Online]. Available: https://mises.org/wire/australias-gun-laws-and-homicide-correlation-isnt-causation.

[376] J. R. L. Jr, "National Post," 2018. [Online]. Available: https://nationalpost.com/opinion/opinion-the-evidence-simply-doesnt-support-calls-for-gun-bans-in-canada.

[377] J. R. L. Jr, "Real Clear Policy," 2017. [Online]. Available: https://www.realclearpolicy.com/articles/2017/05/03/murder_isnt_a_nationwide_problem_110234.html.

[378] "Guardian," 2017. [Online]. Available: https://www.theguardian.com/australia-news/2017/jun/18/australias-rate-falls-to-record-low-of-one-person-per-100000.

[379] "Disaster Center," [Online]. Available: http://www.disastercenter.com/crime/nhcrime.htm.

[380] "Library of Congress," [Online]. Available: https://www.loc.gov/exhibits/creating-the-united-states/interactives/bill-of-rights/beararms/enlarge1-transcribe.html.

[381] "Cornell Law School," [Online]. Available: https://www.law.cornell.edu/wex/second_amendment.

[382] "Disaster Center," [Online]. Available: http://www.disastercenter.com/crime/.

[383] S. McPherson, "The Future of Freedom Foundation," [Online]. Available: https://www.fff.org/explore-freedom/article/gun-control-

britain-failed/.

[384] W. Cummings, "USA Today," 2018. [Online]. Available: https://www.usatoday.com/story/news/world/2018/04/09/london-mayor-knife-control/500328002/.

[385] R. McMaken, "Mises Institute," 2015. [Online]. Available: https://mises.org/wire/gun-control-what-happened-england-ireland-and-canada.

[386] D. Kopel, "Dave Kopel," [Online]. Available: http://davekopel.org/2A/Mags/The-Failure-of-Canadian-Gun-Control.htm.

[387] "Gun Facts," [Online]. Available: https://www.gunfacts.info/gun-policy-info/crime-and-guns/.

[388] S. Adams, "Samuel Adams Heritage Society," [Online]. Available: http://www.samuel-adams-heritage.com/quotes/freedom-liberty.html.

[389] J. Williams, "The Washington Post," 1991. [Online]. Available: https://www.washingtonpost.com/archive/opinions/1991/10/13/japan-the-price-of-safe-streets/03115e40-267d-4cf4-9520-61ebcb73f9d3/.

[390] T. Otake, "The Japan Times," [Online]. Available: https://www.japantimes.co.jp/news/2017/05/30/national/social-issues/preventive-efforts-seen-helping-2016-saw-another-decline-suicides-japan-21897/#.XpDuNqhKiUk.

[391] G. A. Mauser, "Public Polucy Sources," 2003. [Online]. Available: https://s3.amazonaws.com/tld-documents.llnassets.com/0007000/7275/failedexperimentguncontrol.pdf.

[392] T. Jefferson, "Founders Online," [Online]. Available: https://founders.archives.gov/documents/Jefferson/98-01-02-1702.

[393] A. d. Tocqueville, "Democracy in America," 1862, p. 392.

[394] A. B. Powell, "Guns Part 2," p. 2013.

[395] "Tenth Amendment Center," [Online]. Available: https://tenthamendmentcenter.com/legislation/2nd-amendment-preservation-act/.

[396] E. Smith, "CNBC," 2019. [Online]. Available: https://www.cnbc.com/2019/10/22/vicente-fox-legalizing-drugs-is-the-way-to-combat-cartels.html.

[397] "Liberty (Not the Daughter But the Mother of Order)," 1906, p. 8.

[398] T. Jefferson, "Founders Online," [Online]. Available: https://founders.archives.gov/documents/Jefferson/01-12-02-0348.

[399] M. L. K. Jr, "Dr. Wheeler," 1963. [Online]. Available: https://web.cn.edu/kwheeler/documents/Letter_Birmingham_Jail.pdf.

[400] T. Gomez, "The Firearm Blog," [Online]. Available:

https://www.thefirearmblog.com/blog/2014/03/26/80-ar-15-receiver-determination-letter-atf/.

[401]  J. Howerton, "The Blaze," 2014. [Online]. Available: https://www.theblaze.com/news/2014/01/21/anti-gun-senator-is-being-mocked-relentlessly-after-he-warned-of-30-caliber-clip-in-embarrassing-video.

[402]  T. Oppenheimer, "Reason," [Online]. Available: https://reason.com/2014/03/19/video-ares-armor-ceo-tries-to-reason-wit/.

[403]  "WeaponsMan," [Online]. Available: http://weaponsman.looserounds.com/?p=38842.

[404]  M. Gaddy, "Gun Owners of America," 2003. [Online]. Available: https://gunowners.org/op0304/.

[405]  M. Smith, "Independent institute," 2013. [Online]. Available: https://blog.independent.org/2013/02/27/gun-companies-cease-sales-to-government-in-states-where-second-amendment-is-not-respected/.

[406]  M. Opelka, "The Blaze," 2013. [Online]. Available: https://www.theblaze.com/news/2013/02/23/gaining-momentum-now-42-gun-companies-have-stopped-selling-to-law-enforcement-in-anti-2nd-amendment-states.

[407]  "Laws of Alaska," [Online]. Available: http://www.legis.state.ak.us/PDF/28/Bills/HB0069Z.PDF.

[408]  "Gun Owners of America," 2019. [Online]. Available: https://gunowners.org/gun-owners-of-america-funds-challenge-to-national-firearms-act-in-u-s-supreme-court/.

[409]  "Cornell Law School," [Online]. Available: https://www.law.cornell.edu/wex/jury_nullification.

[410]  "Wikipedia," [Online]. Available: https://en.wikipedia.org/wiki/Jury_nullification.

[411]  M. Hudetz, "Las Cruces Sun News," 2019. [Online]. Available: https://www.lcsun-news.com/story/news/local/new-mexico/2019/02/15/nm-sheriffs-fight-gun-bills-sanctuary-county-resolutions/2886741002/.

[412]  E. Goldman, "Anarchism and Other Essays," Mother Earth publishing associatio, 1910, p. 83.

[413]  A. Rand, "Philosophy: Who Needs It," Penguin, 1984.

[414]  "Justia US Supreme," [Online]. Available: https://supreme.justia.com/cases/federal/us/92/542/.

[415]  "Hathi Trust," [Online]. Available: https://catalog.hathitrust.org/Record/010448105.

[416]  "The Glyptodon," [Online]. Available: https://theglyptodon.wordpress.com/2012/08/21/polio-caused-by-ice-cream/.

Made in the USA
Middletown, DE
05 May 2020

92900096R00191